Cotswold Way

44 large-scale maps & guides to 48 towns and villages

PLANNING – PLACES TO STAY – PLACES TO EAT

CHIPPING CAMPDEN TO BATH

TRICIA & BOB HAYNE

TRAILBLAZER PUBLICATIONS

Contents

INTRODUCTION

Cotswold Way

History 9 – Geology 10 – How difficult is the path? 12
How long do you need? 12 – When to go 13

PART 1: PLANNING YOUR WALK

Practical information for the walker

Route finding 17 – Accommodation 18 – Food and drink 22
Money 23 – Other services 25 – Taking dogs along the path 25
Disabled access 25 – Walking companies 26 – Information for
foreign visitors 26

Budgeting 29

Itineraries

Which direction? 31 – Suggested itineraries 32 – Side trips 32
Village and town facilities 34 – The best day and weekend walks 36

What to take

Keep your luggage light 38 – How to carry it 38 – Footwear 39
Clothes 39 – Toiletries 40 – First-aid kit 40 – General items 40
Camping gear 41 – Money 41 – Travel insurance 41 – Maps 42
Sources of further information 42 – Recommended reading 42

Getting to and from the Cotswold Way

Getting to Britain 44 – National transport 45
Local transport 47 – Public transport map 49

PART 2: MINIMUM IMPACT & OUTDOOR SAFETY

Minimum-impact walking

Economic impact 51 – Environmental impact 52 – Access 53

Health and outdoor safety

Health 56 – Outdoor safety 58 – Weather information 58
Walking alone 58

PART 3: THE ENVIRONMENT & NATURE

Conserving the Cotswolds

Government agencies and schemes 60
Voluntary campaigning and conservation organisations 61

Flora and fauna

Trees and shrubs 62 – Wild flowers 63 – Butterflies 66 – Birds 66
Mammals 70 – Reptiles 72

DON 2019

PART 4: ROUTE GUIDE AND MAPS

Using this guide   Trail maps 73 – Accommodation 74

Chipping Campden 75

Chipping Campden to Broadway 81 (Broadway 81)

Broadway to Winchcombe 89 (Stanton 92, Stanway 92, Wood Stanway 94, North Farmcote 94, Hailes 94, Winchcombe 96)

Winchcombe to Cleeve Hill 101 (Postlip 101, Cleeve Hill 102)

Cleeve Hill to Leckhampton Hill 105 (Cheltenham 105, Prestbury Hill Reserve 110, Ham Hill 110, Charlton Kings 112, Near Dowdeswell Reservoir 112, Seven Springs 115)

Leckhampton Hill to Birdlip 115 (Ullenwood 115, Around Crickley Hill 115, Birdlip 119)

Birdlip to Painswick 119 (Little Witcombe 120, Cranham Corner and Painswick Hill 120, Painswick 122)

Painswick to Stonehouse 127 (Edge 127, Randwick/Westrip 128, Stonehouse 130)

Stonehouse to Penn Wood 130 (King's Stanley 130, Middleyard 132, Ebley 132, Selsley 132)

Penn Wood to Dursley 134 (Nympsfield 134, Uley 134, Dursley 136)

Dursley to Wotton-under-Edge 141 (Stinchcombe Hill 142, North Nibley 142, Wotton-under-Edge 146)

Wotton-under-Edge to Old Sodbury 149 (Alderley 150, Hillesley 150, Hawkesbury Upton 150, Horton 152, Little Sodbury 154, Old Sodbury 154)

Old Sodbury to Cold Ashton 157 (Coomb's End 157, Tormarton 157, South of the M4 158, Pennsylvania 162, Cold Ashton 162)

Cold Ashton to Bath 163 (Weston 165)   **Bath** 168

APPENDICES & INDEX

Map key 184 **Waypoints** 185 **Walking with a dog** 187 **Index** 189

DISTANCE CHART 194

OVERVIEW MAPS & PROFILES 197

Contents

ABOUT THIS BOOK

This guidebook contains all the information you need to walk the Cotswold Way:

- All standards of accommodation, from campsites to luxurious guesthouses
- Walking companies offering both self-guided and guided tours
- Suggested itineraries for all types of walker
- Answers to all your questions: when to go, degree of difficulty, what to pack and approximate cost of the whole walking holiday

When you're all packed, boots on and ready to go, there's plenty of information to get you to and from the Cotswold Way, and 44 detailed maps (1:20,000) together with nine town/village plans to help you find your way along it. The route guide section includes:

Cotswold Way 'The Beginning and the End' original marker post in Chipping Campden.

- Walking times in both directions
- Reviews of accommodation including campsites, hostels, B&Bs and guesthouses
- Cafés, pubs, tea shops, restaurants, and shops for buying supplies
- Rail, bus and taxi information for villages on or near the path
- Town plans of Chipping Campden, Broadway, Winchcombe, Cheltenham, Painswick, Dursley, Wotton-under-Edge and Bath
- Historical, cultural and geographical background information
- GPS waypoints

❏ MINIMUM IMPACT FOR MAXIMUM INSIGHT

We do not inherit the earth from our ancestors: we borrow it from our children. **Native American proverb**

By their very nature, walkers tend to be both interested in and concerned about the natural environment. This book seeks to reinforce that interest and concern. There are sections devoted to minimum-impact walking and conservation, with ideas on how to broaden that ethos, as well as a detailed, illustrated chapter on wildlife.

There can be few activities as 'environmentally friendly' as walking. By developing a deeper ecological awareness through a better understanding of nature, and by supporting rural economies, sensitive forms of transport and low-impact methods of farming and land use, we can all do our bit to ensure that the environment remains in safe hands for generations to come.

Photos – Front cover and p3: Broadway's St Michael and All Saints' Church nestles at the foot of the Cotswold Hills. (© TH). **Page 1**: Open walking across Dodington Park. (© TH). **Contents pages**: Approaching Belas Knap above Winchcombe. (© BH).

INTRODUCTION

Asked to conjure up an image of a quintessential Cotswold scene, most people will come up with some combination of a village of honey-coloured houses set against a backdrop of sheep grazing in hillside fields, demarcated by seemingly endless dry-stone walls. For once, the reality and the picture-postcard image still coincide, at least in part. Nevertheless, to walk the Cotswold Way is to discover a far more complex – and arguably more

For once, the reality and the picture-postcard image still coincide...

rewarding – environment, where wide tracts of arable land unfold over the hills, and ancient beech woods line the Cotswold escarpment.

With the Cotswold villages of tourist brochures along the early part of the route, and the architectural glories of Georgian Bath that await the walker in the south, it's soon clear that Cotswold limestone has been hugely influential in defining the landscape. As you head south, so the stone of the houses gradually fades, from Stanton's golden cottages to the palest ivory of Painswick's villas. Simple parish churches, towering follies and stately homes make their mark, too, all constructed of the same stone. Yet it's not just the stone that

Stanton's golden-stone cottages encapsulate the quiet beauty of a Cotswold village.

hints at the region's history. You won't get far without coming across any number of humps, lumps and bumps, relics of earlier inhabitants who left their mark in burial mounds, hill forts, monasteries and even villas right across the trail. Their chosen spots were often some of those most revered by today's walkers: wide-open expanses on windy hilltops with views west to the wide River Severn and the Malvern Hills.

Almost the entire trail runs through the Cotswolds Area of Outstanding Natural Beauty

Almost the entire trail runs through the Cotswolds Area of Outstanding Natural Beauty, crossing fields still bounded by hedges and walls, and hills where sheep have grazed for centuries. In the early years, merchants grew rich on the bounty that was sheep's wool, their fortunes invested in the foundation of towns from Chipping Campden to Dursley. Where grazing has ended, human intervention has ensured that at least some of the rich grassland can remain a haven for the wild flowers, birds and insects that previous generations took for granted.

Thoughtfully, the Cotswold Way crosses all these places – and perhaps that's the greatest advantage of a man-made trail. While earlier walkers must have taken a direct route on pilgrimage to the abbey at Hailes, today's hikers on the Cotswold Way find themselves twisting and turning along a trail that effectively showcases the very best that the region can offer. That that includes

historic castles, more than a passing nod to the Arts and Crafts Movement, and some excellent pubs, is to the benefit of all.

History

HISTORY OF THE TRAIL

The Cotswold Way runs for 102 miles (163km) through the Cotswold Hills from Chipping Campden in the north to the Georgian city of Bath. The route was originally devised as a long-distance footpath by members of the Ramblers' Association (now called Ramblers) and was established in conjunction with the Cotswolds AONB in 1970.

Its development as a national trail was approved in 1998, but it was not until May 2007 that the trail was formally launched, one of just 15 in England and Wales at that time. During the transition, several changes were made to the route, and others are still in the offing, although for the most part the original paths remain open.

Below: Bath's grand Royal Crescent greets the walker on the final stretch of the walk. (© TH)

INTRODUCTION

The path is the responsibility of the National Trail Officer, under the auspices of the Cotswold Way National Trail Office (see box p42).

GEOLOGY

Look at a geological map of England and it is immediately clear that the origins of the present-day Cotswolds lie in the Jurassic period. Such maps show a continuous swathe of Jurassic-age rocks, formed between 199 and 145 million years ago, extending all the way from Dorset to the Yorkshire coast, with the most complete and impressive outcrop making up the Cotswold Hills.

Cotswold stone is an oolitic limestone ... formed in the shallow seas of the Jurassic

Cotswold stone is an oolitic limestone, a sedimentary rock that was formed primarily in the warm shallow seas of the Jurassic. It is comprised of a large number of almost spherical granules, or oolites, packed closely together,

---

❑ **Dry-stone walls**

Dry-stone walls

The dry-stone walls that are so evocative of the Cotswolds are created from irregularly shaped blocks of the local limestone. Deceptive in their simplicity, they require a considerable level of skill to build, with an expert able to complete around six or seven yards (6-7m) a day.

Some beds of Cotswold stone break down naturally into layers of around two or three inches (50-75mm) thick. Typically, the wall is created from two parallel lines of stone, gradually coming together as they near the top. Stones on each side of the wall are fitted together like a jigsaw, laid sloping outwards to draw water away from the centre. Smaller pieces of stone, and offcuts, are used to fill the central cavities, adding strength and durability to the whole wall.

and its origins explain the regular occurrence in the rock of fossils, such as sea urchins. Occasional falls in sea level, however, resulted in dry land where dinosaurs roamed, leaving behind both their footprints and their bones. While most walkers will see little difference between the rocks at various places along the trail, to the geologist there are marked distinctions according to the stages at which the sediments were deposited and compressed. In addition, while the surface rock of the Cotswold range is predominantly limestone, the underlying structure is more usually of clays, silts and sands. It is the precise structure of these rocks that both determines the wildlife that populates the hillside and influences the buildings you will see in each part of the region.

Gloucestershire Geology Trust (💻 www.glosgeotrust.org.uk) is committed to studying and conserving the region's geological heritage, and to recording regionally important geological sites. The trust publishes a series of trail guides (£2 each) entitled *Gloucestershire Uncovered*, which include Cleeve Hill Common, Leckhampton Hill and Crickley Hill.

INTRODUCTION

Finally, a layer of slats, or 'combers', is laid along the top at right angles to the wall. The whole is usually around 3ft (1m) high, and some 20in (50cm) at the base, tapering to around 16in (40cm) at the top.

It is estimated that there are some 4000 miles (6000km) of dry-stone walls across the whole of the Cotswolds AONB. Weather, vegetation and accidents take their toll, so regular maintenance is essential. As a result of a revival of interest in traditional crafts, it is possible to go on a course to learn the basics, or to take part as a volunteer to help preserve the region's existing walls. For more information, contact the Cotswolds Conservation Board (who run the Cotswolds AONB, see p60) or the Dry Stone Walling Association of Great Britain (💻 www.ds wa.org.uk).

INTRODUCTION

How difficult is the path?

Familiarity with the Cotswolds – or at least with the tourist areas in the north – might lead to a sense that the Cotswold Way is little more than a walk in the park. While it would be unreasonable to suggest that it is seriously challenging, it would be equally wrong to underestimate the quite literal ups and downs of a route that takes you from just above sea level to 1066ft (325m) and back over a distance of around 100 miles.

If, as is often suggested, you plan to complete the route in seven days, you're looking at an average of nearly 15 miles, or six to seven hours' actual walking, every day. Some of those hills are steeper than you might expect from a casual glance at the landscape and poor weather can exacerbate what would otherwise be fairly straightforward. It makes sense, then, to have a reasonable level of fitness before you set off, if only to make sure that what should be an enjoyable week or so's walking doesn't turn into a test of endurance.

How long do you need?

This is the great imponderable. Is it reasonable – as many hikers do – to walk the path from end to end in a week? Well yes, but it's a qualified yes. If you have just seven days' holiday but need two of those to get to and from the trail, you'll be faced with walking 20 miles a day, which isn't for the faint hearted. If, on the other hand, you can spend most of those seven days on the trail, a

The route is well signposted so you shouldn't get lost; look for the acorn logo. (© TH).

week is realistic. That said, averaging almost 15 miles a day won't leave much time for exploring the villages on the route, taking time out for a cream tea in Broadway, or a pint of **So while the world reckons that this is a week's walk, give it eight days and you'll be adding in time to breathe**

Donnington's at The Mount Inn in Stanton, or exploring Selsley Common for orchids. You might find yourself casting a wistful backward glance at old churches as you march purposefully past the lych gate, or promising yourself you'll come back to do justice to Hailes Abbey, or Dyrham Park, or even to Bath. So while the world reckons that this is a week's walk, give it eight days and you'll be adding in time to breathe.

If time is really short, you could reasonably leave out the last section, perhaps south of Cold Ashton and down Lansdown Hill into Bath (pp36-8). That isn't to say this isn't worthy of walking – far from it. But Bath is a destination in its own right, so the chances are that you could justify returning on another occasion. **See p33 for some suggested itineraries covering different walking speeds**

Plenty of people can't spare the time to walk from end to end in one go, but still get that sense of achievement by building up the miles over a series of day or weekend walks until they've completed the route. Alternatively, you could simply sample the highlights (though lowlights are few); see p33 for some recommendations.

When to go

SEASONS

Autumn that name of creeper falling and tea-time loving,
Was once for me the thought of High Cotswold noon-air   **Ivor Gurney**, *Old Thought*

While English weather is hardly predictable, at least some generalisations can be made. Statistically, the months when the weather is least likely to be inclement are May to September, but statistics – as we all know – can be very misleading. The air temperature at this time is generally at its warmest, with frosts unlikely from the end of May. Rain, though, is another factor. Some years can see continuous rain for several weeks and parts of the path will become impassable. While it's tempting to think that this is only likely to happen in winter, the last widespread flooding in Gloucestershire was in the summer of 2007, with 2008 running a close second. Conversely, April and October often bring days that are bright and breezy, when the walking and the surroundings are at their best.

Spring

The weather in spring is as unpredictable as the rest of the year. In **April**, it can be warm and sunny on odd days, but seldom for sustained periods. Although the spring of 2007 upset all the record books, conditions are more likely to be

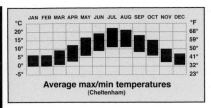

Average max/min temperatures
(Cheltenham)

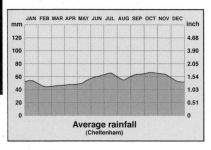

Average rainfall
(Cheltenham)

changeable, with blustery showers and cold spells reminding you that winter has only just passed. On the other hand, the days are long, and less rain falls on average in spring than at any other time of the year. This, coupled with the milder weather of **May** and **June**, and the proliferation of wild flowers early in the year, makes it one of the best times to tackle the trail.

Summer

July and **August** are the traditional holiday months and the conditions can be especially good for walking, with generally mild temperatures and still many hours of daylight. This, however, is also the time when the Cotswolds experience a surge in visitors, especially around the tourist honeypots of Broadway and Bath. Fortunately, most of the trippers won't be out in the fields and on the hills, so here at least you can leave the hordes behind.

Autumn

Many connoisseurs consider autumn, especially early autumn, the best time of year for walking. **September** and **October** can be lovely months to get out on

---

❏ FESTIVALS AND ANNUAL EVENTS

The following events may need to be considered when planning your walk since all will affect the availability and sometimes price of accommodation in their area. Two with a particularly strong impact locally are The Festival in Cheltenham in March, and Badminton Horse Trials in May. In addition to the following annual fixtures, it's as well to be aware that weekend events held at the **Prescott Speed Hill Climb** (🖥 www.prescott-hillclimb.com) outside Winchcombe between about April and October can put a lot of pressure on the town's resources.

February
● **Cheltenham Folk Three** (🖥 www.cheltenhamtownhall.org.uk/whats-on/festivals) Folk music comes to town for three days in mid February.

March
● **Bath Literature Festival** (🖥 bathfestivals.org.uk/literature) Ten days at the beginning of March see Bath's literary scene come alive. Literary greats such as Antonia Fraser, Kazuo Ishiguro and Andrew Motion were among those at the 2015 event.
● **The Festival, Cheltenham** (🖥 cheltenham.thejockeyclub.co.uk) Formerly known as the National Hunt Festival, this four-day event in mid March is one of the racing

the trail, especially when the leaves begin to turn. That said, although the air temperature usually remains relatively mild, October can see the first frosts and rain is an ever-present threat.

Winter
Only the very hardiest of souls will attempt the Cotswold Way in winter. The days are shorter; once the clocks have gone back at the end of October, until mid March, you will need to be at your destination by 4.30-5pm to avoid walking in the dark. Cold weather, wind and driving rain are not the best recipe for a day's walking, although a crisp winter morning takes a lot of beating.

DAYLIGHT HOURS

If you're planning to walk in autumn, winter or early spring, you'll need to take into account how far you can walk in the available daylight. It will not be possible to cover as many miles or to be out for as long as you would in the summer. The table (right) gives the sunrise and sunset times for the middle of each month at latitude 52° North, which runs through the Cotswold Hills, giving a reasonably accurate pic-

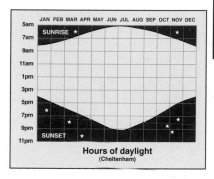

Hours of daylight
(Cheltenham)

ture for daylight along the Cotswold Way. Depending on the weather, you should get a further 30-45 minutes of usable light before sunrise and after sunset.

calendar's highlights – both in racing terms and socially – culminating in every jump jockey's dream, the Cheltenham Gold Cup. Tickets are hard sought after and accommodation throughout the area is often booked a year ahead. If you have no choice but to walk in this week, make sure you plan well ahead.

April/May
● **Wotton-under-Edge Arts Festival** (🖳 www.wottonartsfestival.org.uk) This ten-day festival takes place around the end of April and early May.
● **Cheltenham Jazz Festival** (🖳 www.cheltenhamfestivals.com) A week of jazz is celebrated at the end of April/early May.

May
● **Annual Cheese Rolling** Cooper's Hill (🖳 www.cheese-rolling.co.uk) There's still strong support for this wacky village event, traditionally held on the last May Bank Holiday Monday; see box p119.
● **Badminton Horse Trials** (🖳 www.badminton-horse.co.uk) Hugely important among the riding fraternity, this five-day event takes place east of the trail near Old Sodbury in early May. Accommodation is limited in this area, and guesthouses, pubs and hotels for miles around get prebooked months in advance: you've been warned!

(cont'd overleaf)

FESTIVALS AND ANNUAL EVENTS

May (cont'd from p15)

● **Chipping Campden Music Festival** (⌨ campdenmusicfestival.co.uk) A local two-week festival dedicated to classical music, based in the town's St James's Church.

● **Cotswold Olimpicks**, Dover's Hill, Chipping Campden (⌨ www.olimpickgames .co.uk) Friday after the last May Bank Holiday, followed the next day by the Scuttlebrook Wake; see box p81.

● **Winchcombe Walking Festival** (⌨ www.winchcombewelcomeswalkers.com) A series of graded walks and evening events taking place from Friday to Sunday over the penultimate weekend in May.

● **Winchcombe Festival of Music & Arts** (⌨ winchcombefestival.co.uk) A week-long celebration of local talent held at the end of May.

June

● **Bath International Music Festival** (⌨ bathfestivals.org.uk/music) For two weeks at the end of May and early June, the festival showcases music ranging from classical to jazz and folk.

● **Cheltenham Science Festival** (⌨ www.cheltenhamfestivals.com) Held over six days in mid June.

● **Cheltenham Food and Drink Festival** (⌨ garden-events.com) Three days of foodie heaven in Montpellier Gardens; mid to late June.

● **Cotswold Way Relay** (⌨ www.cotswoldwayrelay.co.uk) It might be best to avoid walking on the last Saturday in June. For details, see box p31.

July

● **Cheltenham Music Festival** (⌨ www.cheltenhamfestivals.com) Popular two-week festival at the beginning of July with international artists playing an eclectic mix of primarily classical music.

● **Cotswold Beer Festival** (⌨ www.gloucestershirecamra.org.uk/cbf) One of CAMRA's national beer festivals, usually held at Postlip Hall outside Winchcombe over the last weekend in July.

● **Cheltenham Cricket Festival** (⌨ www.gloscricket.co.uk/cricket/cheltenham-cricket-festival) Founded in 1872, the festival is held in the grounds of Cheltenham College around the end of July/early August.

August

● **Artburst** (⌨ www.painswickartsfestival.com) Painswick's inaugural Art Festival in 2015 looks set to continue during the first week in August.

● **Frocester Beer Festival** (⌨ www.frocesterbeerfestival.com) Two days of tasting, music and camaraderie, held near Stonehouse; August Bank Holiday weekend.

September

Cheltenham Comedy Festival (⌨ cheltenhamcomedy.com) A week of fun and laughter towards the end of September.

October

● **Cheltenham Literature Festival** (⌨ www.cheltenhamfestivals.com) This ten-day festival in mid October goes from strength to strength, attracting authors as diverse as Salman Rushdie, Terry Wogan and Steve Backshall.

● **Dursley Walking Festival** (⌨ www.dursleywelcomeswalkers.org.uk) A four-day festival focusing on walks around the little town of Dursley.

(Opposite) Open views from the trail near Beckbury Camp. (© TH).

(Overleaf) Folly near Little Sodbury. (© TH).

Practical information for the walker

ROUTE FINDING

Having opened as a national trail only in 2007, it's
no surprise that the Cotswold Way is clearly signposted along almost its entire length. On the few
occasions – usually in a field or a wood – where
there might be some ambiguity, the maps in this
guide should quickly put you straight.

The waymark throughout your walk is the
National Trails' acorn symbol, to be found on
stiles, kissing gates, fingerposts and guideposts.
Sometimes as an alternative you will find the standard yellow or blue footpath or bridlepath roundel
overprinted with the words 'Cotswold Way', and
the authorities in Bath have devised a more discreet sign, a metallic acorn on a black background.

Using GPS with this book

*I never carried a compass, preferring to rely on a good sense of direction. I
never bothered to understand how a compass works or what it is supposed to do.
To me a compass is a gadget, and I don't get on well with gadgets of any sort.*

Alfred Wainwright

While modern Wainwrights will scoff, more open-minded walkers will
accept GPS technology as an inexpensive and well-established, if non-
essential, navigational aid. With a clear view of the sky, GPS receivers
will within a minute of being turned on establish your position and alti-
tude anywhere on earth in a variety of formats, including the British
Ordnance Survey grid system, to an accuracy of within a few metres.

One thing must be understood, however: treating a GPS as a
replacement for maps, a compass and common sense is a big mistake. Although current units are robust, it only takes the batteries to
go flat or some electronic malfunction to leave you floundering,
potentially in the dark. A GPS is merely a navigational aid or backup
to conventional route finding and, in almost all cases, is best used in
conjunction with a paper map. All a GPS does is stop you exacerbat-
ing navigational errors or save you time in correcting them.

(Opp): The traditional Cotswold Lion is distinctive for its unkempt fringe. (BH).

The maps in the route guide include numbered waypoints; these correlate to the list on pp185-6, which gives the latitude/longitude position in a decimal minute format as well as a description. Typically, a waypoint has been given for most of the high spots and significant places of interest along the route, as well as for several of the towns and villages. You can download the complete list of these waypoints for free as a GPS-readable file (that doesn't include the text descriptions) from the Trailblazer website: ▭ www.trailblazer-guides.com (click on GPS waypoints).

It's anticipated that you won't tramp along day after day, ticking off the book's waypoints as you pass them, because the route description and maps are more than adequate most of the time. Only when you're **unsure of your position**, or which way to go, might you feel the need to turn on the unit for a quick affirmation.

It's also possible to buy state-of-the-art **digital mapping** to import into your GPS unit, assuming that you have sufficient memory capacity, but it's not the most reliable way of navigating and the small screen on your pocket-sized unit will invariably fail to put places into context or give you a feel for the bigger picture.

Despite these possibilities, almost everyone who has ever walked the Cotswold Way has done so without GPS, so there's no need to rush out and buy one. The route is exceptionally well waymarked and with the maps in this guide there is little chance you will get lost. That said, it offers a good opportunity to try out new technology before tackling something more navigationally challenging.

ACCOMMODATION

The Cotswold Way is generally well served with bed-and-breakfast and pub accommodation, but there are one or two places, particularly between the Cheltenham area and Dursley, where the options are quite limited and you may be faced with up to a mile further at the end of the day's walk. That said, most places listed in this guide are either on or within easy reach of the trail. Campers, though, will find themselves with quite a challenge and may have to combine camping with the odd night at a B&B. A comprehensive selection of places to stay is given in each section of the route guide (Part 4), though do bear in mind that even the most long-standing establishments can change hands, or close, without warning.

Although smoking in enclosed public spaces is banned in England, places to stay are able to designate rooms for smokers. In practice, however, very few B&Bs do this, so check if it is important to you (see box p27).

Booking

It's best to reserve your accommodation in advance, especially at peak periods and weekends, when there can be stiff competition for beds, and in winter, when several B&Bs close for the season. Very few B&B owners appreciate someone turning up on the doorstep without warning and you don't want to find yourself with nowhere to stop. The suggested itineraries on p33 should help with planning ahead.

Most hotels and some B&Bs offer online or email booking, but for some you will need to contact them by phone. In many cases you will be asked for a deposit of around 50%, rising to 100% for one-night bookings, which is generally non-refundable if you cancel at short notice. While larger places may take credit or debit cards, some via PayPal, many B&Bs accept only cheques or payments by bank transfer for the deposit, with the balance settled by cash or cheque. Do remember to take your cheque book!

If you do have to cancel, be sure to give as much notice as you can so they can offer your room to someone else.

Prices

Prices given in this guide are, unless otherwise stated, per person with breakfast for one night, reflecting the increasing trend even in family-run B&Bs to operate on this basis. Few places along the Cotswold Way offer single rooms so most charge a supplement on the per person rate. However, the occasional place still charges per room, regardless of the number of people and the odd one or two charge more for a twin room than for a double – which may not seem logical to ordinary mortals.

The trend towards flexible pricing according to the time of year, the time of the week, and the occurrence of festivals, is spreading beyond hotels to pubs and even B&Bs, especially in tourist hotspots; this makes it difficult to generalise about rates so do ensure you check the rate before confirming a reservation. Booking early can make a big difference, especially out of season. Conversely, during festivals or at similar times, rates can be extortionate.

For hotels in particular, do check whether or not breakfast is included, and watch out for hidden extras such as service charge and VAT.

For a guide to rates, see under Hostels (below), B&Bs (pp20-1), Pubs (p21), and Hotels (p21).

Camping

Man is born free under the stars, yet we lock our doors and creep to bed.
Robert Louis Stevenson

There are few official campsites along the Cotswold Way, especially along the northern part of the trail between Winchcombe and the Ebley Canal area. **Wild camping** is not permitted anywhere, which is no help to those who prefer the great outdoors to a B&B. It may be worth asking at a farm along the route if you can pitch a tent in a field, but please don't just turn up and risk it. Farmers used to be more amenable to the odd inconspicuous tent but attitudes have changed and if you were discovered you would certainly not be made welcome.

Rates for camping range from £3.50 to £10 per person per night, so it still remains the most economical way to walk the trail – though if you're more into glamping, you're looking at up to £30 a head.

Hostels

Cheap hostel-style accommodation along the Cotswold Way itself is available only in Bath, although there at least you'll have a choice, with beds from £15 a night. The city's youth hostel, where accommodation discounts are available to

PLANNING YOUR WALK

members of the **Youth Hostels Association** (YHA; ☎ 01629-592700, 💻 www.yha.org.uk) and **Hostelling International** (💻 www.hihostels.com), is a good mile east of the centre, so a fair trek for walkers. The cost of annual YHA membership – which automatically entitles you to membership of Hostelling International – is £15-20 per person, or £5-10 for those under 26, with 'household' membership at £25-30 for two adults living at the same address, and children under 18 travelling with them. The price difference depends on the method of payment. Members are entitled to a discount of up to £3 per night.

B&Bs and guesthouses

Although historically there is a distinct difference between a guesthouse and the more personal B&B, the edges are becoming increasingly blurred. Traditionally, those staying in a B&B, where overnight visitors are limited to no more than six at any one time, will find themselves very much as guests in a private house. Establishments accommodating greater numbers have to be registered as a guesthouse.

Staying in **B&Bs** brings you into contact with local people in a way that hotels and guesthouses can't. For anyone unfamiliar with the concept, you get a bedroom in someone's home along with a cooked breakfast the following morning. The accommodation is invariably clean and comfortable, traditionally with the emphasis on floral patterns and chintz – although things are changing fast and rooms in many B&Bs along the Cotswold Way compete with the best for style and elegance. If one night you find yourself in a modern bungalow, the next could be in a picture-perfect cottage, or on a working farm. **Guesthouses**, which effectively bridge the gap between B&Bs and hotels, may be more structured in approach – although in reality, especially in some of the towns along the trail, you may have no idea whether you're in a B&B or a guesthouse. What matters is a warm welcome, a comfortable room, and – ideally – someone who understands that walkers tend to have muddy boots and wet clothes.

Where visitor numbers are high, such as in Bath or Broadway, you may well find that a minimum two-night stay is imposed, which can cause problems for walkers. Others simply charge a higher rate for one-nighters. Such restrictions are most likely to be the case at weekends or in the height of the tourist season.

What to expect For most long-distance walkers, tourist-board star-rating systems have little meaning. At the end of a long day you'll simply be glad of a place with hot water and a smiling welcome. It is these criteria that have been used for places included in this guide, rather than whether a room has tea- and coffee-making facilities, a shaver point or TV – though many of them do.

In the trend towards making rooms **en suite**, many places have carved out a tiny area for a shower and a loo. Yet a larger room with a bathroom across the corridor, often for your own private use, could well be preferable – and the option of a hot bath has significant appeal if you're cold and wet; establishments with baths are indicated in this guide with a ☕ symbol.

Finding anywhere with a **single** room isn't easy and those there are tend to be pretty small. A **double** room is supposed to have one double bed, and a **twin** room two singles, but sometimes the two are interchangeable, allowing greater flexibility. Some places have rooms that can sleep three (**triple**), four (**quad**) or more – these rooms come in a variety of arrangements (see p74) but can also always sleep just two people.

Some B&Bs and guesthouses have a **sitting room** exclusively for guests' use, a real bonus at the end of a day when retiring to your room instead of relaxing in a comfy chair can seem something of an anti-climax. Others will welcome guests to sit out in the **garden** on a summer's evening.

An **evening meal** is sometimes on offer at the more isolated establishments, though you should always pre-book this or you could go hungry. If you're expecting a meal, but are delayed, do ring ahead. Nobody wants to serve (or eat) dried-up lasagne and limp salad. If meals are not available, many owners will offer you a lift to the nearest pub if it's too far to walk.

Rates The image of B&B as a cheap option is no longer valid; costs have soared in recent years. Expect to pay £30-50pp per night based on two sharing a room; for single occupancy you may need to pay £50-90. See p19 and p30.

Transport Where places offering accommodation are not right on the Cotswold Way, B&B owners may offer to collect walkers at an agreed rendezvous point and deliver them back to the trail next day. It's a service that is usually provided free of charge, but do check first. It is important to agree lift arrangements at the time of booking and, if possible, to phone ahead to warn of your impending arrival at the pick-up point – or of any delays, of course.

Pubs

Many pubs offer B&B accommodation and some supply every modern convenience – including luxuries such as four-poster beds. Obviously they tend to be less personal than B&Bs, but for some walkers that's a bonus – and you don't have far to go to the bar, either. Of greater concern for most people is that pubs can be quite noisy, especially at weekends, so bear this in mind if you fancy an early night.

In general, pub prices along the Cotswold Way are similar to those at B&Bs (see above). In tourist areas many pubs – like B&Bs – charge extra at weekends (including Friday night), whereas at more business-orientated establishments prices may drop at weekends.

Hotels

At first glance a hotel may not seem the obvious venue for a walker. Muddy boots and a rucksack might seem at odds with the surroundings and having something suitable to change into could pose a problem, but if you can get over that hurdle, you're down to issues of cost and style.

Most hotels charge per room rather than per person, and while some will negotiate a rate for single occupancy, this is by no means the norm. (See Prices, p19). While you might expect to pay at least £40pp based on two sharing a room (and at least £60 for single occupancy), many hotels charge more, and during festivals or at similar times rates can be extortionate.

Airbnb

The rise and rise of Airbnb (🖳 www.airbnb.co.uk) has seen private homes and apartments opened up to overnight travellers on an informal basis. While accommodation is primarily based in cities, the concept is spreading to tourist hotspots in more rural areas, but do check thoroughly what you are getting and the precise location. While the first couple of options listed may be in the area you're after, others may be far too far afield for walkers. At its best, this is a great way to meet local people in a relatively unstructured environment, but do be aware that these places are not registered B&Bs, so standards may vary, yet prices may not necessarily be any lower than the norm.

Holiday cottages

The inclusion of holiday cottages is outside the scope of a guide dedicated to walkers on the move. However, for those who would prefer to stay at a fixed base, covering different parts of the route each day, self-catering may be the perfect option. Typically, cottages are let on a weekly or fortnightly basis, with prices starting at around £350 a week for four people in the low season. For details, contact the relevant tourist information centre (see box p42). If you're after something more individual, you could try one of the properties owned by the Landmark Trust (see p62).

FOOD AND DRINK

The Cotswolds area isn't known for its haute cuisine. Historically at least, this is a region of simple, farmhouse fare, based on good ingredients, rather than fine cooking. In Bath you'll come across a few regional specialities (see box p117), but elsewhere savvy travellers seek out the delights of Old Spot pork, Cotswold honey, or Double Gloucester cheese. Tea rooms do a fine trade in cream teas, too, though it would be stretching a point to suggest that this is typical of the region.

Breakfast and lunch

A **breakfast** fry-up of bacon, eggs and sausages is considered *de rigueur* by many walkers – and supplied by nearly all good B&B hosts. Most offer a buffet of cereals and fruit juice and toast as well, perhaps with the addition of yoghurt and fresh fruit, so if a 'full English' isn't for you, you'll always be able to fall back on something lighter.

Unless you're planning to stop at a pub or café en route, you will probably need a **packed lunch**. Many B&B owners – indicated in this guide by the (Ⓛ) symbol – will provide one from around £6, and some will also fill your flask with coffee or tea. If you don't fancy breakfast, it's worth asking if you could have a packed lunch instead. Alternatively you could pick up the makings of a picnic lunch at village shops along the trail: rolls, cheese, apples and cereal bars survive well in a rucksack for a couple of days. Be careful to plan ahead, though, as there are sections of the walk when you won't come across any shops at all. In any event, you should always carry some form of high-energy food in case of emergency (see p41).

Evening meals

Perhaps more than any other national trail, the Cotswold Way is abundantly supplied with **pubs** and **inns**, not to mention some pretty exclusive **restaurants**.

❏ **Real ale along the trail**

Much of the beer found in pubs along the path is pasteurised and manufactured in millions of gallons for distribution throughout the UK. Known as keg beer, it has been reviled by real ale drinkers in its time but is invariably smooth and tastes the same wherever you are. However, traditional real ale, the product of small-scale local breweries, is always in demand. Real ale continues to ferment in the cask so can be drawn off by hand pump or a simple tap on the cask itself. Keg beer, on the other hand, has the fermentation process stopped by pasteurisation and needs the addition of gas to give it fizz and sparkle.

Keep an eye out for pubs displaying the CAMRA sticker, which shows they have been selected by the Campaign for Real Ale (💻 www.camra.org.uk). This invaluable organisation, which publishes the annual *Good Beer Guide*, has been largely responsible for the revival of independent breweries in the UK. Their 'LocAle' initiative encourages pubs to stock at least one locally brewed ale and has been taken up by an increasing number of landlords along the trail. Many also have a selection of guest ales from surrounding counties to add variety. Some of the **local brews** you'll find along the Cotswold Way are those by Donnington, Goffs, Cotswold Spring, Battledown, Wickwar, Severn Vale, Stanway, Uley, Stroud, Bath Ales, and Abbey Ales. You'll come across offerings from the Hereford-based Wye Valley Brewery, too, while the Cornish contingent is represented by Sharp's. All create good pints, but try the brews above 4% ABV for better taste and flavour.

Whether you're after a quick half at lunch or putting your feet up in the evening, there's no shortage of pubs with good-quality beer. Scanning the pumps at the *Crown & Trumpet* (see p88) in Broadway you'll spot ales from the small brewery at Stanway House, such as Stanney Bitter and Broadway Artists. Broadway comes up trumps at the *Horse and Hound* (p88) too, where you could strike lucky with a pint of Purity's Mad Goose. An evening meal at *The Mount Inn* (see p92) at Stanton washed down with a pint of Donnington's is hard to beat, or if you time it right a lunch break at *The Edgemoor Inn* (see p127) offers Wickwar's BOB amongst others, or their latest bottled ale – Cotswold Way. While wandering around Painswick, drop into the *Royal Oak* (see p126) for a selection from the Stroud or Butcombe breweries. Well worth a short detour is *The Old Crown* (see p136) at Uley which, as well as supporting its own local brewery, offers an ever-changing choice of other beers; if it all gets too much you can stay overnight, too.

Further south you arrive at ale-seekers' heaven, *The Old Spot* (see p141) in Dursley, voted the CAMRA Pub of the Year in 2007, and still maintaining high standards. It offers a wonderful array of bitters, including Old Ric from Uley (named after owner Ric Sainty, who died in 2008). The *Beaufort Arms* (see p150) at Hawkesbury Upton has an ever-changing range; continuing along the trail, *The Dog Inn* (see p154) at Old Sodbury has Sharp's Doom Bar.

Celebrations should be in order on reaching Bath (see p179), where you'll be spoiled for choice. Try *The Star Inn* or *The Old Green Tree* for a pint of Bellringer (Abbey Ales), or seek out a pint of Gem (Bath Ales) at *The Salamander*. The *Volunteer Rifleman's Arms* is another good choice, but the medal winner is arguably to be found at *The Raven*, where they have their very own brew from Blindmans Brewery, near Frome: Raven's Gold.

Where B&Bs are off the beaten track, most owners will provide an evening meal by prior arrangement, or will drive you to the nearest pub. Occasionally, however, you'll have to fend for yourself, which could involve considerable extra mileage at the end of a long day.

Aside from the ubiquitous pub grub, the choice on menus continues to widen and almost everywhere will have at least one vegetarian option. If you're keeping a strict eye on costs, stick to pubs rather than restaurants, or look for fixed-price menus – often available early in the evening before the place gets busy.

Alternatively, there are numerous **takeaways** in towns along the route, from fish and chips, pizza parlours and kebab joints to Indian and Chinese cuisine.

Self-catering

There are enough shops along the path to allow you to buy supplies reasonably frequently so, in general, you should not need to carry food for longer than a couple of days. Most village shops are open seven days a week, often from 8am to 8pm or even later, taking full advantage of casual trade and the sale of alcohol. Fuel for camp stoves may not always be available though, and, while Camping Gaz and meths can usually be found in the towns, it makes sense not to let supplies run low.

Drink

During licensing hours you can get a pint of beer (see box p23), or any other drink, in licensed premises. The key lies in the words 'during licensing hours'. Gone are the days when pubs were permitted to sell alcohol only during limited hours between 11am and 11pm Monday to Saturday and from noon on Sundays. Instead, each landlord has to apply for a licence relating to the maximum number of hours in which drinking is permitted on the individual premises. As a result, hours are far more flexible and while many pubs in rural areas still close during the afternoon on weekdays, if not at weekends, you've at least a chance of finding a thirst-quenching pint when you want it.

Note that the opening times given for pubs in Part 4 are usually those for which food is served, not necessarily the full licensing hours.

Drinking water Carry at least a litre of water and top it up at public toilets during the day: these are marked on the trail maps in Part 4. Alternatively, ask locally; most people are happy to fill a bottle of water, though it's only fair to buy something first in a pub or café. Drinking from streams is not advisable.

MONEY

Plan your money needs carefully. It makes sense to carry cash for day-to-day spending and to pay for campsites. Most pubs, and all but the smallest village shops, accept debit or credit cards, but in B&Bs payment in cash or by cheque is still the norm. Even those that have facilities for card payments will often levy an extra charge.

If you're planning to stick to cash start with about £200 and expect to replenish along the way. All the towns you pass through have ATMs, either in banks, post offices, or in supermarkets. Cash can also be drawn at post offices against many UK bank accounts: for details, see 🖥 www.postoffice.co.uk. Note that you need to have your cheque book or debit card with you and your PIN number. Travellers' cheques can be exchanged in banks, foreign exchange bureaux and the larger hotels, but not (as in the USA) in shops or restaurants, so these are of least use to the walker.

For more on money, see p41; for budgeting, see pp29-30.

OTHER SERVICES

Many of the villages and all the towns along the trail have at least one public **telephone**, a small **shop** and a **post office**, or a post office counter. Apart from getting cash, post offices are also handy for sending home unnecessary equipment that may be weighing you down. In Part 4 mention is given to other services that may be of use to the walker such as **outdoor equipment shops**, **launderettes**, **internet access**, **surgeries** (medical centres) and **pharmacies**, and **tourist information centres**. The latter can help, among other things, with finding and (sometimes) booking accommodation.

TAKING DOGS ALONG THE COTSWOLD WAY

There is no reason why your dog shouldn't accompany you on the Cotswold Way, provided you act responsibly and keep it under control at all times. The deal with dog mess is the same on a national trail as it is in the local park: clear it up. In Part 4 of this guide, the symbol 🐕 indicates that dogs are usually welcome, though you should still always check ahead; some may accept only small dogs, for example. Few B&Bs charge for dogs but hotels often do, with rates varying from £5 a night to £20 per stay. Hostels generally don't accept dogs at all, with the exception of assistance dogs.

For more on planning a walk with man's best friend, see pp187-8.

DISABLED ACCESS

Many areas of the trail are inaccessible to the majority of wheelchair and scooter users, and those of limited mobility, either because the terrain is unsuitable or because of the not inconsiderable number of kissing gates to be negotiated. Some sections, however, are more forgiving – particularly near country parks which also have nearby parking.

The Cotswolds Conservation Board (see p60) offers a series of 15 walks within the Cotswolds AONB. Entitled *Walks on Wheels*, they can be downloaded from the website. Another initiative involves the hire of off-road mobility scooters at Crickley Hill Country Park. Known as Trampers, the scooters can be hired between April and September, on completion of a short training session, and can be used on any of four waymarked trails. For more on countryside access for the disabled, contact Disabled Ramblers (🖥 www.disabledramblers.co.uk).

WALKING COMPANIES

For walkers wanting to make their holiday as easy and trouble-free as possible there are several specialist companies offering a range of services, from baggage carrying to fully guided group tours.

Baggage carriers/accommodation booking

The thought of carrying a heavy pack puts a lot of people off walking long-distance trails, but on the Cotswold Way it need not be an issue.

Using a **baggage-carrying service** to deliver your bags to your accommodation each night will leave you free to walk unencumbered (well, with just a day pack) during the day. Charges vary, but expect to pay around £10 for the first bag for each leg of the journey, with discounts usually offered for additional bags.

❏ Information for foreign visitors

● **Business hours** Most **shops and supermarkets** are open Monday to Saturday 8am-8pm (sometimes up to 15 hours a day) and on Sunday from about 9am to 5 or 6pm, though main branches of supermarkets generally open 10am-4pm or 11am-5pm; the Spar chain usually displays '8 till late' on the door. Occasionally you'll come across a local shop that closes at lunchtime on one day during the week, usually a Wednesday or Thursday; this is a throwback to the days when all towns and villages had an 'early closing day'. Main **post offices** are open at least from Monday to Friday 9am-5pm and Saturday 9am-12.30pm, but hours at rural offices, such as Painswick, may be considerably shorter. **Banks** typically open at 9.30am Monday to Friday and close at 3.30 or 4pm, though in some places they may open only two or three days a week and/or in the morning only. **ATMs** (**cash machines**) located outside a bank, shop, post office or petrol station are open all the time, but any that are inside will be accessible only when that place is open.

   Pub hours are less predictable; although many open daily 11am-11pm, opening hours in rural areas and during quieter periods (early weekdays, or in the winter months) are often more limited: typically Monday to Saturday 11am-3pm & 5 or 6-11pm, and Sunday 11am/noon-3pm & 7-10.30pm. The last entry time to most **museums and galleries** is usually half an hour, or an hour, before the official closing time.

● **Money** The British pound (£) comes in notes of £50, £20, £10 and £5, and coins of £2 and £1. The pound is divided into 100 pence (usually referred to as 'p', pronounced 'pee') which come in 'silver' coins of 50p, 20p, 10p and 5p, and 'copper' coins of 2p and 1p. Up-to-date currency **exchange rates** can be found on 🖳 www .xe.com/ ucc, at some post offices, and at most banks and travel agents.

● **Holidays** Most business premises close on **bank holidays**: 1 January, Good Friday and Easter Monday (March/April), the first and last Monday in May, the last Monday in August, Christmas Day and Boxing Day (25-26 December). **School holidays** in England vary slightly, especially if Easter is very early or late, but are generally as follows: one week in late October, two weeks over Christmas and the New Year, a week in mid February, two weeks around Easter, one week late May/early June (to coincide with the bank holiday on the last Monday in May) and six weeks from late July to early September. Private school holidays fall at the same time, but tend to be slightly longer.

● **Travel insurance and EHICs** Britain's National Health Service is free at the point of use for UK residents only. All visitors to Britain should be properly insured,

Alternatively, some of the **taxi** firms listed in Part 4 will provide a similar service on request, or you could make an arrangement with your B&B host, some of whom handle baggage transport themselves. Prices vary widely, depending on the mileage involved and the individual concerned, but generally you can expect to pay at least £20 a day, which makes a specialised baggage carrier much better value.

● **Carryabag** (☎ 01242-250642, 🖳 www.carryabag.co.uk; Cheltenham) Linked to Compass Holidays (see p28); can also arrange parking in Cheltenham for the duration of your walk and transfers to and from the trail.

● **Cotswold Luggage Transfers** (☎ 01386-840688, 🖳 www.luggage-trans fers.co.uk; Volunteer Inn, Chipping Campden; see p78) May be able to offer off-road parking in Chipping Campden while you walk.

including comprehensive health coverage. EC residents can obtain essential health treatment during a temporary visit to Britain on production of a valid EHIC card. For details, contact your national social security institution.

● **Weights and measures** Following a European Commission directive, milk in Britain may still be sold in pints (568ml), as may beer in pubs, though most other liquids including petrol (gasoline) and diesel are now sold in litres. Road distances will also continue to be given in miles (1.6km) rather than kilometres. Most food is sold in metric weights (g and kg) but the imperial weights of pounds (lb) and ounces (oz) are frequently displayed too. The population remains divided between those who still use inches and feet and those who are happy with centimetres and millimetres; you'll often be told that 'it's only a hundred yards or so' to somewhere, rather than a hundred metres or so. The weather – a frequent topic of conversation – is also an issue: while most forecasts predict temperatures in °C, many people continue to think in terms of °F.

● **Time** During the winter, the whole of Britain is on Greenwich Meantime (GMT). The clocks move forward one hour on the last Sunday in March, remaining on British Summer Time (BST) until the last Sunday in October.

● **Smoking** There has been a ban on smoking in all enclosed public areas in England since 2007. Although guesthouses, hostels and hotels may designate one or more bedrooms where the occupants can smoke, the ban remains in place in all other areas, even in a private home such as a B&B. Should you be foolhardy enough to light up in an indoor public place, you could be fined £50, but it's the owners of the premises who carry the can if they fail to stop you, with a potential fine of £2500.

● **Churches** Although some churches are open to visitors during daylight, many nowadays are kept locked for security reasons. If you'd like to take a look around, it is worth seeing if there is a note about a keyholder, or – if you are staying in a town or village – asking locally who you could contact.

● **Telephone** From outside the UK the international country access code for the UK is ☎ 44, followed by the area code minus the first 0, and then the number you require. Within the UK, to call a number with the same code as the phone you are calling from, the code can be omitted: dial the number only. It is cheaper to ring at weekends (from midnight on Friday till midnight on Sunday), and after 7pm and before 7am on weekdays. If you're using a mobile phone that is registered overseas, consider buying a local SIM card to keep costs down. See also p41 for details about using a public phone.

● **Emergency services** For police, ambulance or fire, dial ☎ 999 or ☎ 112.

PLANNING YOUR WALK

● **Sherpa Van** (☎ 01748-826917 for baggage transfer only; ☎ 01609-883731, 🖥 www.sherpavan.com; Richmond, N Yorks) Minimum two bags. Also provides an **accommodation-booking** service.

Self-guided walking holidays The following companies provide customised packages for walkers, which usually include detailed advice and notes on itineraries, maps, accommodation booking, daily baggage transfer and transport at the start and end of your walk.

● **Celtic Trails** (☎ 01291-689774, 🖥 www.celtic-trails.com; Chepstow)
● **Compass Holidays** (☎ 01242-250642, 🖥 www.compass-holidays.com; Glos)
● **Contours Walking Holidays** (☎ 01629-821900, 🖥 www.contours.co.uk; Derbyshire)
● **Cotswold Journeys** (☎ 01242-254353, 🖥 www.cotswoldjourneys.com; Cheltenham) Covers only some sections of the Cotswold Way.
● **The Cotswold Walking Company** (☎ 01242-604190, (🖥 www.thecotswold walkingcompany.com; Glos)
● **Cotswold Walks** (☎ 01386-833799, 🖥 www.cotswoldwalks.com; Worcs)
● **Discovery Travel** (☎ 01904-632226, 🖥 www.discoverytravel.co.uk; York)
● **Explore Britain** (☎ 01740-650900, 🖥 www.explorebritain.com; Co Durham)
● **Footpath Holidays** (☎ 01985-840049, 🖥 www.footpath-holidays.com; Nr Warminster, Wilts)
● **Freedom Walking Holidays** (☎ 07733-885390, 🖥 www.freedomwalking holidays.co.uk; Goring-on-Thames)
● **Let's Go Walking** (☎ 01837-880075 or ☎ 020-7193 1252, 🖥 www.letsgo walking.com; Devon)
● **Load Off Your Back** (☎ 01707-331133, 🖥 www.loadoffyourback.co.uk; Welwyn Garden City)
● **Macs Adventure** (☎ 0141-530 5463, 🖥 www.macsadventure.com; Glasgow)
● **Mickledore** (☎ 017687-72335, 🖥 www.mickledore.co.uk; Keswick)
● **Sherpa Expeditions** (☎ 020-8875 5070, 🖥 www.sherpaexpeditions.com; London) Part of the northern section only.
● **The Carter Company** (☎ 01296-631671, 🖥 www.the-carter-company.com; Bucks) Aimed at the luxury end of the market.
● **The Discerning Traveller** (☎ 01743-792622, 🖥 www.discerningtraveller .co.uk; Shropshire) Offer one-week tours along part of the Way
● **The Walking Holiday Company** (☎ 01600-713008, 🖥 www.thewalkinghol idaycompany.co.uk; Monmouth)
● **Walk the Landscape** (☎ 07718-660070, 🖥 walkthelandscape.co.uk; Banbury)
● **Walking the Cotswolds** (☎ 01386-841966, 🖥 www.cotswoldwalking.co.uk; Chipping Camden)
● **Westcountry Walking Holidays** (☎ 0330-350 1348, 🖥 www.westcountry-walking-holidays.com; Norfolk)

Group/guided walking tours Fully guided tours are ideal for individuals wanting to travel in the company of others and for groups of friends wanting the reassurance of a guide. The packages usually include meals, accommodation, transport arrangements, minibus back-up and baggage transfer, as well as a qualified guide. Companies' specialities differ widely, with varied sizes of group, standards of accommodation, age range of clients and professionalism of guides, so it's worth checking carefully before making a booking.

● **Footpath Holidays** (see opposite) Offer tours both for the whole of the Cotswold Way and selected sections.
● **HF Holidays** (☎ 0345-470 8559, 🖳 www.hfholidays.co.uk; Elstree, Herts) Covers Chipping Campden to Wotton-under-Edge.
● **Walk the Landscape** (see opposite) Offer all or part of the way, customised to meet requirements.

For those who would like **to complete the trail in stages**, there is an annual series of guided walks run by the Cotswold Voluntary Wardens. Each of the walks, which take place between May and March, covers about 10 miles, building up over 11 months to the full distance.

For the south to north route, each walk takes place on the first Wednesday of the month, starting in May in Bath, and finishing at Chipping Campden the following March. A coach (for which there is a charge) takes walkers from Winchcombe to the starting point, meets them for a pre-planned pub lunch and collects them at the end. In the other direction, walks are on the first Saturday of each month, with a coach laid on from Bath; participants are asked to bring a packed lunch. You need to commit to the full series of 11 walks, which tend to be booked up months ahead; find out more at 🖳 www.escapetothecotswolds .org.uk/walking/guided-walks.

Budgeting

How you budget for your trip will depend largely on the type of accommodation you use and where you have your meals. If you camp and cook for yourself you will be able to keep costs to a minimum. These escalate as you go up the accommodation and dining scales and will also be affected by the extent to which you use the services offered to guests, such as transportation of luggage, packed lunches and other refinements.

CAMPING

The cost of camping along the Cotswold Way varies from £3.50 to £10 per person, sometimes plus an extra £1 or so for the use of a shower. Living frugally, you could get by on as little as £10-15 per person per night, pitching your tent at official sites and cooking your own food. Most walkers, however, will indulge in the occasional cooked breakfast (around £6), the odd pint of beer (around £3.30), or a pub meal after a long hard day (£9-12), so it's probably more realistic to reckon on about £20 per day. That said, places where you can camp along the Cotswold Way are limited, so you'll almost certainly have to budget for the occasional night in a B&B if you plan to complete the whole trail in one go.

HOSTELS

In reality the only hostels you're going to find along the route are in Bath and (some way off) in Cheltenham, where you'll pay upwards of £15 a night, in some cases including a continental breakfast. Typically prices are highest at weekends and in the summer months, but other price-determining factors include group bookings and local events. Most hostels have some form of self-catering facility; where an evening meal is available you can expect to pay from around £7.50 for a main course.

B&B-STYLE ACCOMMODATION

If you're sharing a room in a B&B, pub or guesthouse, allow around £35-40 per head for an overnight stay including breakfast, perhaps more in the tourist towns over a summer weekend and certainly more if you stay in a hotel. Add on the cost of an evening meal at around £9-16; for a meal with a drink or two expect to pay £15-20. Buying a packed lunch will cost an extra £5 or so. It's therefore best to reckon on about £55-65 per person per day. Those travelling alone can anticipate at least an additional £10-20 a day for a single room, or single occupancy of a double room.

EXTRAS

Don't forget to set aside some money for the inevitable extras, such as batteries, postcards, buses and taxis, drinks, cream teas, snacks and entrance fees – or, rather more crucially, any changes of plan. Around £50-100 should be about right.

Itineraries

All walkers are individuals. Some like to cover large distances as quickly as possible. Others are happy to amble along, stopping whenever the whim takes them. You may want to walk the Cotswold Way in one go, tackle it in a series of days or weekends, or use it as the basis for individual linear walks; the choice is yours. To accommodate these different options, this guide has not been divided up into strict daily sections, which could impose too rigid a structure on how you should walk. Instead it has been designed to make it easy for you to plan the itinerary that suits you. If you need an added spur, consider signing up for the Cotswold Way Hall of Fame which recognises those who have completed the entire walk. You can download a form from the activity website of the Cotswolds AONB (🖳 www.escapetothecotswolds.org.uk/walking).

The **planning map** opposite the inside back cover and the **table of facilities** on pp34-7 summarise the essential information for you to make a plan of your own, in conjunction with the **distance chart** on pp186-7. Alternatively, to make it even easier, see the **suggested itineraries** (see p33) and simply choose your preferred speed of walking. There are also suggestions on pp36-8 for those who want to experience the best of the trail over a day or a weekend. The **public transport map** (p49) may help at this stage.

Having made a rough plan, turn to **Part 4** where you will find summaries of the route, full descriptions of accommodation, places to eat and other services in each town and village, with detailed trail maps.

WHICH DIRECTION?

Most guidebooks to the Cotswold Way assume you will walk from north to south, which is the direction that has been followed in the layout of this book. There are some compelling reasons for this. To start with, although the prevailing wind is from the west, the Cotswolds frequently experience some vicious north-easterlies, and walking into the teeth of these can be decidedly unpleasant. Then there's the fact that the north Cotswolds have more than their fair share of attractive villages and towns with plenty of places to stay and eat – so that distances can be kept shorter in the initial stages, and there's a good choice of restaurants and B&Bs at the end of a walking day. And for those in need of an incentive, what better way to celebrate the end of the walk than by relaxing in Bath's spa?

PLANNING YOUR WALK

❑ **Cotswold Way Relay**

It's been 23 years since the first Cotswold Way Relay and the event continues to attract a considerable number of teams each year. Today, though, improved waymarking along the trail means fewer runners take the 'scenic' route – something that gains considerably in significance when you realise there are no marshals to guide the way.

The record for the fastest ladies' team is held by the organisers, Team Bath Athletic Club, who in 2008 knocked five minutes off the previous time to clock up an impressive 14 hours, 6 minutes and 13 seconds. The senior men's record, though, has stood since 1995 at precisely 11 hours and 55 minutes, set by Stroud & District Athletic Club.

The race starts in Chipping Campden at 7am on the last Saturday in June, finishing at Bath Abbey as evening draws in. It follows the official route of the Cotswold Way, which is divided into 10 stages of varying lengths and difficulty. The shortest, between Dursley and Wotton-under-Edge, covers just 7¼ miles (11.5km), but some runners contend with distances of 12 miles (19km) or more, and one group faces an ascent of 513m into the bargain.

Each stage sees a mass start, triggered by the expected arrival time of the first runner from the previous leg. With the tally in 2015 totalling 100 teams, you might just want to step off the path and let them pass! You'll then have the one-upmanship of taking the time to savour the trail's attractions while others steam past with eyes only on the clock.

Of course, starting from Bath has its advantages, too. Some walkers prefer not to have the sun in their eyes, which can be a deciding factor (although less so than you might think, since the route takes a considerable number of twists and turns). Others may wish to explore one of the quintessential Cotswold villages at leisure once the walk is over. The maps in Part 4 give timings for both directions and, as route-finding instructions are on the maps rather than in the text, it is perfectly straightforward to walk from south to north using this guide.

SUGGESTED ITINERARIES

The itineraries opposite are suggestions only, based on the location of places to stay as well as the attendant distances. How you plan your walk will depend on several factors, from the availability of accommodation to personal interests, as well as the distance you choose to walk each day. Don't forget to add travelling time before and after the walk, and to allow additional time for photography and breaks – or simply to stop and stare.

SIDE TRIPS

Most people embarking on the Cotswold Way do so with the express aim of completing the walk from A to B, and there's certainly enough of interest to justify spending at least a week along the trail. Yet it's always tempting to take off the blinkers occasionally and consider what happens to left and right.

With over 3000 miles (4800km) of footpaths in the Cotswolds AONB alone, and several long-distance trails crossing the region, there's a tantalising number of **side routes** you could follow.

Winchcombe is a great place to get sidetracked, for as well as the Cotswold Way, the town is a junction for several trails. Prime among these is the **Winchcombe Way**, a 42-mile (67km) figure-of-eight route with the focus firmly on the town. Offering the option of an interesting 2-day loop are the **Warden's Way** and the **Windrush Way**, which run over different routes between Winchcombe and Bourton-on-the-Water, covering 13 and 14 miles (21km and 22.5km) respectively. Others include the **Gloucestershire Way**, which meanders for 100 miles (160km) between Chepstow and Tewkesbury, taking in the Forest of Dean and the River Severn.

If the idea of joining up the dots appeals, you could hardly do better than look at the 55-mile (88km) **Wysis Way**. As it crosses the Cotswold Way north of Painswick, it forms a link with two other national trails: Offa's Dyke Path and the Thames Path.

Further south, around Lower Kilcott, the **Monarch's Way** runs alongside the Cotswold Way for a short distance before continuing along its 615-mile (984km) journey between Worcester and Shoreham in West Sussex. The route mirrors that taken by Charles II during his escape to France after the Battle of Worcester in 1651. The journey took the king six weeks to complete – with Parliamentary forces in hot pursuit. It's certainly food for thought.

❏ SUGGESTED ITINERARIES

Few places have a campsite; those that do (as well as B&Bs) have been asterisked.

● Itinerary for slower walkers and those who want to linger

(10 days; shorter route via Middleyard)
Walking 10-11 miles (16-17.5km) a day over 10 days, with two shorter days of 7 miles (11km).

Day	Daily schedule	Miles/km	B&B-style accommodation/ Campsite*
1	Chipping Campden to Stanton	10½/17	Stanton
2	Stanton to Winchcombe	7/11	Winchcombe*
3	Winchcombe to Dowdeswell Reservoir	11/17.5	Dowdeswell Reservoir
4	Dowdeswell to Birdlip	10½/17	Birdlip
5	Birdlip to Painswick	7/11	Painswick
6	Painswick to Middleyard	10/16	Middleyard
7	Middleyard to Wotton-under-Edge	11/17.5	Wotton-under-Edge
8	Wotton-under-Edge to Little Sodbury	11/17.5	Little Sodbury
9	Little Sodbury to Cold Ashton	10.5/16.5	Cold Ashton
10	Cold Ashton to Bath	10/16	Bath

● Itinerary for steady walkers

(8 days; longer route via Selsley Common and Stinchcombe Hill)
Walking 10-14 miles (16-22.5km) a day, with one long day of 17 miles (27km)

Day	Daily schedule	Miles/km	B&B-style accommodation/ Campsite*
1	Chipping Campden to Wood Stanway	12½/20	Wood Stanway, Hailes*
2	Wood Stanway to Prestbury Hill Reserve	13/21	Prestbury Hill Reserve
3	Prestbury Hill Reserve to Birdlip	14/23	Birdlip
4	Birdlip to Selsley	17/27	Selsley
5	Selsley to North Nibley	13½/21.5	North Nibley*
6	North Nibley to Little Sodbury	13/21	Little Sodbury
7	Little Sodbury to Cold Ashton	10½/17	Cold Ashton
8	Cold Ashton to Bath	10/16	Bath

● Itinerary for faster walkers

(7 days; longer route via Selsley Common and Stinchcombe Hill)
Walking 13-17½ miles (21-28km) a day, with one shorter day of 11 miles (17.5km)

Day	Daily schedule	Miles/km	B&B-style accommodation/ Campsite*
1	Chipping Campden to Hailes	15½/25	Hailes*, North Farmcote
2	Hailes to Dowdeswell Reservoir	13/21	Dowdeswell Reservoir
3	Dowdeswell to Painswick	17½/28	Painswick
4	Painswick to Penn Wood	11/17.5	Middleyard
5	Penn Wood to Wotton-under-Edge	14½/23	Wotton-under-Edge
6	Wotton-under-Edge to Tormarton	15/24	Tormarton*
7	Tormarton to Bath	16½/26.5	Bath

PLANNING YOUR WALK

				VILLAGE AND
Place name (Places in brackets are a short walk off the Cotswold Way)	**Distance from previous place directly on Way** approx miles/km (via Selsley & Stinchcombe)	**Cash machine (ATM)**	**Post office**	**Tourist information centre (TIC) or point (TIP)**
Chipping Campden	Start of Cotswold Way	✔	✔	TIC
Broadway	6/9.5	✔	✔	TIC
Stanton	4.5/7			
Stanway	1.5/2.25			
Wood Stanway	0.5/0.75			
(North Farmcote)				
Hailes	3.5/5.5			
Winchcombe	2/3	✔	✔	TIC
Postlip	4/6.5			
Cleeve Hill	2/3			
Prestbury Hill Reserve	1.5/2.5			
(Ham Hill)				
(Charlton Kings)		✔		
Dowdeswell Reservoir	3.5/5.5			
Seven Springs	3/5			
Ullenwood	3.5/5.5			
Crickley Hill	1.5/2.5			
Birdlip	2.5/4			
(Little Witcombe)				
Cranham Corner & Painswick Hill	2/3.25			
Painswick	2.5/4	✔	✔	TIC
(Edge)				
(Randwick/Westrip)				
Stonehouse	7.5/13.5			
(King's Stanley)	(shorter route)	✔	✔	
Middleyard	1/1.5 (shorter route)			
Ebley	1/1.5 (scenic route)			
Selsley	1.5/2.5 (scenic route)			
(Nympsfield)				
(Uley)			✔	
Dursley	7.5/12 (scenic route) 6/9.5 (shorter route)	✔	✔	TIP
Stinchcombe Hill	0.5/1			
North Nibley	3.5/5.5	✔	✔	
Wotton-under-Edge	2/3	✔	✔	TIP
(Hillesley)				
Hawkesbury Upton	7.5/12.5		✔	
Horton	2.5/4			
(cont'd on p36)				

(cont'd on p36)

PLANNING YOUR WALK

TOWN FACILITIES

Eating place	Food store	Campsite	Hostel	B&B-style accommodation	Place name
✔=one; ✔✔=two; ✔✔✔=three +				✔=one ✔✔=two; ✔✔✔=three +	(Places in brackets are a short walk off the Cotswold Way; see opposite for distances)
✔✔✔	✔			✔✔✔	Chipping Campden
✔✔✔	✔			✔✔✔	Broadway
✔				✔✔✔	Stanton
✔					Stanway
				✔✔✔	Wood Stanway
				✔	(North Farmcote)
✔		✔		✔	Hailes
✔✔✔	✔	✔		✔✔✔	Winchcombe
				✔	Postlip
✔✔				✔✔✔	Cleeve Hill
				✔	Prestbury Hill Reserve
				✔✔✔	(Ham Hill)
✔	✔			✔✔	(Charlton Kings)
✔				✔	Dowdeswell Reservoir
✔✔					Seven Springs
✔			✔		Ullenwood
✔					Crickley Hill
✔				✔	Birdlip
✔				✔✔	(Little Witcombe)
✔✔					Cranham Corner & Painswick Hill
✔✔✔	✔			✔✔✔	Painswick
✔				✔	(Edge)
✔✔					(Randwick/Westrip)
					Stonehouse
✔	✔			✔	(King's Stanley)
				✔	Middleyard
	✔				Ebley
✔				✔	Selsley
✔					(Nympsfield)
✔	✔			✔	(Uley)
✔✔✔	✔			✔✔✔	Dursley (scenic route)
					Dursley (direct route)
				✔✔	Stinchcombe Hill
✔	✔	✔		✔✔	North Nibley
✔✔✔	✔			✔✔✔	Wotton-under-Edge
✔					(Hillesley)
✔✔	✔			✔✔	Hawkesbury Upton
		✔			Horton
					(cont'd on p37)

PLANNING YOUR WALK

				VILLAGE AND
Place name (Places in brackets are a short walk off the Cotswold Way)	**Distance from previous place directly on Way** approx miles/km (via Selsley & Stinchcombe)	**Cash machine (ATM)**	**Post office**	**Tourist information centre (TIC) or point (TIP)**
(cont'd from p34)				
Little Sodbury	1/1.5			
Old Sodbury	2/3			
Coomb's End	0.5/1			
Tormarton	1.5/2.5			
(South of M4)				
Pennsylvania	6/10			
Cold Ashton	0.5/1			
Bath	10/16	✔	✔	TIC

TOTAL DISTANCE 102 miles/163km via Selsley and Stinchcombe Hill, or 100.5 miles/161km otherwise

HIGHLIGHTS: THE BEST DAY AND WEEKEND WALKS

Day walks

The suggestions below take in various stretches of the Cotswold Way. In addition, the trail authorities have implemented a series of **circular walks**, ranging from 1½ to 6½ miles and varying in difficulty. Although these walks are in part waymarked with a green roundel stating 'Cotswold Way Circular Walk', these signs are designed merely to complement the detailed and regularly updated route directions that can be downloaded from ⌨ www.nationaltrail.co.uk/cotswold-way/additional-walks.

● **Chipping Campden to Broadway** (see pp81-9) A good 6-mile (9.5km) introduction to the Cotswold Way, taking in two of the trail's most attractive towns as well as some superb views from Dover's Hill and Broadway Tower. If you don't want to retrace your steps, there are buses between the two towns.

● **Broadway to Winchcombe** (see pp89-101) From one of the Cotswolds' most popular villages, this 12-mile (22km) stretch leads to one of the prettiest at Stanton – where there's an excellent pub to break up the day. The route drops down alongside the ruins of Hailes Abbey before continuing to the attractive wool town of Winchcombe. A regular bus service links the two towns.

● **Winchcombe to Cleeve Hill** (see pp101-5) A bracing 6½-miles (10.5km) will see you steadily climbing from Winchcombe up to Belas Knap long barrow (see box p101), and on through woodland to emerge on the edge of Cleeve Hill Common and the highest point of the trail, Cleeve Hill. To return, retrace your

TOWN FACILITIES

Eating place	Food store	Campsite	Hostel	B&B-style accommodation	Place name
✔=one;	* =			✔=one	(Places in brackets
✔✔=two;	limited			✔✔=two;	are a short walk
✔✔✔=three +				✔✔✔=three +	off the Cotswold Way; see opposite for distances)
					(cont'd from p35)
				✔	Little Sodbury
✔✔	✔*			✔✔✔	Old Sodbury
				✔	Coomb's End
✔✔		✔		✔✔✔	Tormarton
	✔			✔	(South of M4)
	✔*			✔	Pennsylvania
✔		✔		✔✔✔	Cold Ashton
✔✔✔	✔		✔	✔✔✔	Bath

steps to the golf club and thence to the road, where a regular bus runs to Winchcombe.

● **Dowdeswell Reservoir to Crickley Hill** (see pp112-17)   This 8-mile (12.5km) walk is ideal for nature lovers, taking in both ancient beechwoods and areas of unimproved limestone grassland, as well as the Devil's Chimney at Leckhampton and some prehistoric sites. Finish at the Air Balloon pub. Public transport at both ends of the walk is via Cheltenham.

● **Crickley Hill to Painswick** (see pp117-21)   More woods characterise this lovely 9-mile (14.5km) walk along the Cotswold escarpment, broken up by Cooper's Hill and Painswick Beacon, and finishing in the attractive town of Painswick. Buses serve both ends of the route.

● **Circular walk around Selsley Common** (see pp132-4)   Start in King's Stanley and link up with the Cotswold Way as it runs along the Stroudwater (Ebley) Canal, and thence to Selsley Common and Middleyard. It's a 5-mile (8km) round trip that takes in some spectacular views, a fascinating Arts and Crafts church, and the two alternative routes along this stretch of the Cotswold Way. A regular bus service goes to King's Stanley.

● **Bath to Dyrham Park** (see pp159-67: ie reverse of the route description)   Climb out of Bath towards the racecourse and the battlefields near Freezing Hill, then continue on to Dyrham Park. It's about 12½ miles (20km), so you might have enough time to explore the house or grounds before getting a taxi back to Bath (there are no buses to Dyrham Park).

PLANNING YOUR WALK

Weekend walks

● **Chipping Campden to Cleeve Hill** (see pp81-105) If there's one walk along the trail that showcases the quintessential Cotswolds, this is it. Villages of Cotswold stone, rolling hills, woodland and some excellent views: they're all in this 24-mile (38.5km) route. Buses serve both ends of the walk.

● **Dursley to Tormarton** (see pp141-58) Most of this 22-mile (35km) walk follows the edge of the Cotswold escarpment, sometimes wooded, at others more open, with numerous small villages and the final stretch through Dodington Park. There are buses at both ends of the route.

What to take

How much you take with you is a very personal decision which takes experience to get right. For those new to long-distance walking the suggestions below will help you strike a sensible balance between comfort, safety and minimal weight.

KEEP YOUR LUGGAGE LIGHT

If there's one maxim that is crucial to long-distance walking, it's 'keep it light'. It is all too easy to take things along 'just in case' but such items can soon mount up. If you are in any doubt about anything on your packing list, be ruthless and leave it at home. You're rarely far from a shop on the Cotswold Way, so if you find you've left out something that turns out to be essential, the chances are you'll be able to pick up an equivalent easily enough.

HOW TO CARRY IT

The size of your rucksack depends on how you plan to walk. If you are staying in B&Bs or pubs, you should be able to get all you need into a 40- to 50-litre pack: large enough for a change of clothes, waterproofs, essential toiletries and first-aid kit, a water bottle, a packed lunch, and ideally a change of shoes. Pack similar things in different-coloured stuff sacks or plastic bags so they are easier to pull out of the dark recesses of your pack, then put these inside a waterproof rucksack liner, or tough plastic sack, to protect everything if it rains. Those camping will also need space for a tent, sleeping bag, cooking equipment, towel and food: 65-75 litres' capacity should be about right.

Whatever its size, make sure before you set off that your rucksack is comfortable. Ideally it should have a stiffened back system and either be fully adjustable or exactly the right size for your back. Carrying the main part of the load high and close to your body with a large proportion of the weight on your hips (rather than on your shoulders) by means of the padded waist belt should allow you to walk in comfort for days on end. Play around with different ways of packing your gear and adjust all those straps until you get it just right. A useful extra is a bum/waist bag or a very light daypack to carry a camera, wallet and other essentials if you go off sightseeing.

Of course, if you decide to use a baggage-carrying service (see pp26-8) you can pack most of your things separately and simply carry a daypack with the essentials for a day's walking.

FOOTWEAR

A comfortable, well-fitting pair of leather or Gore-Tex-lined **boots** is the best footwear you can take and essential if you're carrying a heavy rucksack. In addition to offering proper ankle support, which is particularly important on rough ground, they are most likely to keep your feet dry. Make sure they are properly waxed or waterproofed, both before you set out and during your walk.

Traditionally walkers wear two pairs of **socks**, one thin pair, with a thicker pair on top. Aside from adding warmth, this is a good blister-avoidance strategy, though modern walking socks with two inbuilt layers can do the job just as well. Taking three pairs of socks should be ample.

In summer you could get by with a light pair of trail **shoes** if you're carrying only a small pack, though it's not generally advisable. A second pair of shoes to wear in the evening is well worth taking – they can be useful in case of injury, too. Lightweight trainers are best for the cooler months; in summer sports sandals are equally suitable.

CLOTHES

Wet and cold weather can catch you out even in summer, while spring and summer can be glorious at times, so go prepared for the unexpected. Most walkers pick their clothes according to the versatile layering system, which consists of: a base layer to transport sweat away from your skin; a mid layer or two to keep you warm; and an outer layer or 'shell' to protect you from the wind and rain.

Thermal material is ideal for **base layers** as it draws moisture away from the skin, keeping you drier (and thus warmer when you stop for a break) than a conventional cotton T-shirt. A **mid layer** of micro-fleece is ideal, being both warm and light, with an additional sweater or fleece useful for colder days or when you stop as you can get cold very quickly. Both thermal tops and fleeces have the added advantage that they dry relatively quickly.

All this pales into insignificance when it comes to **waterproofs**. A waterproof jacket is essential year-round and will be much more comfortable (but also more expensive) if it's also 'breathable' to prevent the build-up of condensation on the inside. It can also be worn to protect you against the wind. Waterproof trousers are important most of the year but in summer could be left behind if your main pair of trousers is reasonably windproof and quick-drying. Gaiters are rarely necessary, though they come into their own if you're walking through wet crops.

PLANNING YOUR WALK

Trousers and **shorts** should be light and quick-drying: trousers with zipped legs that convert into shorts can be ideal, especially in summer when the weather can change rapidly. Never wear denim jeans for walking: if they get wet they become heavy, cold and very uncomfortable. In winter, or if you're camping, consider a pair of thermal **longjohns** or thick tights.

What you take in the way of **underwear** is very much a personal preference, but if you want to change every day, you'll need three sets to ensure you always have one dry. Women may find a **sports bra** more comfortable because pack straps can cause bra straps to dig into your shoulders.

A **warm hat** is important at any time of the year, and **gloves**, too, except perhaps in the height of summer. It's surprising how quickly you can get cold if it's raining. In summer a **sunhat** will help to keep you cool and prevent sunburn; **swimming gear** would be useful if you plan to take advantage of one of the pools en route. Finally, don't forget a **change of clothes** for the evenings. While wearing the same kit all week suits some, putting on clean clothes after a shower is a great morale boost – and will probably make you feel more comfortable if you're eating out.

TOILETRIES

Take only the minimum. In addition to **toothpaste** and a **toothbrush**, **sunscreen** is invaluable; you'll need a small bar of **soap** if you're camping. Also take a suitable supply of any **medication** and, for women **tampons/sanitary towels**. A roll of **loo paper** in a plastic bag is handy, as is a lightweight **trowel** if you get caught out far from a toilet (see p53). What you pack in the line of deodorants, razors, hairbrushes etc is a matter of personal preference.

FIRST-AID KIT

Medical facilities in Britain are good so you only need the essentials to cover basic problems and emergencies. Ideally, take a waterproof bag containing the following: **plasters/Band Aids** for minor cuts; **Compeed**, **Moleskin** or **Second Skin** for blisters; a selection of different-sized **sterile dressings** for wounds; **porous adhesive tape**; a **stretch bandage** for holding dressings or splints in place and for supporting a sprained ankle; a **triangular bandage** to make a sling for a broken or sprained arm; **elastic knee support** for a weak knee; **antiseptic wipes**; **antiseptic cream**; **safety pins**, **tweezers** and **scissors**; and **aspirin** or **paracetamol** for mild to moderate pain and fever.

Most importantly, do make sure you have a modicum of first-aid knowledge, or much of your kit will be rendered useless.

GENERAL ITEMS

Essential

Essential items you should carry are a **whistle** to attract attention if you get lost or find yourself in trouble; a **torch** (flashlight) with spare bulb and batteries in case you end up walking after dark; a one- or two-litre **water bottle/pouch**;

emergency food such as chocolate, cereal bars, or dried fruit; a **penknife** and a **watch**. If you're not carrying a sleeping bag or tent you could also consider carrying an emergency plastic **bivvy-bag** – although at no stage on the route are you far from civilisation. A **compass** can be invaluable, especially in poor visibility, but do make sure you know how to use it.

Useful

Many would list a **camera** (and a **spare memory card** or **film** and **batteries**) as essential but a **notebook** or **sketchbook** are other good ways of recording your impressions, and **binoculars** mean you can observe wildlife more easily. A pair of **sunglasses** is useful, as is a **vacuum flask** for hot drinks. A **walking stick** or **pole** helps to take the shock off your knees (some walkers use two poles but this leaves no free hand).

A **mobile phone** is useful, although there are areas without any signal. For this reason, make sure that you always have the wherewithal to call from a public phone box in case you have no signal at the crucial moment. Calls to the emergency services (☎ 999, or ☎ 112) are free of charge, but those urgent calls to book a night's accommodation can catch you out. Calls cost a minimum of 40p, but increasingly you will need a credit, debit, BT or **prepaid phone card** instead. (Insert the card then follow the instructions.)

A **GPS** (see pp17-18) device could also be useful in an emergency, but not as an alternative to a compass: batteries could just fail when most needed.

CAMPING GEAR

If you're camping you will need a decent **tent** able to withstand wet and windy weather; a two- or three-season **sleeping bag**; a **sleeping mat**; a **stove** and **fuel**; **cooking equipment** (a pan with frying pan that can double as a lid/plate is fine for two people); a **bowl**, **mug** and **cutlery** (don't forget a can/bottle opener); and a **scourer** for washing up.

MONEY

The best way to carry your money is as **cash**. There are banks and/or post offices in most of the towns along the path, and ATMs in some others, so withdrawing money along the route with a **debit (or credit) card** is fairly straightforward. Cards are also the easiest way to pay in restaurants, hotels and supermarkets, many of which offer a cash-back facility. For most B&Bs you'll need to pay in cash or – for those with a British bank account – by **cheque**. For more details, see p25.

TRAVEL INSURANCE

Do consider insurance cover for loss or theft of personal belongings, especially if you are camping or staying in hostels, as there may be times when you'll have to leave your belongings unattended. Many British walkers will be covered under their home insurance policy, but it's worth checking this.

For health insurance for visitors from overseas, see box pp26-7.

PLANNING YOUR WALK

MAPS

The hand-drawn maps in this book cover the trail at a scale of 1:20,000, with plenty of detail and information to keep you on the right track. The **Ordnance Survey** (💻 www.ordnancesurvey.co.uk) covers the whole route at a scale of 1:25,000 on four maps within their Explorer series: Nos 179, 168, 167 and 155, each costing £8.99, or £14.99 for the 'weatherproof active' version. Fortunately, none of these is strictly necessary if you pay careful attention to the maps in this

---

❏ SOURCES OF FURTHER INFORMATION

Trail information
Cotswold Way National Trail Office (💻 www.nationaltrail.co.uk/cotswold-way) The website includes news of diversions and the occasional route change as well as details of events and other trail information.

Tourist information offices
Tourist information offices provide all manner of locally specific information for visitors, although generally they are not there to proffer advice. A few – specifically in Bath and Cheltenham – have paid staff and offer an accommodation-booking service (for which there may be a charge). Others along the Cotswold Way are staffed by volunteers who usually have information on accommodation but may not be able to book it for you.

There are tourist offices on or near the Cotswold Way in **Chipping Campden** (see p75), **Broadway** (see p85), **Winchcombe** (see p98), **Cheltenham** (see p108), **Painswick** (see p125), **Wotton-under-Edge** (see p148) and **Bath** (see p169).

Tourist boards
The Cotswolds (💻 www.cotswolds.com) has responsibility for all matters touristic throughout the region. Bath, though, is covered by its own authority, **Visit Bath** (💻 visitbath.co.uk). Another excellent source of information is **The Cotswolds Conservation Board** (see p60).

Organisations for walkers
● **Backpackers Club** (💻 www.backpackersclub.co.uk) Aimed at people who are involved or interested in lightweight camping through walking, cycling, skiing, canoeing, etc. They produce a quarterly magazine, provide members with a comprehensive advisory and information service on all aspects of backpacking, organise weekend trips and also publish a farm-pitch directory. Membership is £15/20 individual/family per year.
● **The Long Distance Walkers' Association** (💻 www.ldwa.org.uk) Annual membership, at £13/19.50 individual/family, includes three copies of *Strider* magazine a year giving details of challenge events and local group walks as well as articles on the subject. Information on 730 long-distance paths is presented in their *UK Trailwalker's Handbook*.
● **Ramblers** (formerly Ramblers' Association; 💻 www.ramblers.org.uk) Looks after the interests of walkers throughout Britain. They publish a large amount of useful information including their quarterly *Walk* magazine (£3.60 to non-members), and have an extensive map library that is free to members. Membership costs £34/45/20.50 individual/joint/concessionary; £10 discount for individual/joint membership if paid by direct debit.

guide, which should help to lighten your load somewhat. That said, it's a good idea for safety's sake to carry the map covering the highest point of the walk, Cleeve Hill Common (Explorer 179). Although the area is not particularly isolated, visibility up there can be seriously compromised when the mist comes down, making it easy to become disorientated and wander dangerously close to the edge of the escarpment. In such conditions a map from which you can take compass bearings is essential.

Another useful option is the **Harvey** map (💻 www.harveymaps.co.uk) which covers the whole route at 1.40,000 on a single, waterproof sheet and costs £13.95. It's also available as a digital download at £12.99.

To save on expense, it's worth noting that members of Ramblers (see box opposite) can borrow maps from their library free of charge.

RECOMMENDED READING
Field guides
There are plenty of good field guides on the market, though deciding which, if any, will justify space in a rucksack is a tough decision. The series published by Collins is unfailingly practical, if a little dated, though for visual appeal – and particularly bird identification – the RSPB's guides come out ahead.
- *Insects of Britain and Western Europe* by Michael Chinery (Collins, 2012)
- *The Mammals of Britain and Europe* by David Macdonald and Priscilla Barrett (Collins, 2005)
- *RSPB Pocket Birds* (Dorling Kindersley, 2012)
- *RSPB What's that Tree?* by Tony Russell (Dorling Kindersley, 2013)
- *Wild Flowers of Britain and Northern Europe* by Richard Fitter, Alastair Fitter and Marjorie Blamey (Collins, 1996)

General reading
- *The Hidden Landscape: A Journey into the Geological Past* by Richard Fortey (Bodley Head, 2010) brings vividly and clearly to life the evolution of a landscape which most of us take for granted.
- *The Arts and Crafts Movement* by Elizabeth Cumming and Wendy Kaplan (Thames & Hudson, 1991) is an accessible introduction to the complexities of the movement (see box p76), from its roots in Britain to continental Europe and the United States.

Biography
No journey through the Cotswolds is complete without Laurie Lee's classic childhood autobiography, *Cider with Rosie* (Vintage Classics, 2002).

Fiction
The novelist Jane Austen lived in Bath for five years and set two of her novels, *Northanger Abbey* and *Persuasion*, in the city. Both can be found in several editions, including Penguin Classics, and afford a rather different perspective on the city and society to that seen by today's visitors.

PLANNING YOUR WALK

More recently, JK Rowling of *Harry Potter* fame hails from the Cotswolds; indeed, the town of Dursley is evoked in the surname of Harry's unpleasant uncle and aunt – though there the connection ends.

If you're into crime fiction, the Cotswold Mysteries by Rebecca Tope, with titles such as *A Grave in the Cotswolds* (Allison and Busby, 2011), should give you something to ponder as you walk along the trail.

Poetry

Most prolific among the poets whose work has been influenced by the Cotswolds is the war poet Ivor Gurney (1890-1937), who was born in Gloucester and served in World War I, before suffering severe mental problems and being confined to an institution. Others include James Elroy Flecker (1884-1915), who was buried in Cheltenham; and WH Davies (1871-1940), known the world over for his poem, *Leisure* (see p53), who made his home in Gloucestershire. Their work can be found in numerous poetry anthologies.

Getting to and from the Cotswold Way

While Bath at the southern end of the trail is easily reached by train, bus, National Express coach or car, getting to and from Chipping Campden is more of a challenge. The nearest railway station is at Moreton-in-Marsh, from where there's a local bus, but taking a train to Stratford-upon-Avon, followed by a bus or taxi, is a viable alternative. For details, see p75 in Part 4 under Chipping Campden and the public transport tables on pp48-50.

Although there are no other railway stations on the trail itself, trains do service Stonehouse, about half a mile (1km) west of the trail where it meets the

---

❏ GETTING TO BRITAIN

● **By air** Most international airlines serve London Heathrow (🖳 www.heathrowair port.com) and London Gatwick (🖳 www.gatwickairport.com). A number of budget airlines fly from many of Europe's major cities to the other London airports: London City Airport (🖳 www.londoncityairport.com); Stansted (🖳 www.stanstedairport .com) and Luton (🖳 www.london-luton.co.uk).

There are a few flights from mainland Europe to Bristol (🖳 www.bristolair port.co.uk) and Birmingham (🖳 www.birminghamairport.co.uk), which are closer to the Cotswold Way than London.

● **From mainland Europe by train** Eurostar (🖳 www.eurostar.com) operates a high-speed passenger service via the Channel Tunnel between Paris/Brussels and London. Trains arrive and depart London from the international terminal at St Pancras station, which itself has connections to the London Underground and to all other main railway stations in London.

For more information on rail travel from Europe contact Voyage-SNCF (🖳 voy ages-sncf.com), your rail network, or Railteam (🖳 www.railteam.eu).

Stroudwater (Ebley) Canal. There is also Cam & Dursley station, almost three miles (4.8km) north of Dursley, with a bus service to the town centre. Connections to Cheltenham, about 2½ miles (4km) west of the trail, are excellent. It is also possible to take the train to Stroud or Gloucester, then transfer by bus from there.

A network of local buses links many of the villages along the Cotswold Way, making it possible – with a bit of planning – to create a series of linear walks without having to retrace your steps.

NATIONAL TRANSPORT

By rail

The rail services of most relevance to walkers along the Cotswold Way are from London Paddington to Moreton-in-Marsh (1½hrs; for Chipping Campden about 3hrs) and from Paddington to Bath (about 2hrs), although there are also trains to Cheltenham Spa from Paddington, with connections from there to Cam & Dursley. A viable alternative to Chipping Campden is the Chiltern Railways service from London Marylebone to Stratford-upon-Avon.

To get to Moreton-in-Marsh from Bath, or vice versa, at the end of your walk, the route with the fewest changes is via Reading.

Fares vary very widely, but significant savings can be made by booking well in advance and by travelling at off-peak times. For the latest on train times, fares and rail information, contact **National Rail Enquiries** (☎ 03457-484950, or – from overseas – ☎ +44 (0)20-7278 5240, 🖳 www.nationalrail.co.uk).

If you think you may need to book a taxi when you arrive, check the relevant place in the route guide or visit 🖳 www.traintaxi.co.uk for details of taxi companies operating at railway stations throughout England. It is also possible to book train tickets that include bus travel to your ultimate destination: enquire when you book your train ticket, or look at 🖳 www.plusbus.info.

PLANNING YOUR WALK

● **From Europe by coach** Eurolines (🖳 www.eurolines.com) works with 32 long-distance coach operators across mainland Europe to provide an integrated network connecting some 500 destinations to the UK, where it links with the National Express network (see p46). Megabus (🖳 megabus.com) also provides services from destinations in mainland Europe to London.

● **From Europe by car** The shortest ferry crossing is between Calais and Dover. An alternative point of embarkation is Dunkerque. There are also numerous other ferry services linking the major North Sea and Channel ports of mainland Europe with ports along Britain's eastern and southern coasts. Both 🖳 www.ferrysavers.com and 🖳 www.directferries.com have a full list of companies and services.

Eurotunnel (🖳 www.eurotunnel.com) operates the shuttle (Le Shuttle) train service for vehicles via the Channel Tunnel between Calais and Folkestone, taking about an hour between the motorway in France and the motorway in Britain. At peak times there are several trains an hour.

❏ **RAIL SERVICES**

Chiltern Railways (☎ 0345-600 5165, 🖳 www.chilternrailways.co.uk)
● London Marylebone to **Stratford-upon-Avon** via Leamington Spa & Warwick, Mon-Sat 6/day, Sun 5/day. Additional services require a change at Solihull or Birmingham.

Cross Country (☎ 0844-811 0124, 🖳 www.crosscountrytrains.co.uk)
● Edinburgh to Bristol via Newcastle-upon-Tyne, York, Leeds, Birmingham New Street & **Cheltenham Spa**, daily approx 1/hr
　　Some services continue to Exeter and Plymouth; others link in to destinations that include Aberdeen, Glasgow, Reading, Southampton and Bournemouth
● Bristol Temple Meads to **Cheltenham Spa** via **Bristol Parkway**, Mon-Sat approx 2/hr, Sun 1/hr

First Great Western (☎ 0345-7000 125, 🖳 www.firstgreatwestern.co.uk)
● London Paddington to Bristol Temple Meads via Reading, Swindon, Chippenham & **Bath Spa**, Mon-Sat approx 2/hr, Sun 1/hr (some services continue to Weston-super-Mare)
● London Paddington to **Cheltenham Spa** via Reading, Swindon, Kemble, Stroud, **Stonehouse** & Gloucester, Mon-Sat approx 1/hr, Sun 8/day (some services require a change at Swindon)
● London Paddington to Worcester via Reading, Oxford, **Moreton-in-Marsh** & **Evesham**, daily approx 1/hr
● Bristol Temple Meads to Gloucester via Bristol Parkway, Yate & **Cam & Dursley**, Mon-Sat approx 1/hr, Sun 6/day

South West Trains (☎ 0345-6000 650, 🖳 www.southwesttrains.co.uk)
● London Waterloo to Bristol Temple Meads via Clapham Junction, Woking, Basingstoke, Andover, Salisbury & **Bath Spa**, Mon-Sat 3/day, Sun 1/day.

By coach

National Express is the principal long-distance bus operator in Britain. Travel by coach is usually cheaper than by train but takes rather longer. Advance bookings can carry significant discounts so it makes sense to book at least a week ahead. The service of greatest use to Cotswold Way walkers is that to Bath, but coaches also run regularly to Cheltenham and Stroud. Local buses connect Cheltenham and Stroud to several points along the trail. See coach services box opposite; note that not all stops are listed.

By car

Chipping Campden lies west of Oxford, so the best access is via the M40 from London or Birmingham, leaving at junction 8 (northbound) or 9 (southbound) to link up with the A44 towards Evesham. The turning to Chipping Campden is the B4081 beyond Moreton-in-Marsh. Getting to **Bath** is infinitely more straightforward: leave the M4 at junction 18, then take the A46.

　　The greater problem is what to do with your car while you are tramping along the trail – and how to get back to it when you reach the end. **Parking** on the road in Bath is not an option, while the maximum stay in the city's multi-storey car

---

❏ **COACH SERVICES**

National Express (☎ 08717-818181, 🖳 www.nationalexpress.com)

327 Scarborough to Bristol via Hull, Nottingham, Leicester, Birmingham, **Evesham**, **Cheltenham**, **Gloucester** & **Stroud**, 1/day

337 Rugby to Teignmouth via Coventry, Warwick, **Stratford-upon-Avon**, **Evesham**, **Cheltenham**, **Gloucester**, Bristol & Exeter, 1/day

403 London Victoria Coach Station (VCS) to **Bath** via **Chippenham**, 10-12/day; some services call at Heathrow Airport & Reading-Calcot

444 London VCS to Gloucester via **Cheltenham**, 8/day
London VCS to Hereford via Oxford, **Cheltenham** & Gloucester, 3/day
London VCS to Worcester via Oxford & **Cheltenham**, 2/day
(1/day calls at Tewkesbury)

445 London VCS to Hereford via Cirencester, **Stroud** & **Gloucester**, 2/day

460 London VCS to **Stratford-upon-Avon** via Coventry, Leamington Spa & Warwick, 3/day

---

parks is seven days, which is tight for all but the fastest of walkers. In Chipping Campden, on-street parking is unrealistic, though the occasional B&B may allow you to park for a week or so, provided you stay with them for a night or two. Given the logistics of returning to their starting point, many walkers choose to leave their car at home, but two of the companies that arrange luggage transfer may be able to store your vehicle and organise transport to, or from, the start/end of the trail (see p27).

LOCAL TRANSPORT

The public transport map on p49 gives an overview of the most useful bus and train routes for walkers. For contact details and the approximate frequency of rail services see box opposite, coach services box above and local buses box pp48-50.

While individual **timetables** are available from operators, more useful is a series of leaflets published by the Cotswolds Conservation Board, entitled *Explore the Cotswolds by Public Transport*. These are updated twice a year, in January and July, and are available online at 🖳 www.escapetothecotswolds.org .uk/visitor-info/gettinghere, or from most tourist information centres along the route. All timetables for bus services operating in, or through, Gloucestershire can be found on 🖳 www.easytraveling.org.uk/gcc.

In addition to the companies listed in the boxes opposite, above and on pp48-50, information can be obtained from the national public transport information line, **traveline** (🖳 www.traveline.org.uk).

Although much of the trail is well served by local bus services, there is little in the way of an integrated service, particularly between the northern and southern parts of the route. Most operators issue timetables twice a year; while these vary less than in some areas, it is important to check ahead to make sure the service you want is running.

❏ LOCAL BUS SERVICES

Note that most local bus companies have no service on a Sunday. However, if there is a Sunday service it almost always operates on a Bank Holiday Monday as well.
   Also, not all stops are listed.

● **Coachstyle** (☎ 01249-782224, 🖳 www.coachstyle.ltd.uk)
41   Malmesbury to Yate via Badminton, Tormarton, **Old Sodbury** & Chipping
   Sodbury, Mon-Sat 4/day

● **Cotswold Green** (☎ 01453-835153)
35   Stroud to **Cam & Dursley station** via **Selsley**, Nympsfield, Uley & **Dursley**,
   Mon-Fri 3/day plus 2/day to Dursley, Sat 3/day
40   Stroud to **Wotton-under-Edge** via Nailsworth, Mon-Sat 4/day
230   Stroud circular route via **Ebley** & **Randwick**, Mon-Sat 3/day

● **First** (☎ 0845-606 4446, 🖳 www.firstgroup.com/bristol-bath-and-west)
1   **Weston** to Coombe Down via **Bath** bus station, Mon-Sat 1-2/hr, Sun 1/hr

● **Johnsons** (☎ 01564-797000, 🖳 www.johnsonscoaches.co.uk)
21   Stratford-upon-Avon to Moreton-in-Marsh via **Chipping Campden**, Willersey
   & **Broadway**, Mon-Sat 4/day
22   Stratford-upon-Avon to Moreton-in-Marsh via **Chipping Campden**,
   Mon-Sat 4/day
24/24A Evesham to Stratford-upon-Avon via **Broadway**, Willersey & **Chipping
   Campden**, Mon-Sat 2-3/day

● **Marchants Coaches** (☎ 01242-257585, 🖳 www.marchants-coaches.com)
606 Cheltenham to Willersey via **Cleeve Hill**, **Winchcombe**, Greet, **Stanton
   Turn** & **Broadway**, Mon-Sat 3-4/day plus 3-4/day to Greet, Sun 1/day to
   Winchcombe, 1/day to Greet & 1/day to Broadway
606S Cheltenham to Stratford-upon-Avon via **Cleeve Hill**, **Winchcombe**, Greet,
   Stanton North Turn, **Broadway** & Willersey, May-Oct Sun & Bank Hol Mons
   2/day plus 2/day to Greet and 1/day to Broadway
W1 & W2 Cheltenham circular routes via **Winchcombe** and **Cleeve Hill**,
   Mon-Sat (13/day each service)

● **Mike's Travel** (☎ 01454-281417)
201 Gloucester to Thornbury via **North Nibley** & **Wotton-under-Edge**,
   Mon-Sat 1/day

● **NN Cresswell** (☎ 01386-48655, 🖳 www.nncresswell.co.uk)
R4 (Rural 4) Willersey to Evesham via **Broadway**, Mon-Sat 4-6/day

● **Pulhams Coaches** (☎ 01451-820369, 🖳 www.pulhamscoaches.com)
801 Cheltenham to Moreton-in-Marsh via Charlton Kings, Lower Dowdeswell,
   Dowdeswell Reservoir (*request only*), Northleach, Bourton-on-the-Water &
   Stow-on-the-Wold, Mon-Sat 8/day, May-Sep Sun 2/day and bank hols 3/day,
   via Dowdeswell, Bourton-on-the-Water & Stow-on-the-Wold
852 Gloucester to Cirencester via **Little Witcombe** (2/day), Witcombe (2/day), Air
   Balloon (Crickley Hill) & **Birdlip**, Mon-Fri 4/day, Sat 3/day

(*continued on p50*)

PLANNING YOUR WALK

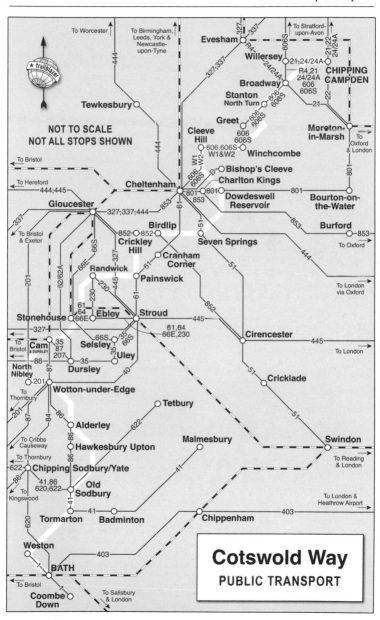

PLANNING YOUR WALK

Cotswold Way
PUBLIC TRANSPORT

❏ **LOCAL BUS SERVICES** *(continued from p48)*

● **Severnside Transport** (STL; ☎ 01454-868544, 🖥 www.severnsidetransport.co.uk)
87 Cribbs Causeway to **Dursley** via **Wotton-under-Edge** & Cam & Dursley
   railway station, Sat 5-6/day
622 Thornbury to Tetbury via Yate, Chipping Sodbury & **Old Sodbury**,
   Mon-Sat 6-7/day

● **Stagecoach West** (🖥 www.stagecoachbus.com)
51 Swindon to Cheltenham via Cricklade, Cirencester, **Seven Springs**,
   Mon-Sat 1/hr, Cirencester to Cheltenham via **Seven Springs**, Sun 5/day
61 Cheltenham to **Dursley** via Cranham Corner, **Painswick**, Stroud, Ebley &
   Stonehouse, Mon-Fri 12/day, Sat 10/day
   Cheltenham to Stroud via Cranham Corner & **Painswick**, Sun 6/day
62/62A Gloucester to **Dursley** via Quedgley, Mon-Sat approx 1/hr, Sun 4/day
64 Stroud to **Stonehouse** via Ebley, Mon-Fri 7/day, Sat 1/hr
66E Gloucester to Stroud via Stonehouse & **Ebley**, Mon-Sat 1/hr, Sun 4/day
66S Gloucester to Stroud via Stonehouse, Bridgend, Leonard Stanley, **King's
   Stanley, Middleyard** & Selsley, Mon-Sat 1/hr, Sun 5/day
88 Bristol to **Dursley** via Berkeley, Mon-Fri 5/day, Sat 3/day
D Hatherley to Bishop's Cleeve via Cheltenham Spa railway station and
   the racecourse, Mon-Sat 6/hr, Sun 2/hr

● **Swanbrook** (☎ 01452-712386, 🖥 www.swanbrook.co.uk)
853 Gloucester to Oxford via Cheltenham, Charlton Kings, Burford & Witney,
   Mon-Sat 2/day, Mon-Fri plus 1/day and Sat 2/day Cheltenham to Oxford

● **Third Sector Services** (☎ 0845-680 5029, 🖥 thirdsectorservices.org.uk
207 **Dursley** to Cam & Dursley railway station, Mon-Fri 1-3/day early morning,
   Sat 2/day in the afternoon

● **Wessex** (☎ 0117-986 9953, 🖥 www.wessexbus.com)
84 Yate to **Wotton-under-Edge** via Chipping Sodbury, Mon-Fri 10/day, Sat 8/day
86 Kingswood to **Wotton-under-Edge** via Yate, Chipping Sodbury, **Old Sodbury**,
   Horton, Hawkesbury Upton, Hillesley & **Alderley**, Mon-Fri 5/day plus 1/day
   Chipping Sodbury to **Wotton-under-Edge**,
   Sat 3/day plus 2/day Kingswood to Chipping Sodbury
620 **Old Sodbury** to **Bath** via Chipping Sodbury & Yate, Mon-Fri 6/day, Sat 4/day

MINIMUM IMPACT & OUTDOOR SAFETY

Minimum-impact walking

Walk as if you are kissing the Earth with your feet
Thich Nhat Hanh, *Peace is every step*

Simply by visiting the Cotswolds you are making a positive impact on the local community – as well as on your well-being. Your presence brings money into the local economy and creates jobs for local people. It ensures that the area maintains a high profile and helps to strengthen the value of local crafts such as dry-stone walling (see box p10) that could otherwise be left to die out. So much for the positives.

On the other side, there is the risk that large numbers of tourists can unwittingly destroy the very place they have come to enjoy. If such tourists adopt a blinkered approach, damage – both environmental and social – is inevitable. But if visitors make the effort to work with local communities to protect the environment, everyone will benefit.

The following guidelines are designed to help you reduce your impact on the environment where you are a visitor, to encourage conservation and to promote sustainable tourism in the area.

ECONOMIC IMPACT

Communities along the Cotswold Way are no strangers to crises, from foot-and-mouth disease to widespread flooding. More generally, political and economic expediency threatens the closure of rural post offices and local hospitals. Yet walkers can play their part in helping to keep such communities economically viable. The watchword is 'local': buy local, support local businesses, encourage local skills, all of which bring significant social, environmental and psychological benefits.

Support local businesses
Rural businesses and communities in Britain have been hit hard in recent years by a seemingly endless series of crises. Most people are aware of the Countryside Code – not dropping litter and closing the gate behind you are still as pertinent as ever – but in light of the economic pressures there is something else you can do: **buy local**.

Look and ask for local produce to buy and eat; not only does this cut down on the amount of pollution and congestion that the transportation of food creates (the so-called 'food miles'), but also ensures that you are supporting local farmers and producers; the very people who have moulded the countryside you have come to see and who are in the best position to protect it. If you can find local food which is also organic so much the better.

It's a fact of life that money spent at local level – perhaps in a market, or at the greengrocer, or in an independent pub – has a far greater impact for good on that community than the equivalent spent in a branch of a national chain store or restaurant. While no-one would advocate that walkers should boycott the larger supermarkets, which after all do provide local employment, it's worth remembering that businesses in rural communities rely heavily on visitors for their very existence.

ENVIRONMENTAL IMPACT

By choosing to walk you have already made a positive step towards minimising your impact on the wider environment. By following these suggestions you can also tread lightly through the Cotswolds.

Use public transport whenever possible
Using public transport rather than private cars benefits both visitors and locals, as well as the environment. Local buses (see pp48-50) service many of the villages through which you'll pass and it's often possible to use them at the end of a day or several days on the trail to get back to a convenient point. Also of use are local taxi firms, which are only too happy to ferry walkers or their luggage around.

Never leave litter
Leaving litter shows a total disrespect for the natural world and others coming after you. As well as being unsightly and unhygienic, litter kills wildlife, pollutes the environment and can be dangerous to farm animals. **Please** remove your rubbish and dispose of it in a bin in the next village. It would be helpful if you were to pick up litter left by other people too.

● **The lasting impact of litter** A piece of silver foil left on the ground takes 18 months to decompose; a plastic bag 10 years; clothes 15 years; and an aluminium can 85 years. Would you want your great-grandchildren to find your discarded lemonade can next to their picnic?

● **Is it OK if it's biodegradable?** Not really. Apple cores, banana skins and the like are unsightly, encourage flies, ants and wasps, and can ruin a picnic spot for others. Orange peel left on the ground takes six months to decompose.

Erosion
● **Stay on the waymarked trail** Please. The effect of your footsteps may seem minuscule but when they are multiplied by several thousand walkers each year they become rather more significant. Avoid taking shortcuts, widening the trail or creating more than one path; your boots will be followed by many others.

● **Consider walking out of season** As the weather warms up, so plants start to grow and walkers appear on the hillsides. Thus areas of the trail subject to the greatest pressure are often prevented from recovering. Walking at less busy times eases this pressure on the environment. It can also be more rewarding, with fewer people on the trail and a more relaxed atmosphere prevalent among local communities.

Respect all wildlife

Care for all wildlife you come across on the path; it has just as much of a right to be there as you. Tempting as it may be to pick wild flowers, leave them so the next person who passes can enjoy them too. Don't break branches off or damage trees in any way.

What is this life if, full of care,
We have no time to stand and stare.
No time to stand beneath the boughs
And stare as long as sheep or cows.
No time to see, when woods we pass,
Where squirrels hide their nuts in grass.
No time to see, in broad daylight,
Streams full of stars, like skies at night.
No time to turn at Beauty's glance,
And watch her feet, how they can dance.
No time to wait till her mouth can
Enrich that smile her eyes began.
A poor life this if, full of care,
We have no time to stand and stare.
William Henry Davies, *Leisure*

If you come across wildlife, keep your distance and don't watch for too long. Your presence can cause considerable stress, particularly if the adults are with young or in winter when the weather is harsh and food scarce. Young animals are rarely abandoned. Never interfere if you find young deer or fledgling birds that are apparently alone; their mother will almost certainly return as soon as you have moved on.

The code of the outdoor loo

As more and more people discover the joys of the outdoors, sorting the toilet issue is of increasing importance. Even the least sensitive of people are offended by loo paper strewn across a path, or by the ill-disguised sight of human excrement. Not only is it offensive to our senses but, more importantly, it can infect water sources.

● **Where to go** Wherever possible wait until you come to a **public toilet**. These are marked on the trail maps in this guide. If you do have to go outdoors, choose a site at least **30m away from running water**. Use a strong stick to **dig a small hole** about 15cm (6") deep in which to bury your excrement. It decomposes quicker when in contact with the top layer of soil or leaf mould; using a stick to stir loose soil into your deposit will speed up decomposition even more. Do not squash it under rocks as this slows down the composting process. If you have to use rocks to hide it make sure they are not in contact with your faeces.

● **Toilet paper and tampons/sanitary towels** Toilet paper takes a long time to decompose, whether buried or not. Like **tampons** and **sanitary towels**, it is easily dug up by animals and could end up in water sources or on the trail. The best method for dealing with such items is to **pack them out**. Put them inside a paper bag, then inside a plastic bag (or two). Then simply empty the contents of the paper bag at the next toilet you come across and throw the bag away.

ACCESS

Rights of way

As a designated national trail, the Cotswold Way is a public right of way, a path that anyone has the right to use on foot provided they stay on the path and do not cause damage or obstruct it in any way. The trail takes in several public rights of way which fall largely into one of three categories:

● A **footpath** (marked with a yellow arrow) is open to walkers only, not to cyclists, horse-riders or vehicles

● A **bridleway** (blue arrow) is open to walkers, horse-riders and cyclists

● A **restricted byway** (purple arrow) is open to walkers, riders and cyclists, but not to motorised vehicles.

That said, not all footpaths are necessarily rights of way. Sometimes a landowner will allow a path across his land to be used for the convenience of walkers, although it may not be recognised as a right of way. This is known as a **permissive path**.

The maintenance of rights of way is down to the landowner in conjunction with the county council through whose area it passes, and sometimes the local authority. Farmers and land managers must ensure that: paths are not blocked by crops or other vegetation, or otherwise obstructed; the route is identifiable; and that the surface is restored soon after cultivation. If crops are growing over the path you have every right to walk through them, following the line of the right of way as closely as possible.

Should you find a path blocked or impassable, report it to the appropriate highway authority.

Right to roam

Following a concerted effort by groups such as the Ramblers (see p42) and the British Mountaineering Council, the principle of access to open countryside and registered common land was finally allowed under the Countryside and Rights of Way Act 2000, affectionately known as CroW. In England, the act came into effect in full in 2005, creating a new right of access to the English countryside for recreation on foot.

There are restrictions, of course: some land (such as gardens, parks and cultivated land) is excluded, and high-impact activities such as driving a vehicle, cycling, and horse-riding may not be permitted. The act also: gives greater

---

❏ **Walking through fields of cattle**

It is very rare that cows will attack walkers but it does happen. Cows get particularly nervous when dogs are about and cows with calves can be even more twitchy. Most of the time they will just watch you pass but very rarely they will wander over out of curiosity. The following guidelines may prove helpful:

● Try not to get between cows and their calves.

● Be prepared for cattle to react to your presence, especially if you have a dog with you.

● Move quickly and quietly, and if possible walk around them.

● Keep your dog close and under proper control.

● Don't hang onto your dog if you are threatened by animals; let it go.

● Don't put yourself at risk. Find another way round the cows and rejoin the footpath.

● Don't panic! Most cows will stop before they reach you. If they follow just walk on quietly.

● Report any problems to the highway authority.

protection to SSSIs (see p61) and AONBs (see p60); lists habitats and species important to biological diversity in England; and covers the conduct of those walking with dogs (see p25). While much of this is only of background interest

❏ THE COUNTRYSIDE CODE

The Countryside Code, originally described in the 1950s as the Country Code, was revised and relaunched in 2004, in part because of the changes brought about by the CRoW Act (see opposite); it was updated again in 2012 and also in 2014. The Code seems like common sense but sadly some people still appear to have no understanding of how to treat the countryside they walk in. An adapted version of the 2014 Code, launched under the logo 'Respect. Protect. Enjoy.', is given below:

Respect other people
• **Consider the local community and other people enjoying the outdoors** Be sensitive to the needs and wishes of those who live and work there. If, for example, farm animals are being moved or gathered keep out of the way and follow the farmer's directions. Being courteous and friendly to those you meet will ensure a healthy future for all based on partnership and co-operation.
• **Leave gates and property as you find them and follow paths unless wider access is available** A farmer will normally close gates to keep farm animals in, but may sometimes leave them open so the animals can reach food and water. Leave gates as you find them or follow instructions on signs. When in a group, make sure the last person knows how to leave the gates. Follow paths unless wider access is available, such as on open country or registered common land (known as 'open access land'). Leave machinery and farm animals alone – if you think an animal is in distress try to alert the farmer instead. Use gates, stiles or gaps in field boundaries if you can – climbing over walls, hedges and fences can damage them and increase the risk of farm animals escaping. Our heritage matters to all of us – Be careful not to disturb ruins and historic sites.

Protect the natural environment
• **Leave no trace of your visit and take your litter home** Take special care not to damage, destroy or remove features such as rocks, plants and trees. Take your litter with you. Litter and leftover food doesn't just spoil the beauty of the countryside, it can be dangerous to wildlife and farm animals. Fires can be as devastating to wildlife and habitats as they are to people and property – so be careful with naked flames and cigarettes at any time of the year.
• **Keep dogs under effective control** This means that you should keep your dog on a lead or keep it in sight at all times, be aware of what it's doing and be confident it will return to you promptly on command. Across farmland dogs should always be kept on a short lead. During lambing time they should not be taken with you at all. Always clean up after your dog and get rid of the mess responsibly – 'bag it and bin it'.

Enjoy the outdoors
• **Plan ahead and be prepared** You're responsible for your own safety: be prepared for natural hazards, changes in weather and other events. Wild animals, farm animals and horses can behave unpredictably if you get too close, especially if they're with their young – so give them plenty of space. See also p53.
• **Follow advice and local signs** In some areas there may be temporary diversions in place. Take notice of these and other local trail advice.

for those walking the Cotswold Way, its impact on the future of walking in the countryside generally will be significant.

Land over which access has been granted may be marked with a circular brown-and-white waymark, depicting a Morph-like creature walking across a hill. For full details and to search a particular area, take a look at 'access and rights of way' on the Natural England website (⌨ www.naturalengland.org.uk).

Health and outdoor safety

HEALTH

Prevention
Water and dehydration You need to drink lots of water while walking – probably more than you think. Many health specialists recommend 2-4 litres a day, depending on the weather and your physique. If you're feeling drained, lethargic or just out of sorts it may well be that you haven't drunk enough. Thirst is not always a reliable indicator of how much you should drink. The frequency and colour of your urine is a more useful guide: the clearer the better.

Sunburn Even on overcast days the sun still has the power to burn. Sunburn can be avoided by regularly applying sunscreen, remembering your lips and ears, and by wearing a hat to protect your face and the back of your neck. Those with fair skin should consider wearing a light, long-sleeved top and long trousers rather than T-shirt and shorts.

Blisters Worn-in, comfortable boots are a must, as are good, well-fitting socks. How many people set out on a long walk in new boots and live to regret it!

Look after your feet, too: air them at lunchtime, keep them clean and change your socks daily. If you feel any 'hot spots' on your feet while you are walking, stop immediately and apply a few strips of zinc oxide tape or one of the commercially available 'blister plasters', and leave on until the area is pain free or the tape/plaster starts to come off.

If you have left it too late and a blister has developed, you can still protect it from further abrasion with one of the 'blister kit' plasters. Popping it can lead to infection. If the skin is broken, keep the area clean with antiseptic and cover with a non-adhesive dressing material held in place with tape.

Joints and muscles If you're susceptible to joint problems – in particular knees and ankles – do invest in a pair of walking poles and use one or both of them, especially during steep ascents or descents. Properly used, they can lessen the impact of long-distance walking on the joints and thus can help to prevent injury. Even the fittest athlete warms up before exercise and stretches afterwards – and it's good practice for walkers. It's surprising how much easier it is to set off in the morning without aching muscles; this, too, lessens the risk of injury.

More serious problems

Hypothermia Hypothermia, or exposure, occurs when the body can't generate enough heat to maintain its core temperature. Since it is usually as a result of being wet, cold, unprotected from the wind, tired and hungry, it is easily avoided by wearing suitable clothing (see pp39-40), carrying and consuming enough food and drink, being aware of the weather conditions, and checking on the morale of your companions. Early signs to watch for include feeling cold and tired with involuntary shivering. If in doubt, find shelter as soon as possible and warm the person up with a hot drink and chocolate or other high-energy food. If possible, give them another warm layer of clothing and allow them to rest.

If the condition is allowed to worsen, strange behaviour, slurring of speech and poor co-ordination will become apparent and the victim can quickly progress into unconsciousness, followed by coma and death. Quickly get the victim out of the wind and rain, improvising a shelter if necessary. Rapid restoration of body warmth is essential and best achieved by bare-skin contact: someone should get into the same sleeping bag as the patient, both having stripped to their underwear, with any spare clothing laid under and over them to build up heat. This is an emergency: send for help.

Hyperthermia At the other end of the scale, hyperthermia occurs when the body is allowed to overheat. **Heat exhaustion** is often caused by water deple- tion and is a serious condition that could eventually lead to death. Symptoms include thirst, fatigue, giddiness, a rapid pulse, raised body temperature, low urine output and, later on, delirium and coma. The only remedy is to re-establish the balance of water. If the victim is suffering severe muscle cramps it may be due to salt depletion. **Heat stroke** is caused by the failure of the body's temper- ature-regulating system and is extremely serious. It is associated with a very high body temperature and an absence of sweating. Early symptoms can be sim- ilar to those of hypothermia, such as aggressive behaviour, lack of co-ordination and so on. Later the victim goes into a coma or convulsions; death will follow if effective treatment is not given. Sponge the victim down or cover with wet towels, then vigorously fan them. Get help immediately.

Dealing with an accident

● Ensure both you and the casualty are out of further risk of danger, but other- wise do not move someone who may be seriously injured.

● Use basic first aid to treat the injury to the best of your ability.

● Try to attract the attention of anybody else who may be in the area: the **emer- gency signal** is six blasts on a whistle, or six flashes with a torch (flashlight).

● If you have to go for help, ideally leave someone with the casualty. If there is nobody else, make sure the casualty is warm, sheltered and as comfortable as possible: leave spare clothing, water and food within easy reach, as well as a whistle and/or torch for attracting attention.

● Telephone ☎ 999 (or ☎ 112) and ask for the police or other rescue service. Be sure you know exactly where you are before you call.

● Report the exact position of the casualty and his or her condition.

❏ **Lyme disease**

Ticks are small blood-sucking creatures that live on cattle, sheep and deer and cannot fly. When you are walking with bare arms or legs through long grass or bracken, small ticks can brush off and attach themselves to you, painlessly burying their heads under your skin to feed on your blood. After a couple of days of feasting they will have grown to about 10mm and will drop off. To avoid this, wear boots, socks and trousers when walking through, or sitting on, long grass, heather and bracken.

There is a very small risk that ticks can infect you with Lyme disease, although one would normally have to be attached to you for 24-36 hours before you were affected. Check your body after a walk and remove any ticks by pinching the head as close to your skin as possible and pulling steadily away from your body, without twisting. Keep the area clean with disinfectant. If you suffer flu-like symptoms, or lasting irritation at the site of the bite for a week or more, see a doctor.

For more information see 💻 www.lymediseaseaction.org.uk.

OUTDOOR SAFETY

The Cotswold Way is not a hazardous undertaking and presents no greater risk than you would encounter on an average day's walk in the countryside. Nevertheless, there are some sensible precautions that can help to prevent problems.

Check the weather forecast (see below) before you set out and go properly equipped (see pp39-40). Be sure to carry plenty of food to last you through the day and at least a litre of water. Drinking from streams is not recommended since they are likely to contain traces of pesticides and other chemicals used on the land. Should the weather close in, take particular care to stay on the route, especially if you are on Cleeve Hill, or one of the other stretches of the Cotswold Way that run along the escarpment. If in doubt, stop and check – using a compass and map, and perhaps a GPS.

Weather information

Anyone familiar with the British weather will know that it can change quickly. What started out as a warm sunny day can be chilly and wet by lunchtime, so don't be fooled. Newspapers, television and radio stations all give the forecast for the day ahead and local people will have plenty of advice on the subject. Weather forecasts can be found online at 💻 www.metoffice.gov.uk and 💻 www.bbc.co.uk/weather.

Walking alone

If you enjoy walking alone you must appreciate and be prepared for the increased risk. Try to tell someone where you are going. One way of doing this is to telephone your booked accommodation and let them know you are walking alone and what time you expect to arrive. If you leave word with someone else, don't forget to let them know you have arrived safely. Carrying a mobile phone is useful, though there's no guarantee of good reception.

THE ENVIRONMENT AND NATURE

Given its route within the relatively narrow range of the Cotswold Hills, the Cotswold Way runs through an unexpectedly broad range of habitats. Among these, grasslands and beechwoods stand out from the dominant farmland, where grazing land and arable farming have created their own habitats. Open moorland contrasts with long-established towns and villages; there's even a river and a canal across the trail. To do justice to the flora and fauna of such an area would take a book several times the size of this one. What follows, then, is a brief description of the animals, birds and plants you may come across – and a few that are there, but which you're unlikely to spot. To find out more, take a look at one of the field guides listed on p43.

While it's interesting in itself to be able to identify individual plants and creatures, far more valuable is to understand their place within their environment and how we, as walkers, can help to protect that fragile relationship. Conservation is part of that relationship, which is why these issues are explored here.

Conserving the Cotswolds

It's the business of government to see that the countryside is preserved for the pleasure and sanity of all of us. The fatal mistake has been to imagine that the interests of the countryside are in some way different from the interests of farmers. The countryside can only be maintained by a healthy agriculture. If farming dies, a most precious part of Britain dies with it. **John Mortimer**

Perhaps John Mortimer had the Cotswolds in mind when he penned these words. He certainly could have done, for farming has been an intrinsic part of these hills for many centuries, shaping the countryside – and the towns and villages – that are seen today.

Yet for all that the Cotswolds draw tourists in their droves, the pressure for development, the economic reality of maintaining small communities, and the red tape imposed on Britain's farmers all conspire against maintaining an equable balance with nature. If it has taken just over 70 years for over 96% of the region's unimproved limestone grassland (that's permanent grassland which has not been regularly cultivated) to disappear, how long will it be before there's nothing left?

There are plenty of organisations that are determined not to let the unthinkable happen, some of them are listed below. Environmental issues are of growing interest on the political field and thanks to the efforts of these groups, many of them voluntary, the fight-back is gaining ground. Their work relies on the active participation of everyone who cares.

GOVERNMENT AGENCIES AND SCHEMES

Primary responsibility for countryside affairs in England rests with **Natural England** (💻 www.naturalengland.org.uk), which bring under one umbrella the work of the former Countryside Agency, English Nature and the Rural Development Council. The organisation is responsible for: enhancing biodiversity, landscape and wildlife in rural, urban, coastal and marine areas; promoting access, recreation and public well-being; and contributing to the way natural resources are managed. One of its roles is to designate national trails, national parks, areas of outstanding natural beauty (AONBs), which afford the second level of protection after a national park, sites of special scientific interest (SSSIs), and national nature reserves (NNRs), and to enforce regulations relating to these sites.

Cotswolds AONB

Now for some statistics. Some 95% of the Cotswold Way national trail falls within the Cotswolds Area of Outstanding Natural Beauty (💻 www.cotswolds aonb.org.uk), the largest of the 37 AONBs in England and Wales. Established in 1966, and extended in 1990, it runs from north to south for 78 miles (126km) and covers a total of 790 square miles (2038sq km).

The area has been inhabited for around 6000 years; today some 139,000 people live within its boundaries. Despite that, more than 80% of the land is still farmland, its fields demarcated by an estimated 4000 miles of dry-stone walls. A further 9% or so is woodland, especially beech, though the walker on the Cotswold Way could be forgiven for thinking that the woods accounted for a significantly higher proportion than this!

Significantly, in terms of the area's natural history, over half of the UK's total Jurassic limestone grassland is to be found here, much of it protected within SSSIs (see opposite). That figure, though, tells only a part of the story. While the region's flower-rich limestone grasslands as a whole covered 40% of the AONB in 1935, that area has shrunk to just 1.5% today. Given that such habitats can harbour almost 400 species of plants and 25 species of butterfly, it's hardly any wonder that conservation of what little remains is such a vital issue.

The Cotswolds Conservation Board (and a team of Cotswold Voluntary Wardens) is responsible for much of the work involved in running the AONB, including the Cotswold Way, from footpath maintenance and hedge-laying to publicity and fundraising. Others lead walks, including an annual series along the Cotswold Way (see p29). A half-yearly newspaper, *Cotswold Lion*, ensures that both local people and visitors are kept informed of what's going on across the region.

Sites of special scientific interest (SSSIs) and national nature reserves (NNRs)

The designation SSSI affords protection to specific areas against anything that threatens their unique habitat or environment. There are more than 80 SSSIs across the Cotswolds, including parts of Cleeve Hill Common (🖳 www.cleeve common.org), Leckhampton Hill, Crickley Hill and Painswick Beacon along the Cotswold Way.

'Triple SIs' are managed in partnership with the owners and occupiers of the land who must give written notice of any operations likely to damage the site and who cannot proceed until consent is given. Many SSSIs are also designated as national nature reserves (NNRs), including several that combine to make up the Cotswolds Commons and Beechwoods NNR.

Geoparks

The European Geoparks initiative was originally set up to help the development and management of deprived areas which nevertheless benefit from a rich geological heritage. The concept has since moved on, with today's geoparks designed to raise awareness of an area and to educate the general public.

The Cotswold Way runs through the Cotswold Hills Geopark (🖳 www.cotswoldhillsgeopark.net), which was established by Gloucestershire Geology Trust (see p11), in partnership with the Cotswolds AONB and Natural England. Currently reaching as far south as Wotton-under-Edge, it may in future be extended to include Bath.

VOLUNTARY CAMPAIGNING & CONSERVATION ORGANISATIONS

Voluntary organisations started the conservation movement back in the mid 1800s and are still at the forefront of developments. Independent of government but reliant on public support, they can concentrate their resources either on acquiring land which can then be managed purely for conservation purposes, or on influencing political decision-makers by lobbying and campaigning.

The **National Trust** (NT; 🖳 www.nationaltrust.org.uk) with its four million members now protects about 247,000 hectares in the United Kingdom. NT properties on or close to the trail include Snowshill Manor (p89), Horton Court (p152), Newark Park (p146) and Dyrham Park (p161), as well as significant tracts of land. Of these, some of the most interesting are Dover's Hill just outside Chipping Campden, and Haresfield Beacon, as well as several areas of woodland.

Recently separated from the governmental body responsible for listed buildings and heritage research (now Historic England), **English Heritage** (🖳 www.english-heritage.org.uk) has gained independent charitable status. It is responsible for the care and preservation of ancient monuments in England, including Hailes Abbey (p96) and several of the long barrows along the Cotswold Way.

THE ENVIRONMENT & NATURE

The **Royal Society for the Protection of Birds** (RSPB; 🖥 www.rspb.org .uk) has more than a million members and around 200 nature reserves, but the nearest to the trail is at Highnam Woods, some 3¾ miles (6km) west of Gloucester.

Rather smaller in scale is the work of **Butterfly Conservation** (🖥 www .butterfly-conservation.org), which owns and manages the 31-hectare Prestbury Hill Reserve, to the south of Cleeve Hill. The two-part reserve, incorporating both Masts Field and the Bill Smyllie Reserve, features a diversity of habitat and is home to some 30 species of butterfly.

The **Woodland Trust** (🖥 www.woodland-trust.org.uk) aims to conserve, restore and re-establish trees, particularly broadleaved species. Their properties along the Cotswold Way include Lineover Wood, Penn Wood, Stanley Wood and Coaley Wood.

In a different mould altogether is the **Landmark Trust** (booking enquiries ☎ 01628-825925, 🖥 www.landmarktrust.org.uk), which works to preserve historic, or architecturally interesting, buildings and to make them suitable for short-term holiday lets. The trust has accommodation options along the trail that include Campden House at Chipping Campden (see p75), Beckford's Tower (see box p163), and two very close to Bath Abbey.

Then there's the work of two other organisations, both important in environmental terms. Those interested in voluntary work may be interested in the **Conservation Volunteers** (TCV; 🖥 www.tcv.org.uk), which encourages people to value their environment and take practical action to improve it. And more broadly there's the **Campaign to Protect Rural England** (CPRE; 🖥 www .cpre.org.uk) – whose name speaks for itself.

Flora and fauna

TREES AND SHRUBS

While the Cotswold Hills are widely revered for their hills and steep cliffs, among their less-sung attractions are the magnificent woods of **beech** (*Fagus sylvatica*) that define the edge of the escarpment. Some veteran species are at least 250 years old, and one – in Lineover Wood south-east of Cheltenham – dates back over 400 years. They are seen at their best in spring, when the soft green of the new leaves adds texture rather than darkness to the woodland panorama. Time is inevitably taking its toll on these old timers, which are threatened by factors such as disease, wind damage and erosion, as well as the vigorous seedlings of other species such as **ash** (*Fraxinus excelsior*).

Also interspersed with the beech are **sycamore** or **sycamore maple** (*Acer pseudoplatanus*), and **oak** (*Quercus robur*), as well as **horse chestnut** (*Aesculus hippocastanum*), **lime** or **linden** (*Tilia vulgaris*) and **birch** (*Betula pubescens*). Another species, the **large-leaved lime** (*Tilia platyphyllos*), is one of the rarest trees in Britain, but there's a bank of them in Lineover Wood, whose name derives from the Anglo-Saxon word for 'lime bank'.

Amongst mixed woodland you will come across trees such as **rowan** or **mountain ash** (*Sorbus aucuparia*), popular with birds who seek out its bright orange berries around August, **silver birch** (*Betula pendula*), **aspen** (*Populus tremula*), **alder** (*Alnus glutinosa*), and **hazel** (*Corylus avellana*). While there are **conifers** to be found, most are incidental to the deciduous trees; there are none of the dark conifer plantations so prevalent in many woodland areas.

In the hedgerows, the white, star-like blossom of the **blackthorn** (*Prunus spinosa*) heralds the beginning of spring, giving way as the year progresses to dark-blue, almost dusty-looking sloes which make great sloe gin. Later, a mass of creamy flowers proclaims the **hawthorn** (*Crataegus monogyna*), whose fruit adds a splash of red in autumn. Then, in early summer, the glory goes to the **elder** (*Sambucus nigra*), with its sweet-smelling clusters of cream flowers which by September have formed into a purplish-black fruit, ripe for making jelly or wine.

WILD FLOWERS [see colour plates opposite p64]

Of speedwell and thistles there are indeed plenty, but Gurney – writing after World War I – does little more than hint at the richness of the flora to be found in

On Cotswold edge there is a field and that
Grows thick with corn and speedwell and the mat
Of thistles, of the tall kind
Ivor Gurney, *Up There*

his native Cotswolds. While much has changed since then, and habitats have declined significantly, there are still wild flowers aplenty along the trail.

Limestone grassland

Until the 1950s, sheep grazed the limestone grasslands that are so characteristic of the Cotswolds (some say the name derived from the Saxon words *wold*, referring to high, open country, and *cod* meaning 'found', but others claim it came from the Cotswold sheep), encouraging a broad range of wild flowers and an attendant population of butterflies and other insects. With changes in agriculture, what was left of this 'unimproved' grassland became overgrown, but several areas are now managed to ensure that this unique habitat can continue to prosper. Over 200 species of wild flower have been identified at Crickley Hill alone, with other similar areas including Leckhampton Hill, Painswick Beacon, Coaley Peak, Selsley Common and Prestbury Hill Reserve, as well as a small patch of ground at Great Witcombe Roman Villa.

Many of the wild flowers that grow in this habitat, such as **cowslips** (*Primula veris*), are also to be found along hedgerows and in fields, but some are specific to this environment. In spring there's the **early purple orchid** (*Orchis mascula*), but it's in summer that the wild orchids really come into their own. Relatively easy to find among colourful patches of **birdsfoot trefoil** (*Lotus corniculatus*), purple **self-heal** (*Prunella vulgaris*) and red or white **clover** (*Trifolium* spp) are the bright pink **pyramidal orchid** (*Anacamptis* *pyramidalis*), and **common spotted orchids** (*Dactylorhiza fuchsii*), which can be pink, pale lilac or white. The **bee orchid** (*Ophrys apifera*), named for its close resemblance to a bee, is a rarity, and is carefully protected where it does grow. Also present are the **fly orchid** (*Ophrys insectifera*) – which does look like a fly – and the rather inconspicuous **musk orchid** (*Herminium monorchis*).

Striking in their summer glory are the tall spikes of startlingly blue **viper's bugloss** (*Echium vulgare*), and the **thistles** (*Cirsium* spp) and **knapweeds** (*Centaurea scabiosa*), their colourful purple flowers a magnet for bees. The delicate **harebell** (*Campanula rotundifolia*) is also at home here, as is the **scabious** (*Knautia arvensis*), their pale-blue flowers contrasting with bold **ox-eye daisies** (*Leucanthemum vulgare*) and the rather less flamboyant **yellow rattle** (*Rhinanthus minor*), named for the sound made by its seeds when they're ripe. Lower down is the **common rock rose** (*Helianthemum nummularium*), its bright-yellow, five-petalled flowers familiar to many gardeners. Look out, too, for the pinkish-purple flowers of wild herbs such as **basil** (*Clinopodium vulgare*), **marjoram** (*Origanum vulgare*) and the ground-hugging **thyme** (*Thymus serphyllum*).

Moorland

Up on the hills and on open spaces such as Cleeve Hill Common you'll come across plenty of **bracken** (*Pteridium aquilinum*), its fronds turning to a crisp brown as the year progresses. Here, too, the bright-yellow flowers of **gorse** (*Ulex europaeus*) brighten up the hillside.

Hedgerows and field boundaries

As the days grow longer and the air begins to warm up, wild flowers start to appear along the hedgerows. Needing little introduction are the more common species which even the uninitiated will soon recognise, such as **primrose** (*Primula vulgaris*), **common dog violet** (*Viola riviniana*), **common speedwell** (*Veronica officinalis*), which can cure indigestion, gout and liver complaints, **bugle** (*Ajuga repans*), **tufted vetch** (*Vicia cracca*), **lesser celandine** (*Ranunculus ficaria*), not unlike the related buttercup, and **red campion** (*Silene dioica*). Here, too, you might find the occasional **green alkanet** (*Pentaglottis sempervirens*) which, with its bright-blue flowers and soft, hairy leaves, is often mistaken for borage, and the tall, deep-purple **honesty** (*Lunaria redivia*), whose flat, translucent seedpods are sought after by flower arrangers.

Later, from May to September, these will be joined by **buttercup** (*Ranunculus acris*), the flowers of which children will use to tell you if you like butter, and the small pink-flowered **herb robert** (*Geranium robertianum*). The **dandelion** (*Taraxacum officinale*) grows almost everywhere, including on waste ground, as does the tall **rosebay willowherb** (*Epilobium angustifolium*). Equally tall is the purple **foxglove** (*Digitalis purpurea*). Its flowers are attractive to bees but the plant is poisonous to humans – although it's from the foxglove that the drug Digitalin is extracted to treat heart disease. Unmistakable is the vivid red splash of the **field poppy** (*Papaver rhoeas*). Then there are the tall white-flowering heads of members of the carrot family such as **cow parsley**

Early Purple Orchid
Orchis mascula

Spotted Orchid
Dactylorhiza fuchsii

Pyramidal Orchid
Anacamptis pyramidalis

Honesty
Lunaria redivia

Field Scabious
Knautia arvensis

Woolly Thistle
Cirsium eriophorum

Rosebay Willowherb
Epilobium angustifolium

Herb-Robert
Geranium robertianum

Black Knapweed
Centaurea nigra

Red Campion
Silene dioica

Rowan (tree)
Sorbus aucuparia

Field Poppy
Papaver rhoeas

Common Dog Violet
Viola riviniana

Dog Rose
Rosa canina

Honeysuckle
Lonicera periclymemum

Ramsons (Wild Garlic)
Allium ursinum

Germander Speedwell
Veronica chamaedrys

Wood Spurge
Euphorbia amygdaloides

Self-heal
Prunella vulgaris

Green Alkanet
Pentaglottis sempervirens

Wood Anemone
Anemone nemorosa

Foxglove
Digitalis purpurea

Bluebell
Hyacinthoides non-scripta

Viper's Bugloss
Echium vulgare

Meadow Buttercup
Ranunculis acris

Rock Rose
Helianthemum nummularium

Gorse
Ulex europaeus

Lesser Celandine
Ranunculus ficaria

Birdsfoot-trefoil
Lotus corniculatus

Marsh Marigold
Caltha palustris

Yarrow
Achillea millefolium

Primrose
Primula vulgaris

Cowslip
Primula veris

Colour photos (following pages)
● **C4 Top left**: The mellow stone church at Wood Stanway (see p94, BH). **Top right**: Broadway Tower (see p85, TH). **Bottom**: Market Hall, Chipping Campden (**left**, TH), the ruins of Hailes Abbey (**centre**, see p96, TH) and Belas Knap long barrow (**right**, p101, TH).
● **C5 Top left**: Cleeve Hill Common (see p101, TH). **Centre**: Flights of fancy abound at Painswick Rococo Garden (see p122, TH). **Bottom**: St Mary's Church, Painswick (**left**, see p122, TH), its Millennium Clock (**centre**, BH) and spectacle stocks (**right**, BH). **Top right**: Lych gate by St Mary's Church, Painswick (TH).
● **C6** Climbing Selsley Common from All Saints' Church, Selsley (see p132, BH).
● **C7** Beech woods are a feature of the Cotswold Way, no more so than in Stanley Wood (TH).
● **C8** The Tyndale Monument (**left**, see p142, TH) offers sweeping views (**top**) across the Cotswolds landscape (BH). **Right**: Dyrham Park (p161, TH), now a National Trust property.
● **C9 Left and bottom**: Limestone circle (TH) in front of Bath Abbey (see p181, BH), marking the finish/start of the Cotswold Way. **Right**: Imposing gateway at Cold Ashton (**centre**, p162), where Sir Bevil Grenville died after the Battle of Lansdown (site shown at **top**, TH).

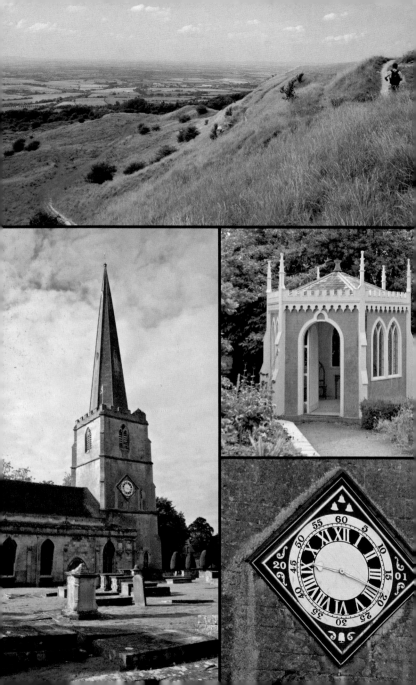

C5

Peacock
Inachis io

Small Tortoiseshell
Aglais urticae

Large Blue
Maculinea arion

Large Garden/Cabbage White
Pieris brassicae

Small Heath
Coenonympha pamphilus

Red Admiral
Vanessa atalanta

Small Garden/Cabbage White
Artogeia rapae

Painted Lady
Cynthia cadui

Small Copper
Lycaena phlaeus

Silver-washed Fritillary *Argynnis paphia*

(*Anthrisus sylvestris*), **yarrow** (*Achillea millefolium*) and **hedge parsley** (*Torilis japonica*).

Summer is when the climbers and ramblers come into their own. Almost everyone is familiar with the common **bramble** (*Rubus fruticosus*), sought out in autumn by blackberry pickers. **Honeysuckle** (*Lonicera periclymenum*), also known as woodbine, makes its appearance growing through hedges and in woodland from June to September, the fruits ripening to red in the autumn. **Hedge bindweed** (*Calystegia sepium*), with its white trumpet-shaped flowers, and the related pink **field bindweed** (*Convolvulus arvensis*) are a common sight during the summer months, as is the pale-pink **dog rose** (*Rosa canina*), which later produces rosehips, an excellent source of vitamin C and used to make a subtle-flavoured jelly. Then there's another autumn beauty, the almost translucent scarlet berries of the **white briony** (*Bryonia cretica*) that tumble in profusion down many a hedgerow. Beware, though: they're extremely poisonous.

Woodland

Spring has to be the best time to walk through the Cotswolds' beech woods. This is when the air is pungent with the smell of densely packed white **ramsons** (*Allium ursinum*), widely known as **wild garlic**. In some places, carpets of **bluebells** (*Hyacinthoides non-scripta*) appear, while others are favoured by **dog's mercury** (*Mercurialis perennis*) – no floral beauty, this, but its bright green leaves make a splendid floor covering. Beneath the still-open tree canopy, the woodland floor is liberally sprinkled with white **wood anemones** (*Anemone nemorosa*), whose petals close up at night and in bad weather. With a similar night-time habit but with more rounded leaves is the smaller **wood sorrel** (*Oxalis acetosella*). The plant with the red stem, dark green leaves and soft green bracts is the **wood spurge** (*Euphorbia amygdaloides*). A little later you might see the occasional patch of **lily-of-the-valley** (*Convallaria majalis*), or the much taller **Solomon's seal** (*Polygonatum multiflorum*).

In darker areas, especially along rocks and walls (look out for them in Penn Wood and Coaley Wood), are **hart's tongue ferns** (*Phyllitis* or *Asplenium scolopendrium*), their long narrow leaves slightly furled; this is the only British fern whose leaves are undivided.

In summer and autumn, there's often the opportunity to supplement a packed lunch with wild **alpine strawberries** (*Fragaria vesca*) and to a lesser extent **wild raspberries** (*Rubus idaeus*). Steer well clear, though, of the poisonous purple fruits of **bittersweet** or **woody nightshade** (*Solanum dulcamara*).

Riverbanks and wet areas

You won't have much opportunity to spot plants along riverbanks as you're walking the trail, but there is the occasional stream, and the alternative route along Stroudwater (Ebley) Canal offers a few water-loving specimens. In summer, the soft cream heads of **meadowsweet** (*Filipendula ulmaria*), which has similar medicinal properties to aspirin, contrast with tall **purple loosestrife** (*Lythrum salicaria*). On the edge of water courses bright-yellow **marsh marigolds** (*Caltha palustris*) may be seen, while on the water itself (take a look on the canal) are large **yellow waterlilies** (*Nuphar lutea*). You might also see the pink **cuckoo flower** (*Cardamine pratensis*) and **ragged robin** (*Lychnis floscuculi*), as well as **watermint** (*Mentha aquatica*), easily identified by its smell, and **hemp agrimony** (*Eupatorium cannabinum*), with its large pink flowers.

BUTTERFLIES [see colour plate opposite p65]

The existence of unimproved limestone grasslands is one of the major features that make butterflies so important to the Cotswolds region. Some 34 species are found in this environment, with the area significant for both the **small blue** (*Cupido minimus*), and the **Duke of Burgundy fritillary** (*Hamearis lucina*). Part of the Cotswolds AONB near Stroud has seen the reintroduction of the **large blue** (*Maculinea arion*), which, along with the **Adonis blue** (*Lysandra bellargus*), had been declared extinct in this area.

Those with a serious interest would be well advised to spend some time at the Prestbury Hill Reserve south of Cleeve Hill, where many species are protected within a reserve managed by Butterfly Conservation (see p62). Some, such as the **large whites** (*Pieris brassicae*) and **small whites** (*Artogeia rapae*), and the nettle feeders like **red admiral** (*Vanessa atalanta*) and **painted lady** (*Cynthia cadui*), are familiar to many of us from our gardens and parks and are easily spotted in many other places. Other, rarer species, such as the **large skipper** (*Ochlodes venata*), **brown argus** (*Aricia agestis*), **chalk-hill blue** (*Lysandra coridon*), **green hairstreak** (*Callophrys rubi*), **dark green fritillary** (*Argynnis aglaja*), **marbled white** (*Melanargia galathea*), **grayling** (*Hipparchia semele*), **small copper** (*Lycaena phlaeus*), **small heath** (*Coenonympha pamphilus*), **speckled wood** (*Pararge aegeria*), **comma** (*Polygonia c-album*), **peacock** (*Inachis io*), **tortoiseshell** (*Aglais urticae*), and **meadow brown** (*Maniola jurtina*), benefit significantly from this protection. Some of these are also found in other reserves, including Leckhampton Hill or at Painswick Beacon. Elsewhere, perhaps in Buckholt Wood (see Map 18), you may be lucky enough to spot the **silver-washed fritillary** (*Argynnis paphia*), the largest of the British fritillaries with a wingspan of almost three inches (70mm).

There may be considerable difference between the male and female of a species, which can be particularly frustrating for the novice attempting to identify a creature that scarcely holds still for a moment. Many of the blue butterflies, for example, take their name from the male; the female is often a rather insignificant brown.

BIRDS

High overhead ran frenzied larks, screaming, as though the sky were tearing apart
Laurie Lee, *Cider with Rosie*

To most of us, the song of a skylark overhead is decidedly more appealing than to Laurie Lee's childhood ears. And fortunately, there are still several places along the Cotswold Way where skylarks can be seen. Of the 86 species of bird that have been identified in the region as a whole, the skylark is considered to be one of 20 that are designated as 'nationally important' – along with the linnet, starling, house sparrow and yellowhammer.

Open farmland and upland areas

Out on the hills is where you'll find the **skylark** (*Alauda arvensis*), which is often heard long before it is seen, its clear song delivered as it soars overhead. Look out for them on Cleeve Hill Common and Selsley Common; they even do an impressive job of drowning out the traffic noise on fields near the M4 south of

SKYLARK
L: 185mm/7.25"

Tormarton. The same environment could throw up the similarly sized **meadow pipit** (*Anthus pratensis*), while two other birds that you're likely to see are the **wheatear** (*Oenanthe oenanthe*), the male of which has a steel-grey back and crown and often bows and flicks its tail and perches on walls or rocks, and the **stonechat** (*Saxicola torquata*), much smaller and darker in plumage and identifiable by its call, a single sharp 'teck'. In autumn, flocks of **redwings** (*Turdus iliatus*) and **fieldfares** (*Turdus pilaris*) arrive from their breeding grounds in northern Europe to feed on wild fruit and berries.

Most easily spotted on hedgerows alongside farmland is the **yellowhammer** (*Emberiza citronella*), its familiar song widely translated as 'little-bit-of-bread-and-no-cheese'. This bright yellow bird with a reddish-brown back is regularly seen at Dover's Hill and Leckhampton Hill, too.

Out on the fields and across the hills is big crow country. You can't miss these gregarious birds, collectively known as corvids, whether the grey-headed **jackdaws** (*Corvus monedula*), the **rooks** (*Corvus frugilegus*), or the **carrion crows** (*Corvus corone corone*). If you doubted their community instincts, look out for jackdaws in particular at Wontley Farm, near Belas Knap, where they have taken over the derelict buildings en masse. In a similar environment you'll find **lapwings** (*Vanellus vanellus*), with their smart crests; during the breeding season the male performs a spectacular display, tumbling through the air to attract its mate.

LAPWING/PEEWIT
L: 320mm/12.5"

Increasingly seen near urban dumps, or anywhere that they can pick up scraps, are **lesser black-backed gulls** (*Larus fuscus*), usually in the company of the noisy and closely related **herring gulls** (*Larus argentatus*). Despite their prevalence, these two still seem entirely incongruous in a rural setting.

In an area where such a large proportion of land is given over to agriculture, the presence of game birds comes as no surprise. **Pheasants** (*Phasianus colchicus*) and

partridges (*Perdix perdix*) are found practically everywhere, so don't be surprised if one suddenly flies up just in front of you, startled at your approach. You may also put up a **snipe** (*Gallinago gallinago*), which has a zig-zag flight when flushed, or in wooded areas the **woodcock** (*Scolopax rusticola*), easily distinguished from the snipe by its larger size and more rounded wings. Its camouflage makes it difficult to observe during the day.

Lording it over them all are the birds of prey. Both the **kestrel** (*Falco tinnunculus*) and the **sparrowhawk** (*Accipiter nisus*) can be seen, but it's the much larger **buzzard** (*Buteo buteo*), with its brown colouring and cruel yellow talons, that attracts most attention. Its mewing cry can send a shiver down the spine as it soars over fields, woods or moorland in search of its prey, anything from a beetle to a rabbit. The buzzard's fierce reputation won't stop other birds from defending their nests: rooks in particular will sometimes gang up to chase it away, although if sufficiently provoked the buzzard could well retaliate. The occasional **red kite** (*Milvus milvus*) is starting to put in an appearance, presumably encroaching west following its successful re-introduction in the Chiltern Hills. It is easily distinguished in flight from other birds of prey by its forked tail.

Woodland

Many of the woodland residents such as the **chaffinch** (*Fringilla coelebs*), **greenfinch** (*Carduelis chloris*), **robin** (*Erithacus rubecula*), **song thrush** (*Turdus philomelos*), **blackbird** (*Turdus merula*), **blue tit** (*Parus caeruleus*) and **great tit** (*Parus major*), are familiar to us from our gardens, although less well known is the **long-tailed tit** (*Aegithalos caudatus*), which is distinguished from other tits by its very long tail: it tends to frequent woodland fringes and clearings.

Of the finches, the **goldfinch** (*Carduelis carduelis*) and **linnet** (*Acanthis cannabina*) are relatively common, too, but you might also spot the **siskin** (*Carduelis spinus*), which is smaller and more streaked than the greenfinch, and more yellow in colour. The **brambling** (*Fringilla montifringilla*), which often mixes with chaffinches in winter, is easily distinguished from them by its distinct white upper rump. The **bullfinch** (*Pyrrhula pyrrhula*) is notable for the male's brilliant red chest; the female is like a monochrome copy of her mate. They feed on berries, buds and seeds in the trees and bushes, their movements slow and deliberate. A much smaller bird is the **goldcrest** (*Regulus regulus*), which is the smallest European bird, recognised by its yellow crown with black edges.

The **willow warbler** (*Phylloscopus trochilus*) and **chiffchaff** (*Phylloscopus collybita*) will keep you guessing since distinguishing between them is quite difficult. The chiffchaff is generally rather browner than the willow warbler and its legs are blackish. More obviously, the willow warbler has the more melodic song.

Even if you're unfamiliar with the **treecreeper** (*Certhia familiaris*), it's not difficult to put a name to this small, brown bird with a curved bill that does exactly that: creeps up trees searching for insects. A similar location might also throw up the **nuthatch** (*Sitta europaea*), with its bluish-grey upper side and pinkish-cream chest, though this species tends to make its way down the trunk head first.

Similar in size, although not in habit, is the **blackcap** (*Sylvia atricapilla*), quite easy to identify not just for the said black head (as well as brown back and lighter chest), but also for its pretty song. Usually a summer visitor, it nests in woods or dense shrubs. Another summer visitor is the inconspicuous **tree pipit** (*Anthus trivialis*); this one happiest on woodland fringes or any rough country, from where it delivers itself into the air, singing as it goes.

Larger and far more conspicuous are members of the woodpecker family. The **green woodpecker** (*Picus viridis*), a striking bird with a bright green body and red head, is also notable for its curious call, a kind of laughing cry that carries a long way. More often heard than seen are the **lesser spotted woodpecker** (*Dendrocopos minor*) and the much larger **great spotted woodpecker** (*Dendrocopos major*), distinctive for its striking black-and-white plumage, with a bright red patch under the tail and – in the male – similarly coloured crown. Both habitually drum on trees, usually to mark their territory and extract insects rather than to bore holes for a nest site.

It is highly likely that you'll see the **magpie** (*Pica pica*) in its handsome black, white and blue plumage, and the colourful **jay** (*Garrulus glandarius*) is becoming more common everywhere; both are highly efficient at cleaning eggs out of birds' nests and even taking young birds. Rarely seen, although its distinctive call is known even to children as the first harbinger of summer, the **cuckoo** (*Cuculus canorus*) is grey or occasionally brown in colour, not unlike a heavy male sparrowhawk. From the dove family, **wood pigeons** (*Columba palumbus*) and **collared doves** (*Streptopelia decaocto*) can be seen – and heard – everywhere.

Finally, there are the birds of the night, of which the one you're most likely to see – even occasionally in the daytime – is the **tawny owl** (*Strix aluco*). It can be quite unnerving to look up from a lunchtime picnic to find you're being observed from on high.

Streams, canals, rivers and reservoirs

Large tracts of open water are not something you'd associate with the Cotswolds, with the notable exceptions of the canal near Ebley, and the parallel River Frome, but reservoirs and the occasional stream or ornamental pond are enough to attract **swallows** (*Hirundo rustica*), **house martins** (*Delichon urbica*) and **swifts** (*Apus apus*). Watch their acrobatics in summer as they swoop low, picking up insects on the wing. You'll also spot these birds further afield, too. House martins often build their nests under the eaves of houses or churches, while swifts can often be seen rising on the currents; look out for them above Selsley Common. Distinctive in flight for its scimitar-shaped wings, the swift cannot perch like the swallow and martin, and spends almost its entire life aloft. The less-common **sand martin** (*Riparia riparia*) nests in colonies in holes in steep riverbanks and cliffs such as those in Witcombe Wood, near the reservoir.

In evidence along the canal are the familiar **mute swans** (*Cygnus olor*), **mallards** (*Anas platyrhynchos*), **coots** (*Fulica atra*) and **moorhens** (*Gallinula chloropus*), but there are other birds around too. The **grey wagtail** (*Motacilla cinerea*) in particular, with a blue-grey head and a bright-yellow underside, can be seen year-round bobbing up and down by the bridge on the river where the stream flows fast.

MAMMALS

You might occasionally spot a **roe deer** (*Capreolus capreolus*) in the woods along the Cotswold escarpment. Small in stature, with an average height of 60-75cm at the shoulder, they are reddish brown in summer, but grey in winter, and have a distinctive white rear end which is conspicuous when the deer is alarmed. Males have short antlers with no more than three points. They are active at dawn and dusk and can sometimes be heard barking. If you come across a young kid apparently abandoned, leave it alone and go away; it's normal behaviour for the mother to leave her kid concealed while she goes off to feed.

An enclosure of **red deer** (*Cervus elaphus*) can be seen at Broadway Tower, but these animals are not found in the wild in the Cotswolds.

Far more visible is the **rabbit** (*Oryctolagus cuniculus*). While many townies consider them to be cute relatives of Peter Rabbit, to the farmer they're a pest, responsible each year for damage to crops that can be counted in the millions. Despite being prey to buzzards, foxes, feral cats, stoats and man, they breed rapidly, bucks mating at four months old and does at three-and-a-half months, so their numbers are on the increase.

The **brown hare** (*Lepus europaeus*) is larger than the rabbit with large powerful hind legs and very long, black-tipped ears. They are found on upland, such as Leckhampton Hill, and rely for escape on their great acceleration, capable of attaining speeds of up to 45mph (70km/h).

Badgers (*Meles meles*) are nocturnal animals and rarely seen during the day, lying up in their underground burrows, or setts. Litters of cubs are born in February. Like rabbits, they are responsible for considerable damage on farmland, but unlike rabbits they are a protected species and cannot be destroyed. There is also some suggestion that cattle can catch the TB virus through contact with badgers.

Red foxes (*Vulpes vulpes*) are becoming common, in spite of occasional persecution by man and the British roads. Readily identifiable by their colour and bushy tail, foxes are shy animals that come out mainly at night to hunt for food. Their supposed habit of killing all the hens in a coop and taking only one is apparently not the result of vicious rage but done to take advantage of abundance while it is available to compensate for times when food is scarce. Although the issue remains controversial, a ban on fox hunting was implemented in 2005.

The ubiquitous **grey squirrel** (*Sciurus carolinensis*) needs no introduction, having driven the native red squirrel into just one or two strongholds since the former's arrival here from North America in the 19th century.

The **weasel** (*Mustela nivalis*), one of Britain's smaller carnivores, is found in a wide range of habitats and is not a protected species. In fact, it may be trapped and killed by gamekeepers out to protect their birds from its claws.

Mainly nocturnal and preferring dry areas, the weasel is smaller than the **stoat** (*Mustela erminea*), the tip of whose tail is always black. Other small creatures that hide away in hedgerows include the nocturnal **hedgehog** (*Erinaceus europaeus*), which curls into a tight prickly ball when startled, as well as **shrews** (*Sorex sp.*), **voles** (*Microtus arvalis*) and **harvest mice** (*Micromys minutus*).

Of the 18 species of **bat** in the UK, several are found in the Cotswolds. The most obvious place to spot them is at Woodchester Mansion (see p134) where six different species roost in the house and grounds. These include the endangered

---

❏ Farm animals

Dotted across the hills, **sheep** seem to take on the colour of Cotswold stone, rather dirty in the rain, but a soft warm cream in the sun, their lambs improbably white. In the Middle Ages, Cotswold sheep, or 'Cotswold Lions' (see photo opposite p17) as they were known, were bred for their long, thick fleeces, which brought immense fortunes to local merchants, enabling them to build the splendid manor houses and imposing 'wool' churches that still grace the region's towns. The animal is distinctive to the layman both for its long coat and a rather unkempt fringe.

Today, because of the widespread crossing of breeds, most of the sheep seen in the fields are cross-breeds, reared primarily for their meat. Yet some of the old breeds are still used, particularly for grazing on Cleeve Hill, so don't be surprised to see the occasional flock of Cotswold sheep.

While the majority of grazing animals in the Cotswolds are sheep, there are still **cattle** to be found, particularly further south along the trail. Many are the familiar black-and-white Friesians, but more conspicuous are the occasional belted Galloways, almost entirely black but with a broad white belt around the girth. Near Stanley Wood you may spot a herd of English longhorn cows, their downward curved horns distinctly different from the norm. The 'local' breed, Gloucester cattle, are distinctive, too, though you'll be lucky to see them. Once bred for Double Gloucester cheese, they have smart, near-black coats (occasionally spotted) enlivened by a bold white streak running from mid spine and through the tail. Other distinguishing features are a black head and legs, and black-tipped horns.

No summary of farm animals in Gloucestershire would be complete without a nod to the **Gloucestershire Old Spot**. Named for the large black spots that dot their otherwise pink skins, these pigs once thrived in the outdoors, foraging on scraps and windfall apples. In fact, the spots are said to be bruises from falling apples in the orchards. They're among the piglets to be seen foraging in the paddock below Stanley Wood, and are immortalised at The Old Spot in Dursley!

Finally, there are the **horses**. Lots of them – though nowadays they scarcely fall into the bracket of farm animals. From children's ponies to thoroughbred racehorses, you'll find plenty that points to man's passion for equines. Riding stables are much in evidence, especially in the north of the region, and many's the day when you'll come across a rider or party of riders as you walk along the trail. With this obvious local involvement, it's no accident that two of the country's biggest events in the horsey calendar, the Cheltenham Gold Cup and Badminton Horse Trials, take place in the Cotswolds.

If you want a closer look at many of these animals and more rare breeds, pay a visit to **Cotswold Farm Park** (☎ 01451-850307, 🖥 www.cotswoldfarmpark.co.uk; mid Feb-Oct daily, 10.30am-5pm, Nov-late Dec 10.30am-4pm), east of Winchcombe, about four miles (6.4km) from the trail at Stumps Cross, off the B4077.

❏ The smaller things in life

While you're looking out for things at ground level, perhaps you'll spot two other

grassland natives that are both now rare, but can still be found in this habitat. The **glow worm** (*Lampyris noctiluca*) was once so common that people could read by the light of several found together. And **Roman snails** (*Helix pomatia*, left) were considered a delicacy by the Romans, which is presumably how they acquired their name. Look out for them around Leckhampton and Crickley Hill, their cream-coloured shells up to two inches wide.

greater horseshoe bat (*Rhinolophus ferrumequinum*), with a wingspan of around 14in (35cm), and its cousin, the **lesser horseshoe bat** (*Rhinolophus hipposideros*), as well as the tiny **pipistrelle** (*Pipistrellus pipistrellus*), which is Britain's most common species of bat – and the smallest, with a wingspan of just 8in (20cm).

REPTILES

The **adder** (*Vipera berus*) is the only venomous snake in Britain but poses very little risk to walkers and will not bite unless provoked or unwittingly disturbed; if you're lucky enough to see one, leave it in peace. Their venom is designed to kill small mammals such as mice and shrews; human deaths are rare.

You are most likely to encounter an adder in spring when they come out of hibernation, and during the summer when pregnant females warm themselves on open ground in the sun. They are easily identified by the striking zigzag pattern on their back and a 'V' on the top of their head behind the eyes.

Grass snakes (*Natrix natrix*) are Britain's largest reptile, growing up to a metre in length. They prefer rough ground with plentiful long grass in which to conceal themselves, laying their eggs in warm, rotting vegetation such as garden compost heaps, the young hatching in August. The body has vertical black bars and spots running along the sides and usually has a prominent yellow collar round the neck. They are sometimes killed by people mistaking them for adders but are neither venomous nor aggressive.

The equally harmless **slow worm** (*Anguis fragilis*) looks like a snake but is actually a legless lizard. It has no identifying marks on the body, which varies in colour from coppery brown to lead grey and is usually quite shiny in appearance. Like lizards, they are able to blink; snakes have no eyelids. They love to sun themselves and are also found in old buildings under stones or discarded roofing sheets. Also present is the **common lizard** (*Lacerta vivipara*), which like other reptiles is partial to sunning itself during the day to warm up its body temperature.

Using this guide

The route guide and maps have not been divided into rigid daily stages since people walk at different speeds and have different interests. The **route summaries** below describe the trail between significant places and are written as if walking the path from north to south. To enable you to plan your own itinerary, **practical information** is presented clearly on each of the trail maps. This includes walking times in each direction, places to stay and eat, as well as shops where you can buy supplies. Further **service details** are given in the text; note that the hours stated for pubs relate, for the most part, to when food is served; most venues serve drinks outside these hours. For **map profiles** see the colour pages at the end of the book. For an overview of this information see **itineraries** (pp30-8) and the village facilities table (pp34-7). The cumulative **distance chart** is on p194.

TRAIL MAPS

Scale and walking times

The trail maps are to a scale of 1:20,000 (1cm = 200m; $3^1/_8$ inches = one mile). Walking times (see box below) are given along the side of each map and the arrow shows the direction to which the time refers. Black triangles indicate the points between which the times have been taken. The time-bars are a tool and are not there to judge your walking ability. There are so many variables that affect walking speed, from the weather conditions to how many beers you drank the previous evening. After the first hour or two of walking you will be able to see how your speed relates to the timings on the maps.

Up or down?

The trail is shown as a dotted line – – –. An arrow across the trail indicates the slope; two arrows show that it is steep. Note that the

---

❏ **Important note – walking times**
Unless otherwise specified, **all times in this book refer only to the time spent walking.** You will need to add 20-30% to allow for rests, photography, checking the map, drinking water etc, not to mention time simply to stop and stare. When planning the day's hike count on 5-7 hours' actual walking.

arrow points towards the higher part of the trail. If, for example, you are walking from A (at 80m) to B (at 200m) and the trail between the two is short and steep it would be shown thus: A– – – >> – – – B. Reversed arrow heads indicate a downward gradient.

Accommodation

Accommodation marked on the map is either on or within easy reach of the trail. Where accommodation is scarce, however, some of the places listed are a little further away. If that is the case, many B&B proprietors will collect walkers from the nearest point on the trail and deliver them back again the next morning, if requested in advance. They may also be happy to transfer your **luggage** to your next accommodation place on the map. Some may make a charge for either or both of these services. Check the details at the time of booking. Details of each place are given in the accompanying text.

The number of **rooms** of each type is stated, ie: **S** = Single, **T** = Twin room, **D** = Double room, **Tr** = Triple room and **Qd** = Quad. Note that most of the triple/quad rooms have a double bed and one/two single beds (or bunk beds); thus for a group of three or four, two people would have to share the double bed, but it also means that the room can be used as a double or twin. See also pp18-19.

Rates quoted for B&B-style accommodation are **per person (pp) based on two people sharing a room** for a one-night stay; rates may well be discounted for longer stays. Where a **single room (sgl)** is available, the rate for that is quoted if different from the rate per person. The rate for **single occupancy (sgl occ)** of a double/twin may be higher and the per person rate for three/four sharing a triple/quad may be lower. Unless specified, rates are for bed and breakfast. At some places the only option is a **room rate**; this will be the same whether one or two people (or more if permissible) use the room. In tourist towns, particularly, you can expect to pay extra at weekends (whereas in the odd business establishment the rate is likely to be higher during the week). Note that some places accept only a two-night stay, particularly at weekends and in the main season.

Your room will either have **en suite** (bath or shower) facilities, or a **private** or **shared** bathroom or shower room just outside the bedroom.

The text also indicates whether the premises have: **wi-fi** (WI-FI); if a bath (🛁) is available either as part of en suite facilities, or in a separate bathroom – for those who prefer a relaxed soak at the end of the day; if a **packed lunch** (Ⓛ) can be prepared, subject to prior arrangement; and if **dogs** (🐾 – see also p25 and pp187-8) are welcome, again subject to prior arrangement, either in at least one room (many places have only one room suitable for dogs), or at campsites. The policy on charging for dogs varies; some places make an additional charge per day or per stay, while others may require a refundable deposit against any potential damage or mess.

Other features

The numbered **GPS waypoints** refer to the list on pp185-6. Generally, other features are marked on the maps when they are pertinent to navigation. In order to avoid cluttering the maps and making them unusable, not all features have been marked each time they occur.

The route guide

CHIPPING CAMPDEN   MAP 1a, p79

It feels fitting to start the trail in Chipping Campden, a beguiling town at the most northern point of the Cotswolds Area of Outstanding Natural Beauty where the classic Cotswold images of warm honey-coloured stone and rolling green hills are so perfectly balanced.

The start – or finish – of the trail has been marked since 2014 by a circular limestone plaque set into the flagstones at the foot of the Market Hall. Designed, like its partner outside Bath Abbey, by artist Iain Cotton, it is engraved with the names of places along the trail, encircled by a line from TS Eliot's 'Four Quartets': 'Now the light falls across the open fields leaving the deep lane shuttered with branches dark in the afternoon.'

Chipping Campden was founded on the wool industry in the 14th and 15th centuries, largely due to one of the country's most successful wool merchants, William Grevel. His home, **Grevel House** [10], still stands on the High St, and to him and other wealthy benefactors the town owes the outstanding, and revered, **St James's Church**. Over two hundred years later, another local worthy, Sir Baptist Hicks, trumped Grevel House with his **Campden House** [5], parts of which are now used by the Landmark Trust (see p62). Hicks was also responsible for the **Market Hall** [20], today owned by the National Trust and still in regular use, and for the **almshouses** [7] in Church St.

Fast forwarding through the centuries brings us to the **Arts and Crafts Movement** (see box on p76), which played an influential role in reversing the town's decline following years of agricultural doldrums. Now tourism is the key to the economy, with plenty of restaurants and a range of accommodation suited to walkers and sightseers alike.

Every year in May the town hosts a two-week music festival (🖳 www.campden musicfestival.co.uk) and – on Dover's Hill – the Olimpick Games (see box p81).

Transport

Access to Chipping Campden is relatively straightforward by road, but by public transport is more challenging. First Great Western operate services to the nearest railway station at Moreton-in-Marsh. Alternatively it's possible to get a Chiltern Railways train to Stratford-upon-Avon from London Marylebone; see box p46.

Johnsons' **bus** Nos 21, 22 & 24/24A (see pp48-50) stop on the High St. On a Sunday, and when there are no buses, you would need to organise a **taxi** (approx £22 one way from Moreton-in-Marsh, £22 from Evesham, or £28 from Stratford-upon-Avon) for the final leg of the journey. If you need to get back to Bath, there is no obvious route by public transport, but a taxi would cost around £110. Taxi firms include: Chipping Campden Cars (mob ☎ 07751-334696, ☎ 01386-840111), Les Proctor (mob ☎ 07580-993492; see Cornerways, Where to stay), and Red Lion Cars (☎ 01386-840760, mob ☎ 07565-226887; see Red Lion Inn Where to stay).

Services

The good **tourist information centre** [19] (☎ 01386-841206, 🖳 www.chippingcamp denonline.org; Apr-mid Nov daily 9.30am-5.30pm, mid Nov-Mar Mon-Thur 9.30am-1pm, Fri-Sun 9.30am-4pm) has its base in the Old Police Station on the High St. In addition to plenty of brochures and leaflets, there is a town guide for £1.50.

Those in search of a **bank** will find a branch of Lloyds [14] on the High St, and an ATM [30] in the car park. The **post**

❏ **Arts and Crafts Movement**
The Arts and Crafts Movement was founded in late Victorian Britain, born of a back-lash against the uniformity which resulted from the Industrial Revolution. Its proponents – practical architects and designers as well as theorists – were largely concerned with restoring a sense of individuality and cohesion to an increasingly fragmented workplace. There was more than a touch of the romantic in their ideals, which included spiritual harmony and a oneness with nature. These aims were to be achieved in part through reuniting the fields of art, craft and design, so that the designer would be brought back in touch with the maker. Authenticity was a key principle, for example with houses to be constructed from naturally occurring materials and fitting into their environment. If buildings and furniture were relatively simple, ornamental pieces such as books and needlework were considerably more elaborate, often drawing on influences not only from the past but from external cultures. Ironically, high-minded intentions to improve the lot of the working man proved unrealistic, since individually crafted work was expensive to produce and out of the reach of all but a privileged few.

The major founders of the movement were the writer and critic John Ruskin, and William Morris, who trained as an architect and was variously a designer, Socialist and author. Although the movement was essentially urban, many of its practitioners moved to the country, and some to the Cotswolds. One of these, the architect CR Ashbee, was the founder in 1888 of the **Guild of Handicrafts**, which he moved from London to Chipping Campden's Silk Mill [36] in 1902. When Ashbee went bankrupt eight years later, his workshop was taken over by the silversmith George Hart, whose great-grandson David now runs the business (see below). The work of Ashbee and eight other craftsmen is featured at **Court Barn Museum** [6] (Apr-Sep Tue-Sun and bank hol Mon 10am-5pm, Oct-Mar Tue-Sun & bank hol Mon 10am-4pm, closed 24 Dec-mid Jan; £5), in a converted barn near the church.

Other places along the trail that are linked to the movement include the **Gordon Russell Design Museum** in Broadway (see p81), **The Wilson Art Gallery and Museum** in Cheltenham (see p108), inspired by William Morris, the **Ashton Beer Collection** in Painswick (see p125), and **All Saints' Church** in Selsley (see p132).

Arts and Crafts visionaries had an impact on gardens, too, typically using topiary hedges used to create a series of 'rooms'. Such influences were important at both **Owlpen Manor** (see box p136) and **Hidcote** (☎ 01386-438333, 🖥 www.nationaltrust .org.uk; end Mar-early Oct daily 10am-6pm, Mar & Oct-daily 10-5pm, mid-end Feb & early Nov-mid Dec weekends only 11am-4pm; £11.50, NT members free), a few miles north of Chipping Campden.

office [23] is across the road, just a few doors down from the tourist office.

Nearby are two small **groceries**: Co-operative food [22] (Mon-Sat 7am-10pm, Sun 8am-10pm), and the One Stop [39] (daily 6am-10pm). More individual fare is to be found at Drinkwater's **greengrocer** [41], Maylam's **Deli** [16] (Mon-Sat 9am-5pm, Sun 11am-5pm), who also prepare sandwiches, the French artisan specialist La Tradition [40], and Toke's [12] (Mon-Fri 9am-6pm, Sat 9am-5pm, Sun 10am-5pm), where bread, cheese and pork pies are lined up beneath racks of wine. Every Friday morning (9-11am) except in January there's an indoor **market** with food and craft stalls in the Town Hall [25].

For something original, don't miss the **Guild** on Sheep St in Silk Mill [36]. Home to several artisans, it boasts a good art gallery, too (daily 10am-5pm), but the real draw is upstairs, where Hart's **silversmith** (🖥 www.hartsilver smiths.co.uk; Mon-Fri 9am-5pm, Sat 9am-noon) has operated since the early 20th century. Commission your own family heirloom, or take time to watch the craftsmen at work. The designs of another silversmith, **Robert Welch** [37] (🖥 www.robertwelch.com; Mon-Sat 9.30am-5.30pm, Sun 10am-4pm), are displayed at the shop bearing his name on Lower High St.

Campden Surgery [27] (☎ 01386-841894; Mon-Fri 8.30am-1.30pm & 2-6pm) is along Back Ends. The **pharmacy** [9] is on the corner of the High and Church streets. There are public **toilets** behind the tourist office (though you'll need 20p to access them), and opposite Silk Mill.

Where to stay

Many walkers starting at Chipping Campden will want to stay a night before setting off the following morning, if only to have a chance to see something of the town. There's plenty of choice – though accommodation does get booked up quickly, especially in the summer and at weekends.

Campers will need to ask at the tourist information centre (see p75) to find out if anywhere is available locally to pitch a tent. Otherwise, the nearest official site is at Hailes (see p94).

A few **B&Bs** are centrally located among the stone cottages of the High St itself. On Lower High St, rooms at *The Old Bakehouse* [34] (☎ 01386-840979, mob ☎ 07717-330838, 🖥 www.theoldbakehouse .org.uk; 2T or D en suite; WI-FI) cost from £45pp, with single occupancy of £80.

Further up the street, two of the tea rooms offer B&B in rooms above the premises: at *Badgers Hall* [21] (☎ 01386-840839, 🖥 www.badgershall.co.uk; 3T or D en suite, 1T private shower room; WI-FI; (L)) there's a minimum stay of two nights; bookings for a single-night stay are accepted only at the last minute. B&B costs from £55pp (sgl occ rates available on request) including a clotted cream tea, but the beamed rooms under the eaves may be cheaper. *Bantam Tea Rooms* [18] (☎ 01386-840386, 🖥 www.bantamtea-rooms .co.uk; 1S/1T/3D, all en suite; ➥; WI-FI) charges £45-50pp (sgl occ £80-90), or £70 for the single. If you stay the night you can leave your car here for the duration of your walk; contact them for details.

On the opposite side of the road is the classy *Seymour House* [11] (☎ 01386-840064, 🖥 www.seymourhousebandb.co .uk; 3D/2D or T, all en suite; ➥; WI-FI) where B&B in very elegant surroundings will set you back £140 for two sharing (sgl occ £90). Another room can be made available for families or groups who are happy to share a bathroom.

South of the main street, two modern options with unfussy rooms sit next to each other on George Lane, with footpath access to the High St. At *Stonecroft* [43] (☎ 01386-840486, 🖥 www.stonecroft-chip pingcampden.co.uk; 1T/1D with interconnecting bathroom, 1D en suite; WI-FI) rates are £40pp (£70 single occupancy). *Cornerways* [42] (☎ 01386-841307, 🖥 www.cornerways.info; 1Tr/1Qd, both en suite; WI-FI) charges £45pp (sgl occ full room rate, three/four sharing £120/150) only accepts advance bookings for at least two nights. They also offer station pick ups: contact Les Proctor (see Transport).

Several of the town's B&Bs lie in the opposite direction, along Aston Rd: solid stone houses with gardens backing on to open countryside. The first, *Cherry Trees* [4] (☎ 01386-840873, 🖥 www.cherrytrees campden.com; 2D/1Tr/1Qd, all en suite; ➥; WI-FI; (L)), is slightly elevated along a narrow track about 150m from the road, with views to Broadway Tower. The balcony room has a double bed as well as a double sofa bed so can sleep up to four people. Rates are £45-57.50pp (sgl occ £75-80, three/four sharing: room rate plus £35pp). They can offer parking if you wish to leave your car here while you walk but they have a two-night minimum stay policy year-round.

Back on Aston Rd itself at No 1 is *The Chance* [3] (☎ 01386-849079, 🖥 www.the-chance.co.uk; 2D or T, both en suite; WI-FI; Feb-Nov), which costs £50pp (sgl occ full room rate); in high season, there is usually a two-night minimum stay policy. Next up, at No 5, is *Taplins* [2] (☎ 01386-840927, 🖥 www.cotswoldstay.co.uk; 2D/1T, all en suite, ➥; WI-FI), under the same ownership as the antiques shop in the town, which perhaps accounts for the Victorian-style roll-

---

CHIPPING CAMPDEN

Where to stay
1 Wolds End House
2 Taplins
3 The Chance
4 Cherry Trees
8 Eight Bells Inn
11 Seymour House
15 Lygon Arms
18 Bantam Tea
   Rooms
21 Badgers Hall
24 Noel Arms
28 Cotswold House
   Hotel & Spa
29 The Kings Hotel
34 The Old
   Bakehouse
35 Volunteer Inn
38 Red Lion Inn
42 Cornerways
43 Stonecroft

**Where to eat and
drink**
8 Eight Bells Inn
13 Orchard Layne
15 Lygon Arms
17 Caminetto
18 Bantam Tea
   Rooms
21 Badgers Hall Tea
   Rooms
24 Noel Arms
26 Michael's
29 The Kings Hotel
31 Huxley's
32 The Campden
   Pantry
33 Butty's
35 Maharaja at
   Volunteer Inn
36 Campden Coffee
   Company
   (in Silk Mill)
38 Red Lion Inn

Other
5 Campden House
6 Court Barn
   Museum
7 Almshouses
9 Pharmacy
10 Grevel House
12 Toke's
14 Lloyds Bank/ATM
16 Maylam's Deli
19 Tourist Information
   Centre
20 Market Hall
22 Co-operative food
23 Post office
25 Town Hall
27 Campden Surgery
30 ATM
36 Silk Mill
37 Robert Welch
39 One Stop
40 La Tradition
41 Greengrocer

---

top bath in one of the rooms. B&B here costs from £39pp, or from £70 for single occupancy.

At *Wolds End House* [1] (☎ 01386-840956, 🖳 www.woldsendhouse.co.uk; 1T or D/1D share bathroom, 1D en suite; WI-FI), B&B costs £37.50pp (sgl occ £65), or £40pp (sgl occ full room rate) for the king-size en suite double.

If a **pub** is more your idea of a con-vivial place to spend the night, Chipping Campden comes up trumps. On Lower High St, almost opposite St Catharine's Church, the 17th-century *Volunteer Inn* [35] (☎ 01386-840688, 🖳 www.thevolun teerinn.net; 5D/4D or T, most en suite; WI-FI) has a couple of rooms where an extra bed can be added, but some rooms are over the bar so can be noisy. B&B costs £30-45pp (sgl occ from £50, three sharing £100), though rates may be negotiable if you turn up on spec. They also offer a lug-gage transfer service (see p27) under the name 'Cotswold Luggage Transfers'.

B&B at the family-run *Red Lion Inn* [38] (☎ 01386-840760, 🖳 www.theredlion inn.org, Lower High St; 1T or D/4D, all en suite; 🍽; 🐾; WI-FI) is normally £37.50-47.50pp (sgl occ £70-94). They also offer a pick-up service from local railway stations, or airports such as Bristol, Heathrow and Gatwick (see Red Lion Cars, p75).

Further along the High Street and not to be confused with its namesake in Broadway, is the *Lygon Arms* [15] (☎ 01386-840318; 🖳 www.lygonarms.co.uk; 7D or T/3Tr, all en suite, 🍽; WI-FI; 🐾;(🄻), a 16th-century coaching inn. Featuring exposed beams and stone walls, its rooms come in at £47.50-77.50pp for B&B (sgl occ £86-110, three sharing £150-170).

Continuing upmarket brings us to the *Eight Bells Inn* [8] (☎ 01386-840371, 🖳 www.eightbellsinn.co.uk; 5D/1D or Qd, all en suite; 🍽; WI-FI), on Church St, a 14th-century hostelry where the rooms, furnished in a sympathetic yet contemporary style, cost £47.50-70pp (sgl occ £75-150;

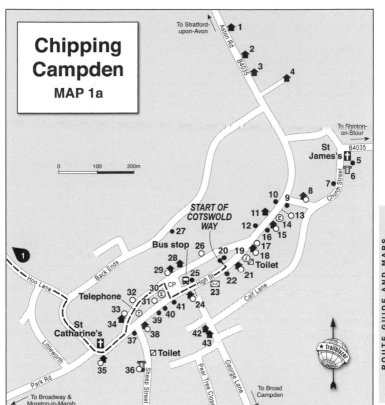

Chipping Campden
MAP 1a

To Stratford-upon-Avon

To Shipton-on-Stour

St James's

START OF COTSWOLD WAY

Bus stop

Telephone

St Catharine's

Toilet

Toilet

To Broadway & Moreton-in-Marsh

To Broad Campden

ROUTE GUIDE AND MAPS

three/four sharing £155/175). Note that at weekends there's a minimum two-night stay.

Smarter still are the **hotels**, of which *The Kings* [29] (☎ 01386-840256, 🖳 www.kingscampden.co.uk; 10D/3D or T in main house and 4D/1D or T in a separate cottage; all en suite; 🛏; WI-FI) has B&B at £57.50-152.50pp, or £97-200 for single occupancy. By prior arrangement it may be possible to leave your car here for the week while you walk.

The *Noel Arms* [24] (☎ 01386-840317, 🖳 www.noelarmshotel.com; 15T or D/12D, all en suite; 🛏; WI-FI; 🐾) charges £75-110pp (sgl occ £140-210). In this rather elevated sphere, there's also

Cotswold House Hotel & Spa [28] (☎ 01386-840330, 🖳 www.bespokehotels .com/cotswoldhouse; 28D or T, all en suite; 🛏; WI-FI; 🐾), which might justify a splurge at the end of a walk. Dynamic pricing makes B&B rates – from £42.50 to £132.50pp for the smaller doubles (sgl occ £75-130), including use of the hydrotherapy pool and steam rooms – something of a lottery, but come in the winter months and you could strike lucky.

Where to eat and drink

Top-quality food with prices to match is done well along Chipping Campden's High St, but there's a good range of more accessible fare as well, especially at lunchtime.

For food on the move, start at *Butty's* [33] (Mon-Fri 7.30am-2pm, Sat 8.30am-1.30pm; WI-FI); there's an all-day breakfast, too, and sandwiches from £3.50. Or try *The Campden Pantry* [32] (Mon-Sat 9am-5pm, Sun 10am-4pm), where sandwiches (including takeaway) from £3.60, soups and salads are served in their café with a courtyard.

If you'd rather linger over tea, coffee or a light lunch, several places fit neatly into the frame. For irresistible cakes, *Bantam Tea Rooms* [18] (see Where to stay; daily 10am-5pm) has an enviable selection, as does the friendly *Badgers Hall Tea Rooms* [21] (see Where to stay; daily 10am-4.30pm). Tucked away down a narrow alley is *Orchard Layne* [13] (daily 10am-4pm), where you can combine coffee and cakes, cream teas or stone-baked pizzas (£5.90-8.50) with a spot of retail therapy in their gift shop. Seating is either at the back of the shop or on an outside terrace. For a serious coffee fix, head straight for the more contemporary but still welcoming *Campden Coffee Company* [36] (💻 www .campdencoffeecompany.co.uk; Mon-Fri 9am-4.30pm, Sat & Sun 10am-4.30pm), in Silk Mill on Sheep St, where coffee beans are freshly ground and the cakes – including gluten free – are home-made. There are smoothies, too, as well as soups, jacket potatoes, baguettes and ice creams.

The town also has some excellent pubs. The *Eight Bells Inn* [8] (see Where to stay; food served Mon-Thur noon-2pm & 6.30-9pm, Fri-Sun noon-2.15pm, Fri & Sat 6.30-9.30pm, Sun 12.15-9pm), which retains the atmosphere of a traditional pub, offers plenty of options. Wherever you eat – in the bar, the restaurant or the courtyard garden – you should eat well, from 'proper' pork pies to upmarket bangers and mash, or try their seasonal menu, with offerings such as jerked chicken, sweet potato chips and pineapple and coriander slaw at £15.85.

At the *Lygon Arms* [15] (see Where to stay; food served daily 11.30am-2.30pm & 6-10pm) the menu features lamb and beef from the family farm, as well as sandwiches, homemade soup and jacket potatoes at

around £6.25. The atmosphere at the *Red Lion Inn* [38] (see Where to stay; food served Mon-Thur noon-2pm & 6-9pm, Fri noon-2.30pm & 6-9.30pm, Sat & Sun noon-3pm & 6-9.30pm), where the sign states 'muddy boots and paws welcome', is relaxed and friendly, and there's a courtyard bar if you'd rather be outside with a pint of IPA. The menu is primarily traditional English, with daily specials that reflect seasonal produce: expect to pay from £10.95 for a main course, with lighter bites at lunch costing around £6.50.

The bar at *The Kings Hotel* [29] (see Where to stay; Mon-Fri noon-2.30pm & 6.30-9.30pm, Sat noon-3pm & 6.30-9.30pm, Sun noon-3pm & 6-9pm) is much classier than the name would suggest, though more intimate than its formal restaurant. Its menu changes regularly, but expect dishes such as broccoli and cauliflower arborio risotto with Cotswold blue brie (£12.50), as well as sandwiches.

The Italian *Caminetto* [17] (Tue-Sat noon-1.30pm & 6-9.30pm) is emphatically not a pizza place (think *saltimbocca alla romana* at £19.20, with pasta mains from £9.75), but it does come well recommended. *Michael's* [26] (💻 www.michaelsmedi terranean.co.uk; Tue-Sat 11am-2.30pm & 7-10pm, Sun noon-3pm) does all things Greek/Mediterranean, albeit at decidedly un-Greek prices. Try *mezedakia* (nine hot/cold hors d'oeuvres for sharing) at £15.50, or moussaka with salad (£15.95).

Close to the car park in the town centre, the convivial *Huxleys* [31] (☎ 01386-849077; 💻 www.huxleys.org; summer Mon-Thur 8.30am-8pm, Fri-Sat to 10pm, Sun 10am-4pm; winter same but Mon-Tue 8.30am-5pm) serves Italian treats from antipasti to panini gustozi (from £7.50). A terrace under willow trees makes a popular summer alternative to the restaurant.

If you fancy a curry, head for the Indian *Maharaja* [35] (see Where to stay; Sun-Thur 5.30-10.30pm, Fri-Sat 5-11pm) at the Volunteer Inn. The pub itself sticks to the beer, which can be savoured in summer in the garden. Otherwise you might be in luck if the *Noel Arms* [24] (see Where to stay) is hosting one of their regular curry nights.

CHIPPING CAMPDEN TO BROADWAY   MAPS 1-3

This first **6-mile (9.6km, 2¾-3¼hrs)** stretch of the Cotswold Way, charac-
terised by agricultural land and open hills, is a great introduction to the trail as
a whole. A gradual ascent leads across farmland to **Dover's Hill**, at 738ft
(225m) the first of many high points along the walk, affording the first of many
superb views. Get your bearings (and your breath) at **Broadway Tower** (see
box p85), the second-highest point along the trail, before the steep descent to
Broadway.

BROADWAY   MAP 3a, p87

Named for its wide central street, once the
main road between Worcester and London,
Broadway is to many tourists (and there are
a lot of them) synonymous with the
Cotswolds.

A broad green at the western end of the
High St sets a somewhat bucolic tone,
enhanced by trees lining the road and rows
of stone cottages, giving rise to an excess of
clichés and tourist shops. And yet, despite
the high number of visitors, the town
retains a considerable charm, particularly
outside the summer months.

Celebrating Broadway's links with the
Arts and Crafts Movement (see box p76),
the **Gordon Russell Design Museum** (☎
01386-854695, 🖳 www.gordonrussellmu
seum.org; Tue-Sun Apr-Oct 11am-5pm,
Nov-Dec & Feb-Mar 11am-4pm; entry £5)
pays tribute to a man who from 1918 committed his working life on this site to
designing and making furniture.

Opened in 2013, the **Ashmolean
Museum Broadway** (☎ 01386-859047, 🖳
www.ashmoleanbroadway.org; Tue-Sun
10am-5pm; £6) harks back to an earlier
period. It is housed in a beautifully preserved 17th-century house, which is no
small part of its attraction. As at the main
Ashmolean in Oxford, it includes a 'cabinet
of curiosities', as well as a fine collection of
18th-century paintings, with an emphasis
on the local area. The top floor showcases
temporary exhibitions featuring artists such
as Whistler.

Somewhat unusually, Broadway's
original parish church of **St Eadburgha**
is marooned in a serene location well over
half a mile (1.10km) to the south, towards
Snowshill. Severely damaged in the 2007
floods, it has now been restored and makes
an interesting detour. Today, its former role
is filled by **St Michael & All Saints**, close
to the town and an attractive backdrop to
the trail as it leaves Broadway.

Transport

[See pp48-50] Several **buses** stop here pro-
viding connections with Stratford-upon-
Avon, Cheltenham and Evesham. The most
useful for walkers is the 606/606S, run by
Marchants.   *(cont'd on p85)*

ROUTE GUIDE AND MAPS

❑ **Olimpick Games**
Chipping Campden displays its frivolous side in the form of Robert Dover's
Olimpick Games (🖳 www.olimpickgames.co.uk), held on Dover's Hill (Map 1, p82)
every May on the Friday after the Whitsun Bank Holiday. Dating back to 1612, it's a
noisy affair, with bands, cannon fire and fireworks, culminating in a torchlit proces-
sion into the town for dancing in the square. If events such as sack races, a tug of war
and even shin-kicking would raise an eyebrow at the Olympics, there's also the more
conventional shot put, part of the Championship of the Hill, as well as wrestling and
cross-country races.

The following day is the **Scuttlebrook Wake**, more of a village fête in style,
with a Scuttlebrook Queen, maypole dancing and colourful floats.

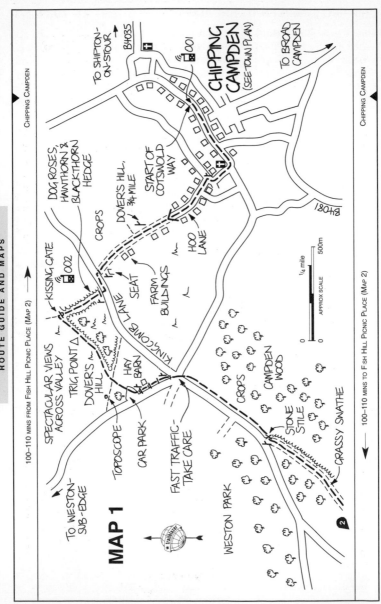

CHIPPING CAMPDEN

CHIPPING CAMPDEN

← 100–110 MINS FROM FISH HILL PICNIC PLACE (MAP 2)

100–110 MINS TO FISH HILL PICNIC PLACE (MAP 2) →

B4035

TO SHIPTON-ON-STOUR

☐☐☐ 001

CHIPPING CAMPDEN
(SEE TOWN PLAN)

TO BROAD CAMPDEN

B4081

DOG ROSES, HAWTHORN & BLACKTHORN HEDGE

START OF COTSWOLD WAY

DOVER'S HILL, ¾ MILE

HOO LANE

CROPS

KISSING GATE

☐ 002

SEAT

FARM BUILDINGS

SPECTACULAR VIEWS ACROSS VALLEY

TRIG POINT △

DOVER'S HILL

HAY BARN

KINCOMBE LANE

TOPOSCOPE

CAR PARK

FAST TRAFFIC - TAKE CARE

CROPS

CAMPDEN WOOD

STONE STILE

GRASSY SWATHE

TO WESTON-SUB-EDGE

MAP 1

WESTON PARK

trailblazer

2

¼ mile

APPROX SCALE

0   500m

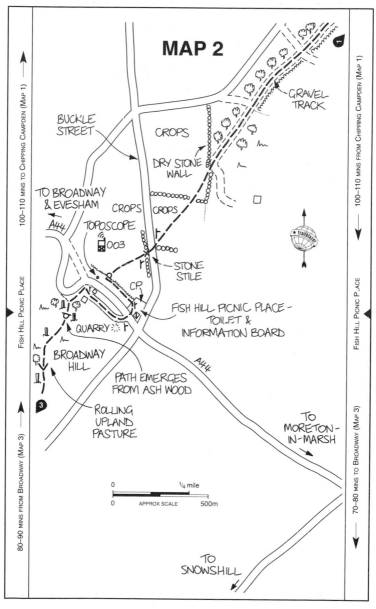

MAP 2

GRAVEL TRACK

BUCKLE STREET

CROPS

DRY STONE WALL

TO BROADWAY & EVESHAM

A44

CROPS   CROPS

TOPOSCOPE
003

STONE STILE

CP

FISH HILL PICNIC PLACE – TOILET & INFORMATION BOARD

QUARRY

BROADWAY HILL

PATH EMERGES FROM ASH WOOD

A44

TO MORETON-IN-MARSH

ROLLING UPLAND PASTURE

0   ¼ mile
0   500m
APPROX SCALE

TO SNOWSHILL

ROUTE GUIDE AND MAPS

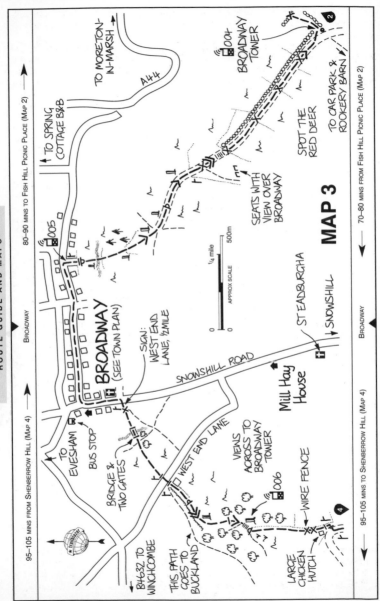

80–90 MINS TO FISH HILL PICNIC PLACE (MAP 2) →

← TO SPRING COTTAGE B&B

TO MORETON-IN-MARSH

A44

1004 BROADWAY TOWER

2

TO CAR PARK & ROOKERY BARN (MAP 2) →

SPOT THE RED DEER

70–80 MINS FROM FISH HILL PICNIC PLACE (MAP 2) ←

SEATS WITH VIEW OVER BROADWAY

1005

MAP 3

¼ mile
500m
APPROX SCALE
0

BROADWAY
(SEE TOWN PLAN)

SIGN: WEST END LANE, ½ MILE

SNOWSHILL ROAD

ST EADBURGHA

SNOWSHILL

BROADWAY

Mill Hay House

← Broadway

95–105 MINS FROM SHENBERROW HILL (MAP 4) →

TO EVESHAM

BUS STOP

B4632 TO WINCHCOMBE

THIS PATH GOES TO BUCKLAND

BRIDGE & TWO GATES

WEST END LANE

VIEWS ACROSS TO BROADWAY TOWER

1006

LARGE CHICKEN HUTCH

WIRE FENCE

4

95–105 MINS TO SHENBERROW HILL (MAP 4) ←

(cont'd from p81) Other services include NN Cresswell's R4 and Johnsons' Nos 21 & 24/24A.

Broadway's **taxi** firms include AJW's Private Hire (mob ☎ 07930-868552, ☎ 01386-642786), Blue Cabs (mob ☎ 07770-175175), Cotswold Horizons (☎ 01386-858599) and Delta Taxis (mob ☎ 07798-767688).

Services

Almost everything in Broadway happens on the High St, though the smart **tourist information centre** (☎ 01386-852937, 🖳 www.beautifulbroadway.com; Mon-Sat Apr-Oct 10am-5pm, mid Feb-Mar & Nov to late Dec 10am-4pm, Sun mid-Feb-Oct 11am-3pm) is set back behind Budgens **supermarket** (daily 8am-9pm). Across the road on the High St itself is the more personal and very well-stocked Broadway Deli

(Mon-Sat 8am-5pm, Sun 9am-3pm), with fresh fruit and veg, bakery bread and all sorts of goodies.

Close at hand is Blandford Books (☎ 01386-858588; hours vary but generally Mon-Sat 10.30am-5.30pm, Sun 11am-4.30pm) stocks a good range of **books** and is particularly strong on local titles. Those browsing for **antiques** will find plenty to delay them along the street, too.

More practically, the **post office** is on the High St, as is a branch of Lloyds **bank**, with an ATM; there's another ATM at Budgens.

For **medical** matters, contact Barn Close Surgery (☎ 01386-853651; Mon-Fri 8.30am-6.30pm) opposite the post office, or the nearby Lloyds **pharmacy**.

A footpath from the High St leads through to the public **toilets** in the car park on Church Close.

❏ Broadway Tower   Map 3

With its turreted top and walls of oolitic limestone, the tall tower that looms into view as you cross the fields on the outskirts of Broadway is an unlikely sight, apparently protecting only the sheep that graze nearby. Built in 1799 as a folly for Lady Coventry by the 6th Earl of Coventry, it sits atop Beacon Hill which, at 1024ft (312m), is the second highest point in the Cotswolds. In its heyday, it was a lively retreat, attracting several Pre-Raphaelite artists, among them the Socialist and artist William Morris (1834-96), who was a regular visitor from his home at Kelmscott. Rejected by the National Trust in 1949, the tower is now in private hands, but it is open to the public (☎ 01386-852390, 🖳 broadwaytower.co.uk; daily 10am-5pm exc 25-26 Dec & 1 Jan; admission £5).

According to Morris's daughter, May, men used to bathe on the roof of the tower, which was described as 'the most inconvenient and the most delightful place ever seen'. Today's visitors can climb up to the roof, too, but only for the scenery: in good weather there are superb 360° views across 13 counties. The ground floor is given over to a shop, while each of the interim floors showcases a series of small exhibitions covering the history of the tower, and its links with both William Morris and the Royal Observer Corps. Some 200m north of the tower, and somewhat incongruous in this setting, is a Cold War nuclear bunker (open weekends and bank holiday Mondays, 45-minute tour £4, or £8 to include entrance to the tower; no under 12s), which used to be manned by the Royal Observer Corps. Rather more in keeping with the rural surroundings is a herd of red deer, which roam peacefully within a small enclosure.

The *Morris & Brown* café in the grounds (daily 10am-5pm exc 25-26 Dec & 1 Jan) opened in 2015, alongside a small but swanky gift shop where you can also buy tickets for the tower. The décor is contemporary, the food likewise: panini and ciabatta from £6.50 are set alongside 'soup of the moment', and dishes that include chipotle chicken salad (£9.90). And lots of tea and cakes.

Where to stay

There's no shortage of places to stay in this picture-postcard village that draws American visitors in their droves. Finding something within a tight budget is much harder – and unless you're planning to walk in the depths of winter, you'd be well advised to book ahead.

A couple of **pubs** offer accommodation. At the pleasant *Horse and Hound* (☎ 01386-852287; 3D/1D or T, all en suite; 🛏; WI-FI; 🐾), at the top of the High St, a room above the pub is from £40pp (£70 for single occupancy).

Rates at the 17th-century *Crown & Trumpet* (See also Where to eat; ☎ 01386-853202, 🖳 www.cotswoldholidays.co.uk; 1T/3D, all en suite; 🛏; WI-FI) are £24-34pp (sgl occ full room rate); at weekends there is a two-night minimum stay.

There are several more traditional **B&Bs** in and around the centre. The Cotswold Way runs right past the gate of *Cowley House* (☎ 01386-858148, 🖳 www.cowleyhouse-broadway.co.uk, Church St; 3D/4T or D/1Qd, most en suite; 🛏; 🐾; WI-FI; ⓛ), which is part 17th century. Just off The Green, so peaceful but central, it has rooms for £39.50-53pp (sgl occ £66-96, three/four sharing: room rate plus £25pp), the higher rate coming with a four-poster bed. Small dogs can be accommodated in one room, which has a private garden. For £7.50 a load they'll even do your laundry.

At the other end of the High St away from any traffic but also on the Cotswold Way, is the award-winning *Olive Branch* (☎ 01386-853440, 🖳 www.theolivebranch-broadway.com; 1S private shower facilities, 3D/2T or D/1Tr/1Qd, all en suite; 🛏; WI-FI; ⓛ), built in 1592 and offering B&B for over 50 years. Today, rooms are fitted out in an elegant but cottagey style (three with a bath) and a range of extras. Rates are £46.50-60.50pp (sgl £70-75, sgl occ £95, three/four sharing: room rate plus £25pp).

Still very central, on Leamington Rd just off the High St, is *Hadley House* (☎ 01386-853486, 🖳 hadley.house; 3T/2D, all en suite; WI-FI; ⓛ), where B&B costs £40-45pp (£55 single occupancy).

Just off this road, on the corner of Colletts Fields and the footpath from Upper High St, is *Dove Cottage* (☎ 01386-859085, 🖳 www.broadway-cotswolds.co.uk/dove-cottage-bb; 1T/1D, both en suite; 🛏; WI-FI; ⓛ), charging from £42.50pp (sgl occ from £50).

To the west of town, in the direction of Evesham, there's a cluster of good-sized B&Bs lining Station Rd. First up, less than quarter of a mile (0.3km) from the trail, is *Whiteacres* (☎ 01386-852320, 🖳 www.broadwaybandb.com; 1Tr/4D, all en suite; WI-FI), with B&B at £37.50-42.50pp, or £60-65 for single occupancy.

The neighbouring *Windrush House* (☎ 01386-853577, 🖳 www.windrushhouse.com; 3D/2T, all en suite; WI-FI; ⓛ) offers a more contemporary décor in the rooms which is reflected in the higher price: from £45pp a night (£75 for single occupancy). Advance bookings at weekends must be for two nights.

Next door again, walkers are particularly welcome at *Apple Tree House* (formerly called Southwold House; ☎ 01386-853681, 🖳 www.appletreebroadway.co.uk; 1S private facilities, 2T or D/4D/1Tr, all en suite, 🛏; WI-FI; ⓛ), where there's a bath in one of the pretty double rooms and a drying cupboard for wet clothes. B&B here costs £40-47.50pp (£58 single, sgl occ £70-85, three sharing £120).

A similar distance further up the road is *Brook House* (☎ 01386-852313, 🖳 www.brookhousebandb.co.uk; 1S & 1D share bathroom, 2D/1Qd, all en suite; 🛏; 🐾; WI-FI; ⓛ), where rates start from £40pp (sgl £50, sgl occ £70, three/four sharing £120/140).

Last of the bunch, about half a mile (0.8km) from the trail, is *The Old Stationhouse* (☎ 01386-852659, 🖳 www.broadwaybedandbreakfast.com; 4D, all en suite, 🛏; WI-FI), occupying the old stationmaster's lodgings down a private drive between the railway bridge and the fuel station. B&B costs £47.50-60pp (sgl occ £80-105) but the minimum stay is two nights.

In the opposite direction lies *Spring Cottage* (off map 3; ☎ 01386-852920, 🖳 juneruddy@googlemail.com; 2D en suite, 🛏; WI-FI), backing onto farmland on the

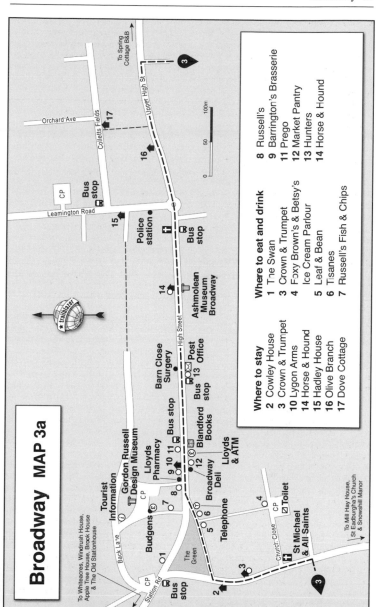

Broadway MAP 3a

Where to stay

2 Cowley House
3 Crown & Trumpet
10 Lygon Arms
14 Horse & Hound
15 Hadley House
16 Olive Branch
17 Dove Cottage

Where to eat and drink

1 The Swan
3 Crown & Trumpet
4 Foxy Brown's & Betsy's Ice Cream Parlour
5 Leaf & Bean
6 Tisanes
7 Russell's Fish & Chips
8 Russell's
9 Barrington's Brasserie
11 Prego
12 Market Pantry
13 Hunters
14 Horse & Hound

quiet Bibsworth Lane. To find it, head east from the trail along Upper High St for about a quarter of a mile (0.4km), then turn left at East House and continue for a similar distance; it's the last house on the right. B&B here costs £37.50pp, or £60 for single occupancy.

For most walkers, the renowned *Lygon Arms* (☎ 01386-852255, 🖥 www.thehotel collection.co.uk/hotels/the-lygon-arms-hotel-cotswolds; 2S/76D but some twins, most en suite; ☞; WI-FI; 🐾) at £69.50-125pp (sgl £90-120; sgl occ rates on request) a night is likely to remain firmly off limits, but at least it puts other places in perspective. Rates can vary a lot and may include breakfast and/or dinner, so it is worth checking their website.

And if you fancy being truly decadent, you could swap your boots for Queen Anne-style splendour at *Mill Hay House* (see Map 3, p84; ☎ 01386-852498, 🖥 www.mill hay.co.uk; 3D, all en suite; ☞) where, from a mere £92.50-120pp (sgl occ £165-220), Annetta Gorton offers a 'gourmet breakfast', though there may be a minimum two-night stay policy at weekends in the high season. It lies on Snowshill Rd less than half a mile (0.65km) south of the trail.

Where to eat and drink

A popular option for lunch or dinner is *The Swan* (☎ 01386-852278, 🖥 www.theswan broadway.co.uk; Mon-Fri noon-10pm, Sat 9am-10pm, Sun 9am-9.30pm), opposite The Green, where comfy chairs & heavy wooden tables feel right at home in the old building. Relaxed and informal, it offers a varied menu, with the likes of West Country beefburgers (£10.50) alongside slow-cooked pork belly and seared scallops with sticky ginger-beer glaze (£18.25). Do book if you want to be sure of a table.

At the *Horse and Hound* (see Where to stay; daily noon-2.30pm & 6-8.30pm), the refurbished bar has a lighter touch but still feels traditional, with at least three guest ales on tap. Their standard lunch menu includes soup (from £4.50) as well as pizzas from £4.95 and more substantial fare (£8.95-16.95). More lively is the *Crown & Trumpet* (see Where to stay; Mon-Thur

noon-2.30pm & 6-9.15pm, Fri-Sun noon-9.15pm) on Snowshill Rd, where there's jazz and blues most Thursday evenings, and contemporary live music on Saturdays. Their Sunday roast costs from £9.95 and they have ales from Stanway Brewery and other local breweries.

Back on the High St, all things Italian loom large at *Prego* (☎ 01386-306670, 🖥 www.pregobroadway.co.uk; daily coffee and cakes 10am-6pm, lunch noon-2.30pm, evening meal 6-9pm, closed Sun in winter), with its cool décor and unpretentious service. Think ciabatta with chips and salad at £4, along with pasta, pizza – and a great cocktail menu. They even do takeaways (noon-2.30pm & 6-7.30pm), if you fancy an evening with your feet up.

Part of the Lygon Arms, but in a separate building, the not-inaccessible *Barrington's Brasserie* (☎ 01386-854418; Wed 6-9pm, Thur noon-2.30pm & 6-9pm, Fri noon-2.30pm & 6-10pm, Sat noon-3pm & 6-10pm, Sun noon-3pm & 6-8.30pm) spills out onto the pavement on sunny days. You can get main meals at lunch and in the evening, from £12, but during the day, from Thursday to Sunday, it also serves the likes of sandwiches or ciabatta with salad and chips from £6.50.

Along a passageway leading from the High St, *Russell's Fish & Chips* (☎ 01386-858435, 🖥 russellsfishandchips.co.uk; daily noon-2.30pm & 5-8.30pm) does exactly what it says, either to eat in or take away and from £9.95. The relaxed sibling of Russell's (see below), it has tables both inside and out, with no traffic fumes to add to the mix. Continuing upmarket, *Russell's* itself (☎ 01386-853555, 🖥 russellsofbroad way.co.uk/restaurant; Mon-Sat noon-2.15pm & 6-9.15pm, Sun noon-2.30pm) offers a fixed-price menu at £14-22 (not available Saturday evening or Sunday). There's an à la carte menu, too, albeit best kept for very special occasions.

Not surprisingly, with so many tourists around, tea is high on the agenda here. Try *Tisanes* (☎ 01386-853296; daily 10am-5pm), on The Green, complete with waitresses in white pinnies and traditional bow window, though the option of gluten-free dishes is rather more contemporary. Further up, on the High St, the popular *Market Pantry* (☎ 01386-858318; Mon-Fri 9am-5pm, Sat 9.30am-5pm, Sun 10am-5pm) serves breakfast, lunch and tea, to include toasties at £6.25 and some innovative tartines (£6.95). Note that it may close earlier in winter. The nearby *Hunters* (☎ 01386-858522; Mon-Fri 10am-4pm, Sat & Sun 10am-5pm) falls into a similar category, its menu including substantial sandwiches from £2.30. More modern but still cosy is the *Leaf & Bean* (☎ 01386-859151;

daily 10am-5pm), whose range of fancy sandwiches include falafel, caramelised onion and salad.

At the bright and efficient *Foxy Brown's* (☎ 01386-852155; daily approx 9.30am-5.30pm but depends on demand), in the precinct leading to the car park, cyclists jostle with shoppers for coffee and home-made cakes. More substantial are quiches and the likes of warm chicken salad (£7.25), or pick up an ice cream in the affiliated *Betsy's Ice Cream Parlour* (similar hours) to enjoy as you continue on your way.

BROADWAY TO WINCHCOMBE   MAPS 3-8

This **12-mile (19.3km, 5½-6½hrs)** stretch should fulfil the expectations of anyone who has leafed through glossy coffee-table books on the Cotswolds. Here are the rolling hills, the fine views and the cottages of time-weathered stone. This is rural England at its best, with **Stanton** the quintessential Cotswold village. Some steep ups and downs bring in several cultural highlights, too: **Stanway House** (see p92); the site of the Iron-Age **Beckbury Camp**, where a stone monument known locally as 'Cromwell's seat' is reputed to mark where Thomas Cromwell watched Hailes Abbey burn; and the ruins of **Hailes Abbey** itself (see box p96) – which are well worth exploring. From Hailes it's an easy and pleasant walk to the fine old wool town of Winchcombe.

ROUTE GUIDE AND MAPS

❏ **Snowshill Manor**   off Map 4, p90
Even those least interested in museums will find something appealing about a man who amassed a collection that ranged from Samurai armour to stringed instruments to boneshaker bicycles. Charles Paget Wade was just such a collector, cramming his house, 2½ miles (4km) south of Broadway, with a seemingly random range of over 22,000 items. Even the gardens, with their terraces, ponds and outdoor rooms, were the subject of his apparently boundless enthusiasm.

Today, Snowshill Manor (☎ 01386-852410, 🖳 www.nationaltrust.org.uk; mid Mar-Oct daily 11am-5.30pm; Nov weekends only grounds 10.30am-3.30pm, guided tour of house 11.15am-2.15pm; admission £11.50, gardens only £6.50, Nov £3, NT members free) is in the hands of the National Trust, which struggles to keep pace with the number of visitors to what is a relatively small house. For walkers along the Cotswold Way, the house is best approached along the footpaths leading east from Shenberrow Farm; it's a distance of around three-quarters of a mile (1.2km). The tea room in the grounds makes a detour particularly appealing, but with timed tickets to visit the house, you may need to be flexible to avoid disappointment.

❏ **Important note – walking times**
All times in this book refer only to the time spent walking. You will need to add 20-30% to allow for rests, photography, checking the map, drinking water etc.

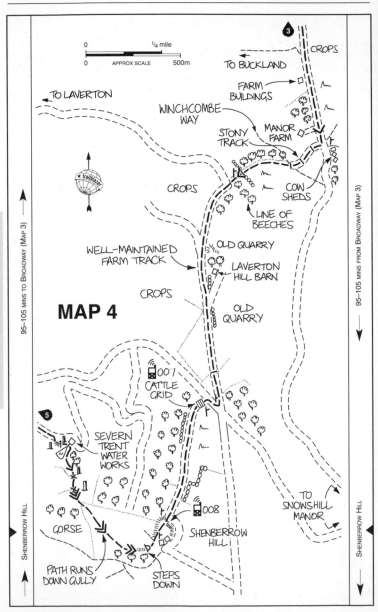

0   ¼ mile
0   APPROX SCALE   500m

3

TO BUCKLAND

CROPS

FARM
BUILDINGS

WINCHCOMBE
WAY

STONY
TRACK

MANOR
FARM

TO LAVERTON

CROPS

COW
SHEDS

LINE OF
BEECHES

WELL-MAINTAINED
FARM TRACK

OLD QUARRY

LAVERTON
HILL BARN

CROPS

OLD
QUARRY

MAP 4

95–105 MINS TO BROADWAY (MAP 3)

95–105 MINS FROM BROADWAY (MAP 3)

007
CATTLE
GRID

5

SEVERN
TRENT
WATER
WORKS

TO
SNOWSHILL
MANOR

008

GORSE

SHENBERROW
HILL

PATH RUNS
DOWN GULLY

STEPS
DOWN

SHENBERROW HILL

SHENBERROW HILL

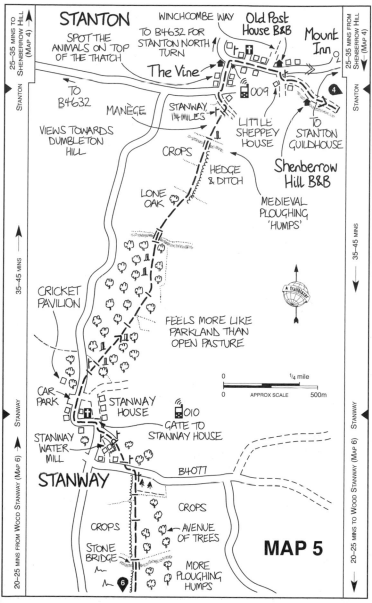

STANTON MAP 5, p91

Broadway may attract the tourists, but for true Cotswold beauty Stanton is hard to beat. At the heart of the village is the **church of St Michael & All Angels**, its tall spire clearly visible in the valley from the surrounding hills.

Marchants' No 606/606S **bus** stops at Stanton North Turn – the most northerly of the junctions on the B4632, about half a mile from the village. As yet there's no bus stop, but if you wave to the driver from either turning, they should stop. See public transport map and table, pp48-50.

There are a few **B&Bs** in the village, all on the trail, and all benefiting from an excellent **pub**, ***The Mount Inn*** (☎ 01386-584316, 🖳 www.themountinn.co.uk; food served daily Apr-Oct noon-2pm, Mon-Sat 6-9pm, Sun 6-8pm; Oct-Apr no food Sun pm or Mon; note that the pub closes in the afternoon). Up a steep hill, yet only a stone's throw from the trail, it boasts an inglenook fireplace, Donnington beers and superb views; evening reservations are strongly recommended. The menu ranges from baguettes to The Mountmans: a cheese, meat and chutney variation on the ploughman's theme (£13), and specials such as confit of duck leg on bubble and squeak with green peppercorn sauce (£15.25).

Within just 200m of the pub is ***Shenberrow Hill*** (☎ 01386-584468, 🖳 www.broadway-cotswolds.co.uk/shenberrowhill; 3D/2T/1Tr, all en suite, ▼; 🐕; WI-FI; Ⓛ), not to be confused with the complex of buildings at the top of Shenberrow Hill (Map 4). B&B costs from £44.50pp (sgl occ from £59, rates for three sharing on request), with some of the rooms (1D/2T) in an annexe.

Right in the heart of the village, ***The Vine*** (☎ 01386-584777, 🖳 www.broadway-cotswolds.co.uk/thevine; 1D/1T/1Tr; ▼; small 🐕; WI-FI; Ⓛ) offers B&B for £42.50pp (sgl occ £65-85, £115 for three sharing); the double and triple have their own shower and washbasin, but share a toilet; the twin is en suite. Guests share a sitting room. The owner specialises in horseriding (☎ 01386-584250).

Equally central is the ***Old Post House*** (☎ 01386-584398, 🖳 www.cotswold-way.co.uk/oldposthouse; 1T en suite, 1S/2T private facilities; ▼; WI-FI; Ⓛ), its gate tucked behind the scarlet phone kiosk that now serves as an information post. Conversion of the old telephone exchange has resulted in a traditional but tasteful twin room, with three further rooms in the main house. Expect to pay £45pp for B&B, or £60 for single occupancy.

Up the hill, about 300m beyond the car park of The Mount Inn, is ***Stanton Guildhouse*** (☎ 01386-584357; 🖳 www.stantonguildhouse.org.uk; 1S/5T/ 1Qd, shared bathroom; ▼; WI-FI; Ⓛ), whose self-contained stone-built house has space for up to 15 guests on a self-catering basis. As the four bathrooms are shared, the house is always let out to one party, with a minimum of six people. B&B (continental breakfast) is available mid-week at £50pp; at weekends, you'll stay on a self-catering basis, with prices on application. Walkers are welcome, but many guests are there to take part in one of the classes, seminars and workshops for which the Guildhouse was founded.

STANWAY MAP 5, p91

If you're passing through in June, July or August on a Tuesday or Thursday between 2pm and 5pm, do drop into the Jacobean **Stanway House** (☎ 01386-584469, 🖳 www.stanwayfountain.co.uk; fountain £4.50, house & fountain £7). Set in a restored 18th-century water garden, with its own tea room, it claims to have the tallest gravity fountain in the world which, at 300ft (91m), normally 'plays' at 2.45pm and 4pm. At other times you'll have to be content with the sight of the imposing gatehouse and the neighbouring church. Spare a glance, too, for the thatched cricket pavilion set on staddle stones near by. It was a gift from *Peter Pan* author JM Barrie, who used to rent the house during the summer months.

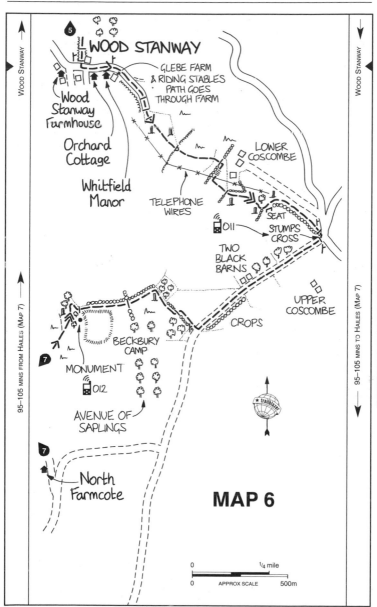

5

WOOD STANWAY

GLEBE FARM
& RIDING STABLES
PATH GOES
THROUGH FARM

Wood
Stanway
Farmhouse

Orchard
Cottage

Whitfield
Manor

LOWER
COSCOMBE

TELEPHONE
WIRES

SEAT
011 STUMPS
CROSS

TWO
BLACK
BARNS

UPPER
COSCOMBE

CROPS

7

BECKBURY
CAMP

MONUMENT
012

AVENUE OF
SAPLINGS

7

North
Farmcote

MAP 6

0   ¼ mile

0   APPROX SCALE   500m

95–105 MINS FROM HAILES (MAP 7)

95–105 MINS TO HAILES (MAP 7)

ROUTE GUIDE AND MAPS

A further attraction on the Stanway estate is the restored **Stanway Watermill** (☎ 01386-584446/69, 🖳 www.stanway mill.co.uk; £3; phone for combined ticket with the house), which opens to visitors at the same times as the house, plus 10am-noon on Thursday all year.

WOOD STANWAY   MAP 6, p93

Blink and you could miss the sleepy hamlet of Wood Stanway, but it does offer a couple of **B&B** options and a swanky boutique hotel. The 17th-century *Wood Stanway Farmhouse* (☎ 01386-584318, 🖳 www .woodstanwayfarmhouse.co.uk; 1D/1T/2Qd, all en suite; 🛁; 🐾; WI-FI; Ⓛ), 30 yards down the road to the right as you come through the gate, has open views across farmland and the hills. B&B costs from £37.50pp (sgl occ £45, three/four sharing rates on request). The nearest pub is 1¼ miles (2km) away in Toddington, but a three-course evening meal around £17pp can be prebooked.

Smaller, but built of similarly age-softened stone, *Orchard Cottage* (☎ 01386-584752, 🖳 annflavellwood@yahoo.co.uk; 1D/1T, en suite; 🛁; WI-FI; Ⓛ) is just a stone's throw away, with B&B for £40pp (single occupancy £45). An evening meal can be provided at £19.50-23.50 if booked in advance.

The village is also the setting for a new upmarket boutique hotel, *Whitfield Manor* (🖳 www.whitfield-manor.com; 10D or T, all en suite; 🛁; 🐾; WI-FI; Ⓛ). Opening in spring 2016, it is set in a traditional old manor house, with six rooms in the main house and four in a stone coach house. At £125pp for B&B (sgl occ from £230), it may be beyond the budget of most walkers, but their **restaurant** (daily 8-10.30am, 12.30-2pm & 7-9pm) will be open to all.

NORTH FARMCOTE   MAP 6, p93

One of a handful of working farms offering B&B within reasonable reach of the Cotswold Way is *North Farmcote* (☎ 01242-602304, 🖳 www.northfarmcote.co .uk; 1D/1T both en suite, 1Tr private bathroom; 🛁; WI-FI; 🐾), in a glorious location just over quarter of a mile (0.2km) from the trail (see Map 7 for access, and follow the sign for Farmcote Herbs). B&B costs £42.50-47.50pp (sgl occ £60, £110-120 for three sharing). If the owners aren't busy they will drive guests to the nearest pub, a couple of miles away at Ford, for an evening meal.

HAILES   MAP 7

Hailes (or Hayles, or Hales) – which really does have three spellings – takes its name from the **abbey** (see box p96).

The trail descends parallel to the orchards of *Hayles Fruit Farm* (☎ 01242-602123, 🖳 www.hayles-fruit-farm.co.uk; 🐾). This has one of the few **campsites** along the entire Cotswold Way that is actually on the trail, so make the most of it. It's a large, fairly level, grassy site, with shower and toilet facilities, where you can pitch a tent for £7.50pp per night. They also have pre-erected bell tents sleeping either three (£30) or five people (£50), the latter with a wood-burning stove. These should be booked in advance. Just up the hill is their excellent **farm shop** (daily 9am-5pm, winter days/hours variable), where you can buy good cakes and delicious apple juice, as well as ice-cream, fresh bread and the makings for a substantial breakfast. There's also a welcoming **tea room and restaurant** (daily 9am-5pm; hot food served noon-3pm); sit by the window to combine your meal with a spot of birdwatching!

If you'd prefer a **B&B**, *Ireley Farm* (☎ 01242-602445, 🖳 www.ireleyfarm.com; 1T private bathroom/2D en suite; 🛁; 🐾 but have to stay in outside building; WI-FI; Ⓛ) could fit the bill. You'll pay from £32pp, with a simple meal available from about £7.50 a head. Access is via a footpath from Hailes of just over half a mile (0.8km); the farm is also within walking distance of Winchcombe Pottery (see p98).

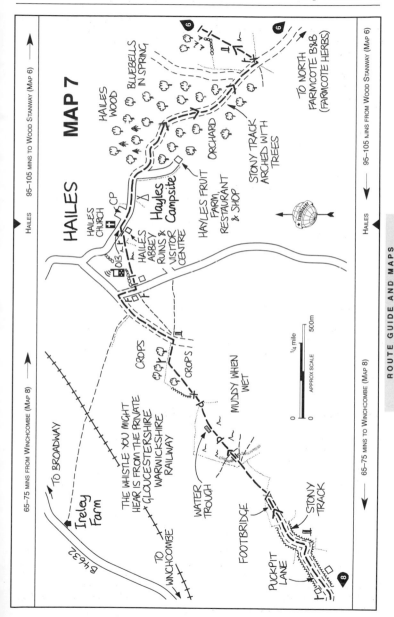

MAP 7

HAILES

HAILES WOOD

BLUEBELLS IN SPRING

6

6

TO NORTH FARMCOTE B&B (FARMCOTE HERBS)

STONY TRACK ARCHED WITH TREES

ORCHARD

HAILES CHURCH

CP

Hayles Campsite

HAILES ABBEY RUINS & VISITOR CENTRE

013

HAYLES FRUIT FARM RESTAURANT & SHOP

★ trailblazer

TO BROADWAY

Ireley Farm

B4632

TO WINCHCOMBE

THE WHISTLE YOU MIGHT HEAR IS FROM THE PRIVATE GLOUCESTERSHIRE WARWICKSHIRE RAILWAY

CROPS

CROPS

MUDDY WHEN WET

WATER TROUGH

FOOTBRIDGE

PUCKPIT LANE

STONY TRACK

8

¼ mile

500m

0

APPROX SCALE

0

❑ Hailes Abbey   Map 7, p95

Hailes Abbey (☎ 01242-602398, 🖳 www.english-heritage.org.uk; daily Apr-Jun & Sep-Oct 10am-5pm, Jul-Aug 10am-6pm; admission £4.70, or £5.20 inc Gift Aid, English Heritage and National Trust members free) dates back to the 13th century. It owes its construction to a vow made by Richard, Earl of Cornwall (1209-72), should he survive a storm at sea during his return from a military campaign. The ship returned safely to harbour, and the earl, son of King John and brother of Henry III (who was responsible for the construction of Westminster Abbey), founded the abbey in 1246.

The site, that of an existing settlement, was chosen carefully. Limestone was readily available for building, there was good grazing for sheep, and a reliable water supply, with which the monks created a series of fishponds. The building itself was an elaborate affair, in contrast with the traditional simplicity of the Cistercian brotherhood – and indeed with the austerity of the earlier parish church, which lies across the road, and is still in use. The importance and grandeur of the abbey lay largely in its possession of the Holy Blood relic, which was housed in its own specially designed shrine and which brought considerable income into the abbey's coffers.

Initially, the population at the new abbey comprised a prior, 20 monks and 10 lay brothers, who moved here from Beaulieu Abbey in Hampshire, but much of the community died in 1361 during a recurrence of the Black Death. The monastery was dissolved in 1539, one of the last to be closed on Henry VIII's orders, and the abbey destroyed. The remainder of the estate was given by the king to Katherine Parr. Later, the buildings were adapted as a country house, but by 1794 that, too, lay in ruins. Today, it is the ruined cloisters that most vividly conjure up some sense of the ordered life once led by the monks. All that remains of the abbey are the footings, yet these – together with artefacts found on the site, on display in the excellent visitor centre – give a powerful indication of the scale and drama of the original building. In the words of St Bernard, *Bonum est nos hic esse*: 'It is good for us to be here.'

WINCHCOMBE   MAP 8a, p99

The ancient Saxon borough of Winchcombe, one-time capital of the kingdom of Mercia, later enjoyed status as a focal point for pilgrims. Its abbey has long since gone, but the town – emphatically not a village – of Winchcombe remains a significant presence in the Cotswolds. For walkers along the Cotswold Way, it's an ideal place to stay or to stop for a bite to eat at one of a number of pubs, restaurants and tea rooms. Even if you're short of time, it's worth taking a look inside the wool church of **St Peter's**.

If you've longer to spare, you might want to check out **Sudeley Castle** (see box p98), or one of two small museums. At **Winchcombe Folk and Police Museum** (🖳 www.winchcombemuseum.org.uk; Apr-Oct Mon-Sat 10am-4pm; £2), next to the **old stocks** and the tourist information office (see p98), exhibits about the town's history rub shoulders with a collection of police paraphernalia.

Those with a nostalgic bent might make time for a trip on the **Gloucestershire Warwickshire Steam Railway** (☎ 01242-621405, 🖳 www.gwsr.com). Axed by Beeching in the 1960s, the line – which skirts the town to the west – was bought in 1981 and restored by volunteers. Steam trains run between Toddington and Cheltenham Racecourse; for timetables and special events, see the website.

The Cotswold Voluntary Wardens lead a heavily oversubscribed annual series of **11 consecutive walks** for those who would like to complete the trail in stages, one of them based from Winchcombe; for details, see p29.

See box p16 for details of the festivals held here in May.

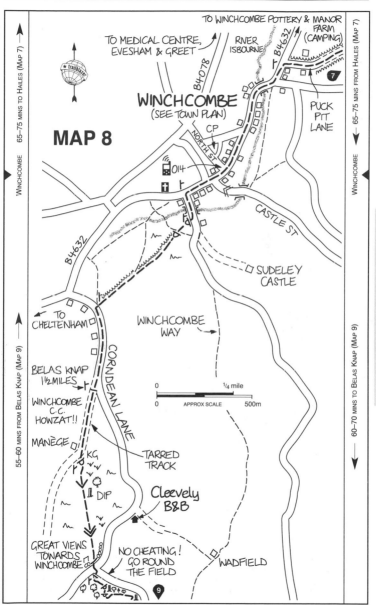

Transport

Winchcombe is well placed on a north–south **bus** route running through the Cotswolds. The 606/606S, operated by Marchants, links Broadway with Cheltenham via Stanton, Winchcombe – including at the war memorial and North St – and Cleeve Hill. Marchants also operates the new W1 and W2 services. For details, see the public transport map and table, pp48-50.

A reliable **taxi** service is run by Taylor's (mob ☎ 07814-570876, ☎ 01242-603651).

Services

There's a small but helpful **tourist information centre** (☎ 01242-602925; Apr-Oct daily 10am-4pm, Nov-Mar Sat 10am-4pm, Sun 10am-3pm), in the old Town Hall, on the corner of North St. Useful websites are ☐ www.winchcombewelcomeswalkers.com and ☐ www.winchcombe.co.uk.

Lloyds **bank** has a branch with an ATM on the High St; on Hailes St there's a **newsagent** that sells drinks and snacks, but most other tourist amenities are found along North St. This lies at right angles to the trail from the tourist information centre and is where you'll find the **post office**, as well as the town's **supermarket**, the Co-op (Mon-Sat 7am-10pm, Sun 8am-10pm), and

several independent shops. Try North's **bakery** for fresh rolls and sandwiches, or the excellent **delicatessen** Food Fanatics (see Where to eat), where sandwiches are made to order or to eat in. There's also an independent **greengrocer** next to the Co-op.

Just over half a mile (1km) north of Puck Pit Lane on the B4632, to the left just after the railway bridge, you'll find **Winchcombe Pottery** (off Map 8, p97; ☎ 01242-602462, ☐ www.winchcombepottery.co.uk; Mon-Fri 8am-5pm, Sat & bank hols 10am-4pm, May-Sep Sun noon-4pm), where traditionally crafted pots are still turned, fired and sold on the premises. There's a **shoe repairer** here, too (☎ 01242-604602; Mon-Fri 8am-1pm), so if your boots need some attention, it's worth going out of your way.

Winchcombe **medical centre** (☎ 01242-602307; Mon-Fri 8.15am-6.30pm) is about a quarter of a mile (0.4km) north of the town, along Greet Rd, and there's a branch of Lloyds **pharmacy** on the High St.

Where to stay

Winchcombe has a good assortment of small pubs and inns and a few B&Bs, most of them fairly central. **Campers**, though, will need to walk some three-quarters of a mile (1.2km) from the trail to *Manor Farm* (off map 8a; ☎ 01242-602423; 🐾) where

---

❏ **Sudeley Castle**   **Map 8, p97**

The history of Sudeley Castle (☎ 01242-602308, ☐ www.sudeleycastle.co.uk; mid Mar-Oct daily 10am-5pm; entry £14.50, 20% discount to English Heritage members) can be traced back as far as King Ethelred, in the 10th century. Although nothing of his manor house remains, the estate's royal connections run like a thread through its chequered past, from Edward IV to Queen Elizabeth I. The buildings visible today, including the Dungeon Tower and St Mary's Church, were constructed by Baron Sudeley from the mid 15th century. It is in the church that Katherine Parr, the sixth of Henry VIII's wives, is buried, having lived at Sudeley following the king's death. A century later, the castle fell into disuse, becoming increasingly dilapidated until it was bought and restored during Victoria's reign by members of the Dent family. The castle today is the private home of their descendants.

Visitors may look round the church and tour the estate, with its beautiful rose gardens, a pheasantry, and a wonderful wooden fort that will make you wish you were 10 years old again. A number of rooms in the castle are also accessible to the public, including the Dent-Brocklehursts' library, the morning room, and Chandos bedroom. A new visitor centre opening in 2016 will incorporate space for a shop and café.

you'll pay £7pp (toilet/shower facilities are available). To get there from the Cotswold Way, turn right at the end of Puck Pit Lane, go under the railway bridge and turn immediately left (past the pottery) to **Greet**. Just before the Harvest Home pub, turn right; the farm is about a quarter of a mile (0.4km) up that road on the left-hand side.

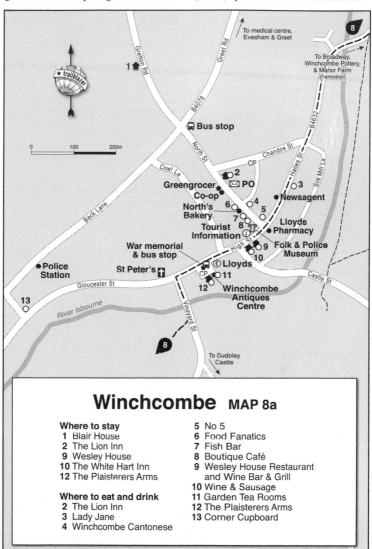

Winchcombe MAP 8a

Where to stay
1 Blair House
2 The Lion Inn
9 Wesley House
10 The White Hart Inn
12 The Plaisterers Arms

Where to eat and drink
2 The Lion Inn
3 Lady Jane
4 Winchcombe Cantonese

5 No 5
6 Food Fanatics
7 Fish Bar
8 Boutique Café
9 Wesley House Restaurant and Wine Bar & Grill
10 Wine & Sausage
11 Garden Tea Rooms
12 The Plaisterers Arms
13 Corner Cupboard

ROUTE GUIDE AND MAPS

Blair House (☎ 01242-603626, 💻 www.blairhousewinchcombe.co.uk; 1T/2D; ✉; WI-FI; 🐾), at 41 Gretton Rd, has an en suite double for £37pp B&B (sgl occ £54). The other rooms share a bathroom and cost £33-35pp; single occupancy of these rooms is £46-50.

For those seeking a more rural setting, the half-timbered *Cleevely* (see Map 8, p97; ☎ 01242-602059, 💻 cleevelybxb@hotmail.com; 1T en suite/1Tr private bathroom; ✉; WI-FI; 🅛), on Corndean Lane, could fit the bill. Just off the trail (and three-quarters of a mile – 1.2km – from the nearest pub, in Winchcombe), it is surrounded by farmland and enjoys glorious views. B&B here is from £35pp (sgl occ £40, three sharing around £100). There may be a minimum two-night stay policy at weekends.

Of the **pubs** and inns, the *White Hart Inn* (☎ 01242-602359, 💻 www.whitehart winchcombe.co.uk; 3T/3T or D/5D, most en suite; ✉; WI-FI; 🅛), on High St, is right on the trail and ideal for walkers, with three designated ramblers' rooms (2T/1D) which share a bathroom and cost £19.50-39.50pp. The other (en suite) rooms are divided into standard (£24.50-49.50pp) and superior (£29.50-59.50pp). Single occupancy of any room costs £34-115. See The Wine & Sausage (Where to eat).

Right next door is the smartly gabled *Wesley House* (☎ 01242-602366, 💻 www.wesleyhouse.co.uk; 4D/1D or T, all en suite; WI-FI; 🅛), more of a restaurant with rooms, charging £37.50-42.50pp (sgl occ £65-80) from Sunday to Thursday. On Friday and Saturday rooms may be booked only as part of a two night B&B package with either an evening meal or Sunday lunch, at £92.50-102.50pp (sgl occ around £135). Rates may be higher during the National Hunt Festival in March (see box p14).

Set back from the main road on Abbey Terrace, near Lloyds Bank, *The Plaisterers Arms* (☎ 01242-602358, 💻 www.plaisterersarms.co.uk; 2T/3D, all en suite; ✉; WI-FI; 🐾) has B&B for around £65 for two sharing, or £40-65 for single occupancy. If you have a dog you will need to bring bedding for it.

Close to the shops on North St is *The Lion Inn* ☎ 01242-603300, 💻 www.the lionwinchcombe.co.uk; 2D or T/5D, all en suite; ✉; WI-FI; 🐾; 🅛), where B&B in comfortably refurbished rooms with a blissful lack of TV costs £55-92.50pp (sgl occ full room rate). For a convivial evening, just head downstairs to the excellent bar.

Where to eat and drink

'Winchcombe welcomes walkers' proclaims the sign, and nowhere more so than in its wide range of places to eat. On Hailes St, you'll be walking past the olde-worlde *Lady Jane* (☎ 01242-603578; Sat-Wed 10am-4.30pm, also Fri in summer). Their menu encompasses afternoon tea as well as lunch; consider soup and a sandwich for £7.95. Round the corner on North St, the licensed deli *Food Fanatics* (see p98; ☎ 01242-604466, 💻 www.food-fanatics.co.uk; Mon-Fri 8am-7pm, Sat to 6pm, Sun 10am-5pm) serves a range of sandwiches, platters and cakes as well as breakfasts; the nearby *Boutique Café* was taken over by new owners after research; it is open but may have been renamed by the time you get here.

Those with an acquisitive nature might be drawn to the *Garden Tea Rooms* at **Winchcombe Antiques Centre** (☎ 01242-300556; Easter to Oct Mon-Sat 11am-5pm, Sun 11am-4pm; Oct to Easter Sat/Sun 11am-4pm only), off the High St, where you'll pass rooms enticingly jammed with antiques to reach the simple basement café for tea and cakes, or a light lunch.

For more hearty fare, try one of the pubs. On the main street is *The Plaisterers Arms* (see Where to stay; Mon-Sat noon-2.30pm & 6-9pm, Sun noon-6pm), which does a good range of baguettes at lunchtime and substantial mains in the evening, not to mention a scrumptious chocolate mousse. They've a lovely garden, too, and as a diversion, no fewer than 28 different gins! Further along is the *Corner Cupboard* (☎ 01242-602303; Mon-Sat noon-3pm & 6-9pm, Sun noon-3pm & 6-8pm), where the Sunday lunch is particularly good and real ales prominent. In a class of its own is *The Lion Inn* (see Where to stay; daily noon-3pm & 6-9pm); the atmosphere is relaxed but the food – from a lunchtime pizza of tuna, fennel, pickled ginger and baby spinach (£12.50) to slowly braised brisket of wagyu beef, mashed potato, French beans and rich beef jus at dinner (£16.50) – is taken very seriously.

The restaurant at the White Hart Inn (see Where to stay), *Wine and Sausage* (🖵 wineandsausage.whitehartwinchcombe.co.uk; food daily 8am-9pm), speaks for itself: come for a range of local sausages (£11) and other fare, washed down with wine – or beer, or cider. They serve breakfast, coffee and afternoon teas, too.

More jazzy is *Wesley House Wine Bar & Grill* (see Where to stay; daily noon-2pm & 6-10pm) which thoughtfully offers a two-course Cotswold Way lunch menu for £12.50. Otherwise soups, salads, fishcakes and a risotto of the day (£11), sit alongside sandwiches (lunchtime only), with cocktails an added bonus. For a special occasion, try their more upmarket sibling, *Wesley House* (Tue-Sat noon-2pm & 7-9.30pm, Sun noon-2pm), or *No 5* (☎ 01242-604566, 🖵 www.5northstreet restaurant.co.uk; Wed-Sun 12.30-1.30pm, Tue-Sat 7-9pm) on North St.

If none of these appeals, Winchcombe also has a couple of takeaways, also along North St: the *Fish Bar* (Tue-Sat 11.30am-2pm, Mon-Sat 4.30-9.30pm); and *Winchcombe Cantonese Chinese Takeaway* (Wed-Mon 5-11pm).

WINCHCOMBE TO CLEEVE HILL   MAPS 8-10

The next **6 miles (9.6km, 3-3½hrs)** take in one of the highlights of the Cotswold Way: **Cleeve Hill Common**, passing the ancient and impressive long barrow of **Belas Knap** (see box below). Considered to be the largest single area of unimproved limestone grassland in Gloucestershire, the common rises to the highest point on the trail, at 1066ft (325m). Wild and windswept, its closely cropped turf is shared by sheep, golfers and walkers, but it's a successful partnership; there is plenty of space for all.

Much of the trail at this point runs along the edge of the Cotswold escarpment, with a grandstand view of **Cheltenham Racecourse** on the plains below. If visibility is poor, take especial care along this stretch; it would be all too easy to stray too close to the edge.

POSTLIP   **MAP 9a, p103**
The Cotswold Way neatly sidesteps the hamlet of Postlip, but the section between Belas Knap and Cleeve Hill Common does skirt around the edge of the privately owned Postlip Hall; see box p16 for details of the Cotswold Beer Festival which is usually held here.

ROUTE GUIDE AND MAPS

❏ **Belas Knap**   **Map 9, p102**

Sheltering in the corner of a field, at the edge of the woods, the ancient long barrow (see box p136), or burial ground, of Belas Knap rises up from the ground rather like a beached whale, some 180ft (55m) long and 18ft (5.5m) high. Dating back to around 2500BC, it was used for successive burials, possibly over several centuries, until it was deliberately blocked. Archaeologists have uncovered the remains of 38 human skeletons, as well as animal bones, flints and pottery. At the northern end, an apparent entrance in fact leads nowhere, but the reason for this is unclear.

The grass-covered mound – for such is its appearance today – is dotted with cowslips and daisies, but you can clearly see the thin layers of stone, neatly stacked like sheaves of paper, that were used in its construction.

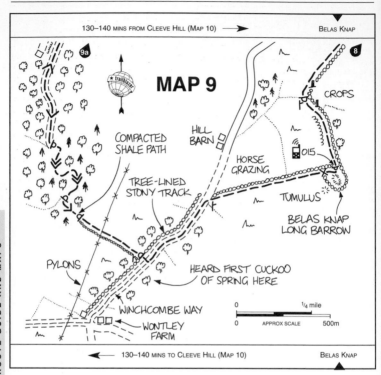

130–140 MINS FROM CLEEVE HILL (Map 10) ⟶
BELAS KNAP

9a

MAP 9

8

CROPS

HILL BARN

HORSE GRAZING

015

COMPACTED SHALE PATH

TREE-LINED STONY TRACK

TUMULUS

BELAS KNAP LONG BARROW

PYLONS

HEARD FIRST CUCKOO OF SPRING HERE

0   ¼ mile

0   APPROX SCALE   500m

WINCHCOMBE WAY

WONTLEY FARM

◀ 130–140 MINS TO CLEEVE HILL (Map 10)
BELAS KNAP

There's a perfectly positioned **B&B** right on the trail here at ***Postlip Hall Farm*** (☎ 01242-603351, 🖳 www.smoothhound .co.uk/hotels/postlip; 1T or D/1D, both en suite; WI-FI; (Ⓛ), but with no evening meal available you may have to walk or consider a taxi to The Rising Sun (see opposite) on Cleeve Hill. The house itself is built of stone and sheltered behind high hedges on a working farm. Rooms cost £42.50pp, or £65 for single occupancy.

CLEEVE HILL   MAP 10, p104
Right by the trail, and up on Cleeve Hill itself, the bar at ***Cleeve Hill Golf Club*** (☎ 01242-672025, 🖳 www.cleevehillgolf club.co.uk; daily 8am-4pm, winter 9am-4pm) is open to non-members for tea, coffee and light lunch.

You can eat in the clubhouse, on the veranda or on the grass looking up to Cleeve Hill and the golf course, choosing from a menu that's available from midday and ranges from baguettes at £4.40 to ploughmans, jacket potatoes and fish & chips at around £7.50.

All three hotels on Cleeve Hill are clustered fairly close together about a quarter of a mile (0.4km) down the hill from the trail, along the busy B4632 but with views across to the Malvern Hills. To avoid walking along the road, you can take one of the footpaths that lead down from the trail, bringing you out at the back of the hotels. First up is the elegant ***Cleeve Hill House***

Hotel (☎ 01242-672052, 🖥 www.cleeve hill-hotel.co.uk; 7D/3D or T, all en suite; 🍷; WI-FI; ⓛ), where you'll need sufficient energy in reserve for the steep steps up to the front door. Some rooms here are suites or have four-poster beds; B&B costs £47.50-55pp (sgl/sgl occ £60-75).

Slightly further down the hill, *Malvern View* (☎ 01242-672017, 🖥 www.malvern view.com; 6D all en suite, 1T private bath-room; 🍷; WI-FI; ⓛ) has rooms of varying styles. Rates are £45-60pp for B&B (around £65 for single occupancy).

Finally, just a couple of hundred yards further down, there's the rather larger *Rising Sun* (☎ 01242-676281, 🖥 www.old englishinns.co.uk/our-locations/the-rising-sun-hotel-cheltenham; 1S/4T/17D/2Tr, all en suite with 🍷; WI-FI; 🐾; ⓛ). B&B rates are complex but range from £25pp to £60pp (sgl occ full room rate); the single is £55-70 and three sharing costs £80-95. Dining (Mon-Fri 7-10am, Sat/Sun 8-10am, daily noon-10pm) is pretty relaxed, whether in the restaurant or bar, outside on the terrace, or in the steep hillside garden – where

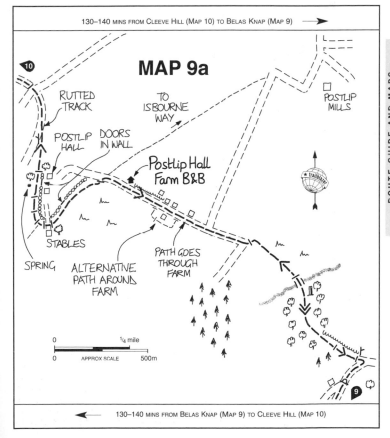

130–140 MINS FROM CLEEVE HILL (MAP 10) TO BELAS KNAP (MAP 9) ⟶

MAP 9a

RUTTED TRACK

TO ISBOURNE WAY

POSTLIP MILLS

POSTLIP HALL

DOORS IN WALL

Postlip Hall Farm B&B

★ trailblazer

STABLES

SPRING

ALTERNATIVE PATH AROUND FARM

PATH GOES THROUGH FARM

0   1/4 mile
0   APPROX SCALE   500m

9

130–140 MINS FROM BELAS KNAP (MAP 9) TO CLEEVE HILL (MAP 10) ⟵

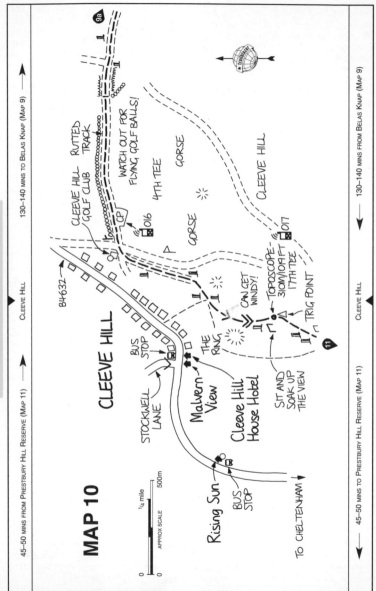

MAP 10

CLEEVE HILL

B4632

9a

CLEEVE HILL GOLF CLUB

RUTTED TRACK

WATCH OUT FOR FLYING GOLF BALLS!

CP

016

4TH TEE

GORSE

GORSE

CLEEVE HILL

GORSE

TOPOSCOPE 310M/1017FT 17TH TEE

017

TRIG POINT

CAN GET WINDY!

BUS STOP

STOCKWELL LANE

THE RING

Malvern View

Cleeve Hill House Hotel

SIT AND SOAK UP THE VIEW

11

Rising Sun

BUS STOP

TO CHELTENHAM

¼ mile

500m

APPROX SCALE

0

0

trailblazer

there's a superb view to distract from the traffic, but you may struggle to keep the plates on the table! As well as lunchtime favourites there's a comprehensive menu with mains averaging £8-12, and a daily specials board. Wednesday night is quiz night.

Marchants' **bus** Nos 606/606S and W1/W2 stop at Stockwell Lane, opposite the first two hotels, and also by the Rising Sun; see the public transport map and table, pp48-50.

CLEEVE HILL TO LECKHAMPTON HILL   MAPS 10-15

The **9¼-mile (15km)** section of the trail that skirts around Cheltenham takes about **4¾ to 5½ hours** to complete. If it seems from on high as though the town goes on forever, much of the walking is across open common land with exceptionally rewarding views. Those interested in natural history are in for a treat, with ancient beeches and large-leaved limes in **Lineover Wood** (Map 13; the word means 'lime bank'), and the protected areas of **Prestbury Hill Reserve** (Map 11; incorporating both Masts Field and the Bill Smyllie Reserve), **Charlton Kings Common** (Map 14) and **Leckhampton Hill** (Map 15), each sheltering several rare flowers and butterflies.

Leckhampton Hill itself is the site of one of the many hill forts (see box, p122) that line the escarpment, and of the much-photographed **Devil's Chimney**. This tall outcrop of rock towers over a disused quarry, giving rise to a legend involving the Devil hurling stones from this spot at worshippers as they made their way to church on a Sunday. More prosaic suggestions as to its provenance include erosion (somewhat unlikely), and the attractive possibility that it was created as a bawdy joke by 18th-century quarry workers. Whatever its history, the chimney has been regularly climbed by local youngsters over the years and even survived an earthquake in the 1920s. Today, it is securely fenced to help protect it from (very real) erosion.

CHELTENHAM   MAP 11b, p109

Cheltenham was swept into the popular consciousness by George III, who first came to take the waters in 1788. Its Regency architecture, with whitewashed houses rather than the natural dressed stone typical of Georgian Bath, continues to attract visitors, but today the town's primary attractions are considerably broader than its architecture or spa waters. Although Cheltenham is some distance from the trail, many visitors to the town will want to sample at least a section of the Cotswold Way, while some walkers along the trail may wish to work the town into their trip in some way, so the information given here is intended as a starting point.

❑ **Walking between Cheltenham and the Cotswold Way   Map 11a, p107**
While the most direct route from Cheltenham to the Cotswold Way is probably along the busy London Rd, this is hardly attractive walking territory. Far more interesting is to head north out of town through the park towards the racecourse, from where a network of footpaths along the edge of Queen's Wood leads up to Cleeve Hill Common – some of it coinciding with the Gustav Holst Way (see p108). If you fancy returning a different way, you can descend along the woodland path to Southam and thence back to the racecourse, a circular trip of just over 5 miles (8.25km).

ROUTE GUIDE AND MAPS

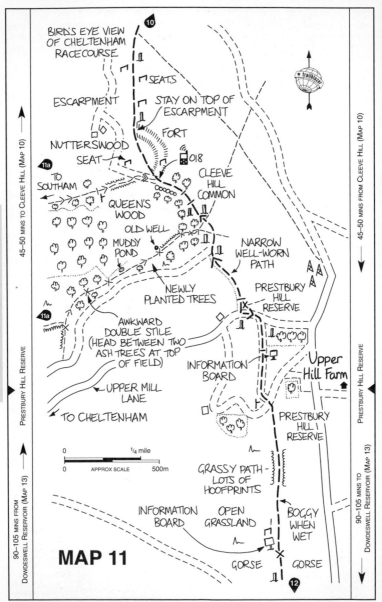

BIRD'S EYE VIEW
OF CHELTENHAM
RACECOURSE

10

SEATS

ESCARPMENT

STAY ON TOP OF
ESCARPMENT

FORT

NUTTERSWOOD
SEAT

018

11a

TO
SOUTHAM

CLEEVE
HILL
COMMON

QUEEN'S
WOOD

OLD WELL

NARROW
WELL-WORN
PATH

MUDDY
POND

PRESTBURY
HILL
RESERVE

NEWLY
PLANTED TREES

11a

AWKWARD
DOUBLE STILE
(HEAD BETWEEN TWO
ASH TREES AT TOP
OF FIELD)

INFORMATION
BOARD

Upper
Hill Farm

UPPER MILL
LANE

TO CHELTENHAM

PRESTBURY
HILL
RESERVE

0   ¼ mile

0   500m
APPROX SCALE

GRASSY PATH -
LOTS OF
HOOFPRINTS

INFORMATION
BOARD

OPEN
GRASSLAND

BOGGY
WHEN WET

MAP 11

GORSE   GORSE

12

45–50 MINS TO CLEEVE HILL (MAP 10)

45–50 MINS FROM CLEEVE HILL (MAP 10)

PRESTBURY HILL RESERVE

PRESTBURY HILL RESERVE

90–105 MINS FROM DOWDESWELL RESERVOIR (MAP 13)

90–105 MINS TO DOWDESWELL RESERVOIR (MAP 13)

trailblazer

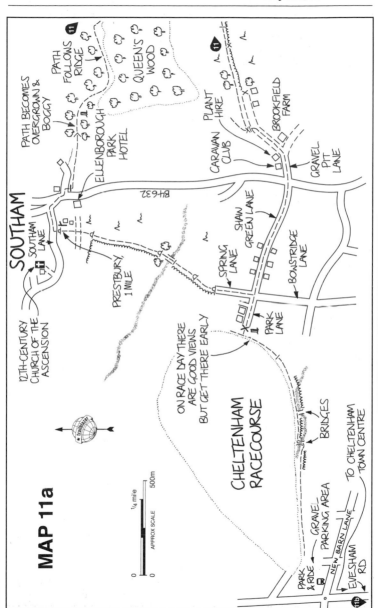

The town's **tourist information centre** (☎ 01242-237431, 🖥 www.visitchelten ham.com; daily 9.30am-5.15pm except main public holidays) is on the ground floor of The Wilson Art Gallery and Museum (see below) on Clarence St.

Cheltenham is also home to several festivals (see box pp15-16), and regularly hosts live concerts. For additional information on these, see 🖥 www.cheltenhamtown hall.org.uk.

What to see and do

Cheltenham was built with pleasure in mind, laid out with wide promenades, formal gardens and elegant houses fronted by intricate metal balconies. The town's Regency architecture can best be viewed by walking in the **Montpellier district** then on through the central area and north alongside Pittville Park. Significant among the buildings is **Pittville Pump Room** which, with its distinctive columns and decorated dome, stands at the head of the park. Completed in 1830, it was restored in 1960, and today remains in regular use for functions. Events permitting, visitors can look around the building and take the spa waters from Wednesday to Sunday, 10am to 4pm.

Following significant development, **The Wilson**, Cheltenham's **Art Gallery and Museum** (☎ 01242-237431, 🖥 www .thewilson.org.uk; daily 9.30am-5.15pm; entry free except for special exhibitions), on Clarence St, reopened to public acclaim in 2013. From the uber-modern entrance hall (housing the tourist information centre; see above) to a new permanent art gallery, their archive department (known as the Paper Store), and space for temporary exhibitions, the improvements are certainly dramatic. Of major importance is an exhibition of furniture, together with silver, textiles, ceramics and paintings, from the Arts and Crafts Movement; don't miss the remarkably intricate piano created by CR Ashbee for his wife. Other artefacts span the period from ancient Egypt to the 20th century, with a small exhibition dedicated to Edward Wilson of Antarctic fame, who was born in the town, and for whom the gallery is named.

Next door, do make time for **The Guild at 51** (☎ 01242-245215, 🖥 www .guildcrafts.org.uk; Tue-Sun 10am-5pm), which continues the Arts and Crafts theme through displays and sales of work by members of the Gloucestershire Guild of Craftsmen.

Further north, **Holst Birthplace Museum** (☎ 01242-524846, 🖥 www.holst museum.org.uk, 4 Clarence Rd; Feb-Jun & Oct-mid Dec Tue-Sat, Jul-Sep Tue-Sat 10am-5pm, Sun 1.30-5pm; entry £5) is set in a small Regency townhouse, displaying a drawing room of that period and a Victorian kitchen. It celebrates the life of the composer Gustav Holst, internationally renowned for his *Planets* suite, which was first performed in London in 1918. Holst was born in this house in 1874, was educated in the town, and returned in the late 1920s, remaining until his death in 1934. The composer's love of his native countryside is celebrated in the waymarked 35-mile (56km) Gustav Holst Way, from Cranham to Wyck Rissington, which in parts runs parallel to the Cotswold Way.

Prestbury Park just north of the town has been home to **Cheltenham Racecourse** (☎ 01242-513014, 🖥 cheltenham.thejock eyclub.co.uk) since 1831. Before that, race meetings were held on Cleeve Hill, where horses are still regularly exercised. The course hosts around 14 meetings a year between October and May, with the highlight being the four-day National Hunt Festival in March (see box pp14-15). A footpath alongside the course affords a close-up view of the races, though be warned: it's a popular spot!

Transport

Cheltenham is well served by trains, coaches and buses.

Both First Great Western and Cross Country **train services** (see box p46) call at Cheltenham Spa, which is about a mile (1.6km) west of the town centre. Stagecoach's D bus service plies frequently between here, Clarence St (but not the bus station) and the Racecourse Park & Ride, making it ideal for walkers heading up onto the Cotswold Way.

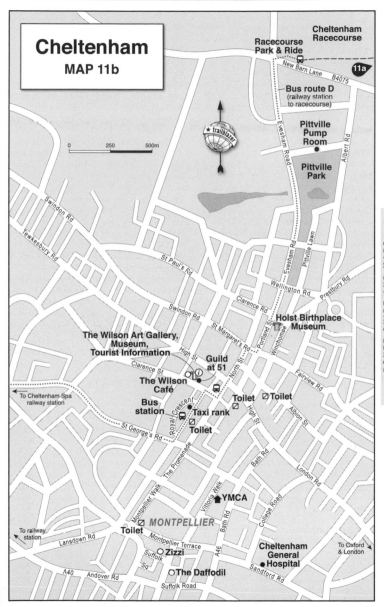

All National Express **coaches** (see box p47), and most other **buses**, go to the Royal Well bus station behind the Promenade. Probably of greatest use to walkers is Marchants' No 606/606S service, but Pulhams' No 801 and Swanbrook's No 853 also call here. Stagecoach's No 51 and 61 stop on the Promenade. For details, see the public transport map and table, pp48-50.

Central Taxis (☎ 01242-228877) are at the **taxi** rank at the bus station.

Where to stay

Details of accommodation in Cheltenham can be obtained from the tourist information centre (see p108). At the budget end of the spectrum is *Cheltenham YMCA* (Map 11b; ☎ 01242-524024, ☐ www.cheltenham ymca.com, 6 Vittoria Walk; 19S/7T/2Tr share facilities/6-bed & 8-bed dorms; ☛; WI-FI), with 24hr access. Single rooms cost £29 a night, or you can stay in a single-sex dorm for £20pp; a twin room is £45, three sharing a room costs £65. All rates include a basic breakfast.

Where to eat and drink

While it is beyond the scope of this guide to cover Cheltenham's restaurants in detail, a couple of places in the attractive Montpellier district should point you in the

right direction. A good start might be *Zizzi* (☎ 01242-252493, ☐ www.zizzi.co.uk/ venue/index/cheltenham, 3 Suffolk Sq; daily noon-10pm). It's part of the relatively predictable pizza/pasta chain, but the star is the setting: a large converted church with stained-glass windows looking down on an outsize pizza oven in place of the altar. A piano in the gallery is played on Friday and Saturday evenings.

Another restaurant with a twist is *The Daffodil* (☎ 01242-700055, ☐ www.the daffodil.com, 18-20 Suffolk Parade; Mon-Sat noon-2.30pm, 3-5pm & 6-10pm), grandly located in the old Art Deco cinema. Where once the audience sat enthralled by the big screen, today's visitors dine in contemporary style, with live jazz on Saturday lunchtime and Monday evenings. They serve afternoon tea, too, and their two-course 'Dailies' menu at £13.95 is available at lunch and early evenings. Booking is advised in the evenings.

During the day, combine a visit to The Wilson Art Gallery and Museum (see p108) with coffee or a light lunch in the contemporary space at *The Wilson Café* (☎ 01242-257441; Mon-Sat 8.30am-5.30pm, Sun 10am-5pm).

WHERE TO STAY AND EAT AROUND CHELTENHAM   MAPS 11-15

PRESTBURY HILL RESERVE
MAP 11, p106

About half a mile (0.8km) from the trail as it heads south of Cleeve Hill Common through Prestbury Hill Reserve is the exceptionally welcoming *Upper Hill Farm* (Map 11; ☎ 01242-235128, ☐ www.upper hillfarm.co.uk; 1T/2D, all en suite; ☛; WI-FI; ﷯; Ⓛ). Sympathetically restored, it

has an elegant guests' lounge and spacious rooms with modern décor. These cost £42.50pp (sgl occ £60). In the evening, the owner will drive walkers to a pub for dinner. If you stay for two nights they will also pick you up from where you walk to (normally around Wood Stanway/Birdlip) and drop you back the next morning.

HAM HILL   MAP 12

Less than half a mile (0.65km) west of the trail is Ham Hill Farm South, where *Old Stable Cottage* (☎ 01242-227003, ☐ www .a1tourism.com/uk/old-stable.html; 1D or T, en suite) charges £45pp, or £55 for single

occupancy. Guests stay in a self-contained building but breakfast is served in the main house. Just a little further down Ham Rd, some three-quarters of a mile (1.25km) from the Cotswold Way, is *Glenfall Farm*

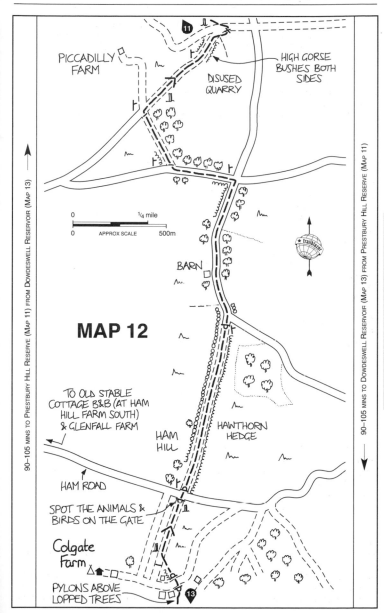

PICCADILLY FARM

DISUSED QUARRY

HIGH GORSE BUSHES BOTH SIDES

0   ¼ mile
0   500m
APPROX SCALE

★ trailblazer

BARN

MAP 12

TO OLD STABLE COTTAGE B&B (AT HAM HILL FARM SOUTH) & GLENFALL FARM

HAM HILL

HAWTHORN HEDGE

HAM ROAD

SPOT THE ANIMALS & BIRDS ON THE GATE

Colgate Farm

PYLONS ABOVE LOPPED TREES

← 90–105 MINS TO PRESTBURY HILL RESERVE (MAP 11) FROM DOWDESWELL RESERVOIR (MAP 13)

90–105 MINS TO DOWDESWELL RESERVOIR (MAP 13) FROM PRESTBURY HILL RESERVE (MAP 11) →

ROUTE GUIDE AND MAPS

B&B (☎ 01242-520302, 🖥 www.glenfall farm.co.uk; 2D/1D or T/1T, most en suite; ☕; WI-FI; ⓛ). B&B comes in at £42.50-46.25pp; for single occupancy you'll pay £70-75. The twin room has a private bathroom. In the evening, the owner is happy to give walkers a lift to the nearest pub for dinner.

Continuing along the Cotswold Way, you'll come to *Colgate Farm* (mob ☎ 07549-297996, ☎ 07980-607867, 🖥 www .colgatefarm.co.uk; 2D/1T, all en suite; WI-FI; 🐾), a working farm with both **B&B**

(£50pp) and **camping** (£10pp). Guests in the double rooms, which include a self-contained log cabin, cook their own breakfast from supplies provided; those in the twin room have breakfast in the main house.

In the evening, subject to prior arrangement, you can have a home-cooked meal in the farmhouse. Campers will find hot showers, free WI-FI, and firepits with free wood. There's even bike hire (£15/day) if you still have any energy after all that walking.

CHARLTON KINGS   off MAP 13

A couple of places on London Rd offer B&B within less than a mile (1.6km) of the trail. Closest is *Charlton Kings Hotel* (☎ 01242-231061, 🖥 www.charltonkingshotel .co.uk; 2T/2D or T/5D/1Tr, all en suite; ☕; WI-FI; 🐾; ⓛ), some three-quarters of a mile (1.2km) to the west. Rates vary, but walkers can expect to pay £47.50-57.50pp (sgl occ £69 and £135 for three sharing) for B&B in comfortable modern rooms, including a triple room with three single beds.

In the evening (daily 6-9pm), bar snacks such as sandwiches, paté and bowls of excellent chilli con carne (£8) are available. For something more substantial, the nearest pub is about three-quarters of a mile (1.6km) closer to Cheltenham.

Almost opposite, a narrow lane leads across the River Chelt to *Detmore House* (☎ 01242-582868, 🖥 www.detmorehouse .com; 1T/2D/1Tr, all en suite; ☕; WI-FI; ⓛ), set amid fields and an orchard. B&B here costs from £47.50-55pp (£135 for three sharing, sgl occupancy from £75).

Almost next to the hotel is East End Service Station, where there's an **ATM** and small Mace **shop** (daily 7am-9.30pm), though you'll find more variety at East End Stores across the road (Mon-Sat 7am-8pm, Sun 8am-7pm).

Pulham's No 801 **bus** service calls here as does Swanbrook's No 853; for details see pp48-50.

NEAR DOWDESWELL RESERVOIR   MAP 13

At the foot of the hill leading down towards the reservoir, welcoming hot and cold **drinks and snacks** (75p-£1.50) await the weary at the former B&B, Langett. At the bottom of the hill, the old Reservoir Inn has morphed into an Indian restaurant with rooms, *Koloshi* (☎ 01242-516400, 🖥 www .koloshi.co.uk; 1D/1T, both en suite; ☕; WI-FI; 🐾; ⓛ; restaurant Tue-Sun noon-2.30pm & 5.30-10pm). You'll pay

£37.50pp for B&B in the double room, or £47.50pp in the larger room, but do note that the restaurant is closed on a Monday.

Pulham's No 801 **bus** stops outside the restaurant on request. Since there is no official bus stop here, if you want to be picked up be sure to stand somewhere conspicuous and where it can safely pull over – just outside the restaurant car park is best. For details, see pp48-50.

Symbols used in text   🐾 Dogs allowed subject to prior arrangement
☕ Bathtub in at least one room   ⓛ packed lunch available if requested in advance

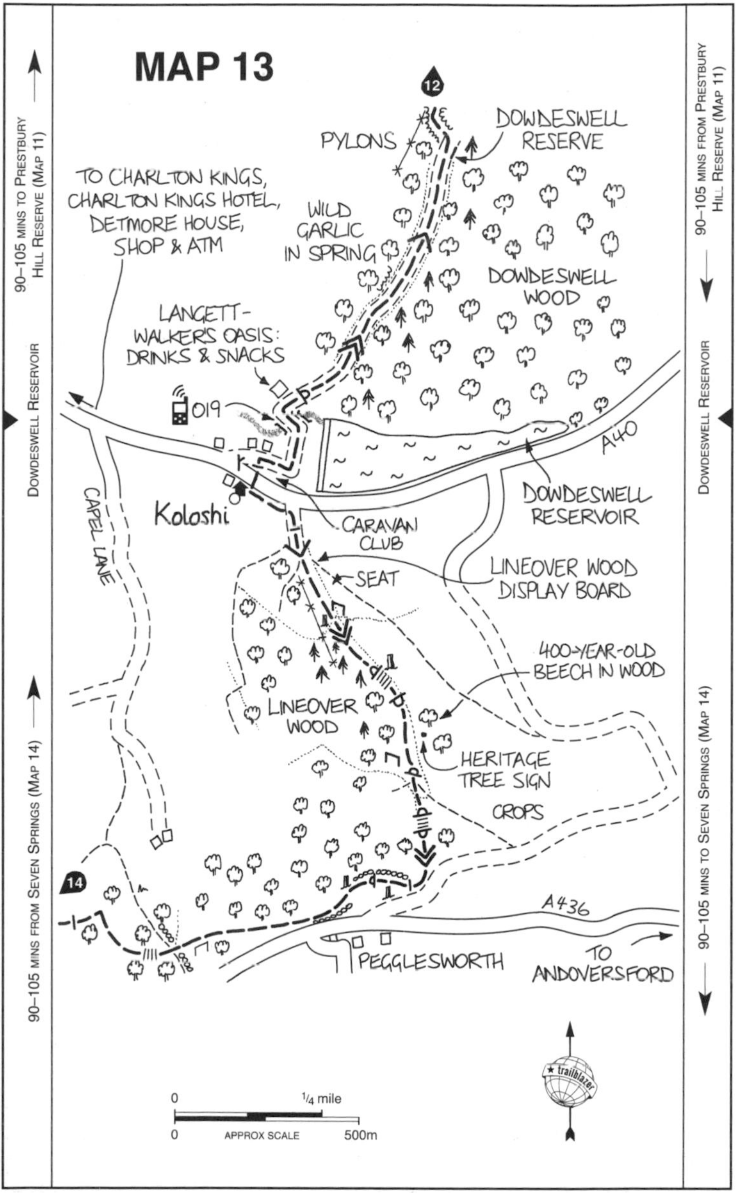

MAP 13

90–105 MINS TO PRESTBURY HILL RESERVE (MAP 11)

DOWDESWELL RESERVOIR

90–105 MINS FROM SEVEN SPRINGS (MAP 14)

12

PYLONS

DOWDESWELL RESERVE

WILD GARLIC IN SPRING

DOWDESWELL WOOD

TO CHARLTON KINGS, CHARLTON KINGS HOTEL, DETMORE HOUSE, SHOP & ATM

LANGETT-WALKERS OASIS: DRINKS & SNACKS

019

Koloshi

CAPEL LANE

CARAVAN CLUB

SEAT

LINEOVER WOOD

A40

DOWDESWELL RESERVOIR

LINEOVER WOOD DISPLAY BOARD

400-YEAR-OLD BEECH IN WOOD

HERITAGE TREE SIGN

CROPS

14

PEGGLESWORTH

A436

TO ANDOVERSFORD

90–105 MINS FROM PRESTBURY HILL RESERVE (MAP 11)

DOWDESWELL RESERVOIR

90–105 MINS TO SEVEN SPRINGS (MAP 14)

ROUTE GUIDE AND MAPS

0   ¼ mile

0   APPROX SCALE   500m

★ trailblaze

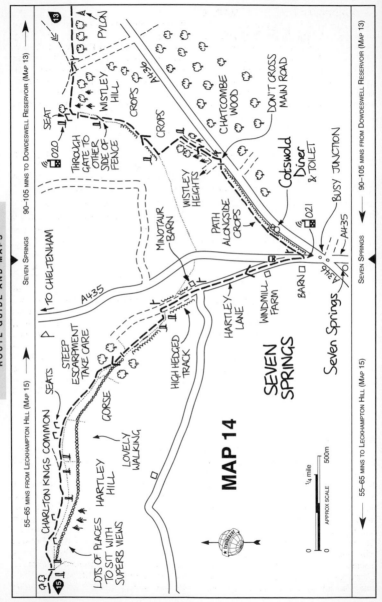

MAP 14

SEVEN SPRINGS

Seven Springs

PYLON

SEAT

WISTLEY HILL

CROPS

CROPS

CHATCOMBE WOOD

DON'T CROSS MAIN ROAD

020

THROUGH GATE TO OTHER SIDE OF FENCE

WISTLEY HEIGHTS

Cotswold Diner & TOILET

TO CHELTENHAM

A435

MINOTAUR BARN

PATH ALONGSIDE CROPS

021

BUSY JUNCTION

A436

A435

STEEP ESCARPMENT TAKE CARE

HIGH HEDGED TRACK

HARTLEY LANE

WINDMILL FARM

BARN

CHARLTON KINGS COMMON

SEATS

GORSE

LOVELY WALKING

HARTLEY HILL

LOTS OF PLACES TO SIT WITH SUPERB VIEWS

15

¼ mile   500m

0

APPROX SCALE

0

SEVEN SPRINGS   MAP 14

There is really little more than a pub and a small roadside diner at this busy junction, but Stagecoach's **bus** No 51 (see pp48-50) calls frequently at the bus stop here.

Set in a layby off the A436 is the *Cotswold Diner* (Mon-Fri 7.30am-3pm, exc bank hols), a converted but comfortable bus offering warmth and succour to weary walkers. Stop for tea or coffee, breakfast or baguettes, and even ice cream in the summer months. More permanent is the *Seven Springs* (☎ 01242-870219, 💻 www.hungry horse.co.uk; Mon-Fri 10am-10pm, Sat-Sun 10am-9.30pm; WI-FI). Part of the Hungry Horse chain, it has a huge menu at bargain prices, with glossy pictures to match; finesse is not the order of the day. Alongside pub favourites from £5.29, there are baguettes, wraps and hot dogs.

LECKHAMPTON HILL TO BIRDLIP   MAPS 15-17

From Leckhampton Hill it's a fairly straightforward 5¾-mile (9.25km) walk to Birdlip, taking about 2¾ to 3¼ hours. The route primarily follows the line of the escarpment, with attendant views in good weather. If you're less lucky, warming up at the Air Balloon pub (see below) is an appealing prospect; it's worth lingering at **Crickley Hill** (see below), both to explore the hill fort and surrounding area and for the excellent visitor centre – when it's open, that is.

ULLENWOOD   MAP 15, p116

The good people at the National Star College in the grounds of Ullenwood Manor have set up a couple of ventures that are perfect for walkers along the Cotswold Way. **Campers** will find relative comfort in the four wooden camping pods at *Ullenwood StarGlamping* (01242-527631, 💻 www .nationalstar.org/visit-us/star-camping; 🐾; Ⓛ by prior arrangement). As well as two pods sleeping one or two people, and a third up to four (£30 for one or two people, £35/40 for three/four), there's Shire House which is double bedded (£45). Expect toilets and showers, of course, but you'll need to bring your own sleeping bags, towels etc.

On the same site is the *StarBistro* (☎ 01242-535984; Mon-Fri 11am-4pm; WI-FI), which serves coffee, lunch and afternoon tea during the week, except on bank holidays. The bistro is staffed by youngsters with disabilities from the college, working with a resident chef. There is also a small **shop** on site selling souvenirs, sandwiches and snacks.

AROUND CRICKLEY HILL
          MAP 16, p117

Popular locally with families and dog walkers, **Crickley Hill Country Park** covers 143 acres (58 ha) protecting both the site of an ancient hill fort (see box p122) and a natural environment which attracts a broad diversity of birds, butterflies and wild flowers, including the rare bee orchid (see p63). The introduction of scooter hire for those with limited mobility is an added bonus. There's a good visitor centre here (Apr-Sep afternoons only) and picnic tables, but no café. The toilets are open longer (Apr-Sep daily 6am-9.30pm, Mar & Oct 6am-7pm, Nov-Feb 6am-6pm); just push the door hard!

For somewhere to eat, head for *Air Balloon* (☎ 01452-862541, 💻 www.old englishinns.co.uk; Mon-Sat 11am-9pm, Sun noon-9pm), a big, friendly pub with a garden, which is especially popular on Sundays. The menu covers the full works, from value meals at £4.99 to steaks (£11.29-15.49), not to mention sandwiches and jackets (until 5pm, Mon-Sat), plus coffee, tea and lots of puds. (cont'd on p119)

ROUTE GUIDE AND MAPS

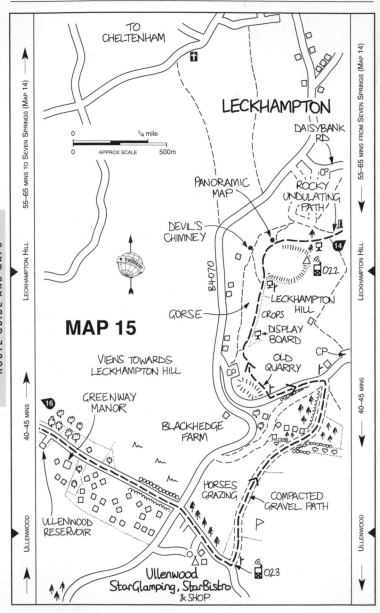

TO CHELTENHAM

LECKHAMPTON

DAISYBANK RD

55-65 MINS TO SEVEN SPRINGS (MAP 14)

55-65 MINS FROM SEVEN SPRINGS (MAP 14)

¼ mile

APPROX SCALE

500m

PANORAMIC MAP

ROCKY UNDULATING PATH

CP

14

DEVIL'S CHIMNEY

B4070

O22

LECKHAMPTON HILL

LECKHAMPTON HILL

GORSE

CROPS

DISPLAY BOARD

CP

MAP 15

OLD QUARRY

CP

VIEWS TOWARDS LECKHAMPTON HILL

16

GREENWAY MANOR

40-45 MINS

40-45 MINS

BLACKHEDGE FARM

ULLENWOOD RESERVOIR

HORSES GRAZING

COMPACTED GRAVEL PATH

P

ULLENWOOD

ULLENWOOD

O23

Ullenwood StarGlamping, StarBistro & SHOP

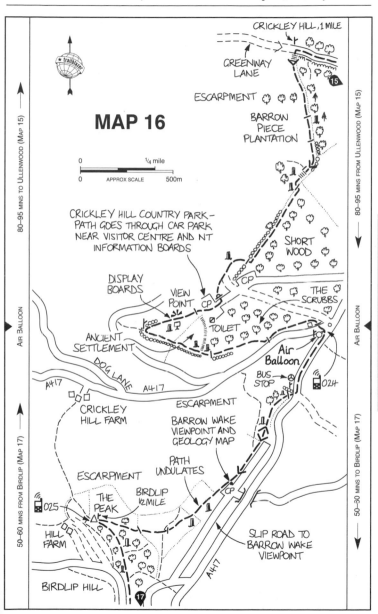

CRICKLEY HILL, 1 MILE

GREENWAY LANE

ESCARPMENT

BARROW PIECE PLANTATION

15

MAP 16

0   1/4 mile

0   APPROX SCALE   500m

CRICKLEY HILL COUNTRY PARK – PATH GOES THROUGH CAR PARK NEAR VISITOR CENTRE AND NT INFORMATION BOARDS

SHORT WOOD

THE SCRUBBS

DISPLAY BOARDS

VIEW POINT

CP

CP

TOILET

ANCIENT SETTLEMENT

Air Balloon

DOG LANE

A417

A417

BUS STOP

024

CRICKLEY HILL FARM

ESCARPMENT

BARROW WAKE VIEWPOINT AND GEOLOGY MAP

ESCARPMENT

PATH UNDULATES

025

THE PEAK

BIRDLIP 1/2 MILE

CP

SLIP ROAD TO BARROW WAKE VIEWPOINT

HILL FARM

A417

BIRDLIP HILL

17

80–95 MINS TO ULLENWOOD (MAP 15)

AIR BALLOON

50–60 MINS FROM BIRDLIP (MAP 17)

80–95 MINS FROM ULLENWOOD (MAP 15)

AIR BALLOON

50–30 MINS TO BIRDLIP (MAP 17)

ROUTE GUIDE AND MAPS

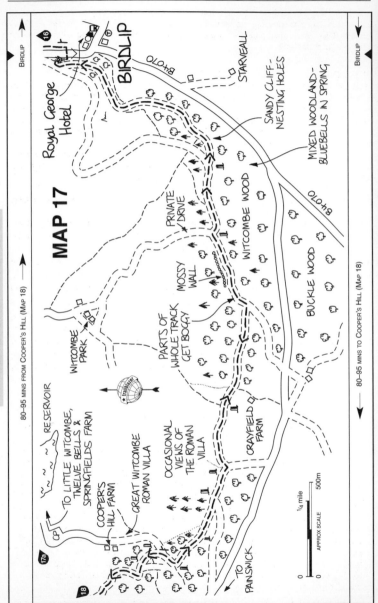

BIRDLIP

BIRDLIP

80–95 MINS FROM COOPER'S HILL (MAP 18)

80–95 MINS TO COOPER'S HILL (MAP 18)

MAP 17

17a

18

Royal George Hotel

BIRDLIP

STARVEALL

SANDY CLIFF – NESTING HOLES

MIXED WOODLAND – BLUEBELLS IN SPRING

B4070

B4070

WITCOMBE WOOD

BUCKLE WOOD

PRIVATE DRIVE

MOSSY WALL

PARTS OF WHOLE TRACK GET BOGGY

WITCOMBE PARK

RESERVOIR

TO LITTLE WITCOMBE, TWELVE BELLS & SPRINGFIELDS FARM

COOPER'S HILL FARM

GREAT WITCOMBE ROMAN VILLA

OCCASIONAL VIEWS OF THE ROMAN VILLA

CRAYFIELD FARM

TO PAINSWICK

¼ mile

500m

APPROX SCALE

trailblazer

(cont'd from p115) Pulhams' No 852 **bus** stops near the pub heading northbound towards Gloucester. See public transport table and map, pp48-50.

If you're planning to stop in this area, note that Little Witcombe (see p120) is almost as close to Birdlip Hill as it is to Cooper's Hill.

BIRDLIP   MAP 17

Although the Cotswold Way passes within 200m of Birdlip, it is easy to miss the tiny village entirely. But negotiate the steep and busy road and you'll come to the stone-built *Royal George Hotel* (☎ 01452-862506, 🖳 www.oldenglishinns.co.uk/our-locations/the-royal-george-hotel-birdlip; 26D/8T, all en suite; 🖤; WI-FI; 🐾). B&B rates vary daily and are usually best for

online bookings, but expect to pay £25-50pp (sgl occ £40-100); special deals are regularly available. **Meals** (daily noon-10pm) can be taken in the restaurant, or more informally in the bar or garden, or on the terrace.

Pulhams' No 852 **bus** stops here about 100m up the road from the hotel; see public transport table and map, pp48-50.

BIRDLIP TO PAINSWICK   MAPS 17-20

For much of the next **6¾ miles (10.9km, 3¼-3¾hrs)** you'll continue along the Cotswold escarpment through a woodland fringe, which opens out occasionally to reveal hillside areas such as **Cooper's Hill** (site of the annual cheese-rolling competition, see box p15), and tantalising glimpses north-west to the Malvern Hills. Be particularly careful to follow the waymarked path up here, and not to wander off the edge of the escarpment in misty weather; the rough picket fence would do little to break a fall.

Painswick Beacon, site of an Iron-Age hill fort (see box p122) follows, before you reach one of the trail's architectural highlights: **Painswick**. It was east of the town, in the Slad Valley, that the three-year-old Laurie Lee was famously 'set down from the carrier's cart', thus beginning his evocative autobiographical work, *Cider with Rosie*. While the world has moved on, many of the views along this part of the route are probably little changed – at least superficially – since Lee's childhood.

❏ **Cheese rolling**   Map 18, p121
Picture the scene at Cooper's Hill near Brockworth on the Whitsun Bank Holiday Monday at the end of May. At the top, a group of contestants is set on chasing a giant Double Gloucester cheese down the almost sheer hillface for no other reason than to win the cheese – and the glory. Add in the unpredictable English weather and it's a spectacle that will gladden the heart of anyone who thought British eccentricity was dying out. It's a risky affair, with paramedics kept busy throughout the five races, but that hasn't stopped the proceedings – yet.

In 2010, as international popularity threatened to swamp this once strictly village event, the official line was that it was cancelled for safety reasons. While it looked like the end, participants were less easily convinced. Cheese rolling has a long history in this neck of the woods, and local rivalries are not that easily put down. The event went ahead anyway, as it has done every year since, so if you're timing your walk at the end of May, be prepared to share the hill with some 4000 spectators. For details, see 🖳 www.cheese-rolling.co.uk.

LITTLE WITCOMBE   MAP 17a,

A steep walk down from the trail brings you to **Great Witcombe Villa** (Map 17), which was constructed during Roman times, but abandoned around the 5th century AD. The foundations are still clearly visible, but almost as interesting is an unmown section of grass which in summer yields numerous wild flowers, including the pyramidal orchid (see p63 and photo opposite p64).

About 1¼ miles (2km) from the trail – or the villa – the Bickell sisters have been welcoming **B&B** guests to *Springfields Farm* (☎ 01452-863532; 2S/1D; shared bathroom ➤; 🐾; Ⓛ) since the war. It's an old-fashioned place, warm and welcoming, with a cosy guest lounge, a garden and an excellent breakfast. B&B costs £25pp.

Just a short walk across the main road is the *Twelve Bells* (☎ 01452-862521, 🖳 www.beefeater.co.uk; Sun-Thur noon-10pm, Fri-Sat noon-11pm; WI-FI), part of the Beefeater chain. The adjacent *Premier Inn* (☎ 0871 527 8458, 🖳 www.premierinn.com; 37D, all en suite; ➤; WI-FI) is a dependable choice, with some of the rooms having space for additional children (though not adults). Pricing varies widely, so a room rate (whether one or two share) of £50-100 is just a rough guide. If you book online and well in advance you may pay as little as £29, albeit generally only for a Sunday night, and non-refundable/amendable 'saver' rates are £39. Breakfast – taken at the pub – is all you can eat and costs £6.25 for a continental breakfast, or £8.75 for a full English cooked to order. They also have a 'meal deal' at £22.99, which includes a two-course evening meal and drink and an all-you-can-eat breakfast.

Pulhams' No 852 **bus** stops here; see public transport table and map, pp48-50.

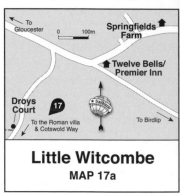

Little Witcombe
MAP 17a

CRANHAM CORNER AND PAINSWICK HILL
MAP 18 & MAP 19, p123

Not so much a village as a point on the map where the road to Cranham (and the Cotswold Way) meets the A46, Cranham Corner is nevertheless served by a **bus**, Stagecoach's No 61. See public transport table and map, pp48-50. The village itself, almost a mile (1.3km) east of the trail, was a favourite with Gustav Holst (see p105), who composed the music here for *In the Bleak Midwinter*.

A short walk from the trail on the A46 is the independent *Royal William* pub (☎ 01452-813650, 🖳 www.royalwilliam.co.uk), where a wide-ranging menu is served daily noon-9pm. Take your pick from burgers and baguettes, salads and steaks, and more, washed down with real ale.

Pretty well on the trail, some three-quarters of a mile (1.3km) north of Painswick, is the exceptionally friendly *Hortons* at Painswick Golf Club (☎ 01452-812180, 🖳 www.painswickgolf.com; Tue-Sun 10am-4pm approx, depending on golf commitments; WI-FI; 🐾). Open for lunch and tea, with real ales, Sunday roasts and gargantuan slices of homemade cake, it has a sunny balcony with glorious views over the Slad valley.

If a spot of wildlife appeals, or a hot drink, **Prinknash Bird and Deer Park** (Map 18; ☎ 01452-812727, 🖳 www.thebirdpark.com; daily Mar-Oct 10am-5pm, Nov-Feb 10am-4pm; £7.80) might appeal. It's located west of the trail, off the A46, and is home to both deer and an array of exotic birds.

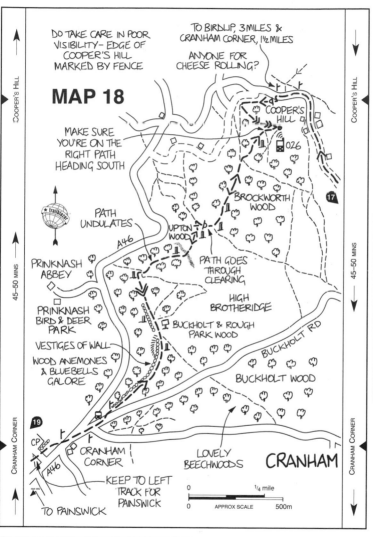

MAP 18

DO TAKE CARE IN POOR VISIBILITY– EDGE OF COOPER'S HILL MARKED BY FENCE

TO BIRDLIP, 3 MILES & CRANHAM CORNER, 1½ MILES

ANYONE FOR CHEESE ROLLING?

COOPER'S HILL

026

MAKE SURE YOU'RE ON THE RIGHT PATH HEADING SOUTH

BROCKWORTH WOOD

17

PATH UNDULATES

UPTON WOOD

PATH GOES THROUGH CLEARING

A46

PRINKNASH ABBEY

PRINKNASH BIRD & DEER PARK

HIGH BROTHERIDGE

BUCKHOLT & ROUGH PARK WOOD

VESTIGES OF WALL

WOOD ANEMONES & BLUEBELLS GALORE

BUCKHOLT RD

BUCKHOLT WOOD

19

CP

CRANHAM CORNER

LOVELY BEECHWOODS

CRANHAM

KEEP TO LEFT TRACK FOR PAINSWICK

A46

TO PAINSWICK

0   ¼ mile

0   APPROX SCALE   500m

COOPER'S HILL

45–50 MINS

CRANHAM CORNER

ROUTE GUIDE AND MAPS

❑ **Important note – walking times**
All times in this book refer only to the time spent walking. You will need to add 20-30% to allow for rests, photography, checking the map, drinking water etc.

❑ Hill forts

Painswick Beacon (see Map 19), also known as Kimsbury Camp, is just one of 35 Iron-Age hill forts that have been identified in Gloucestershire, this one dating back to around 400BC. From the layman's perspective, it is arguably the fort that gives greatest vent to the imagination along the Cotswold Way, with steep sides leading up to the fort area from where there are extensive views. Although golf has been played here since 1891, and quarrying has left its mark, the outline of the fort on the ground can still clearly be seen. Today, steps have been cut into the hill to prevent further damage to the ramparts.

Other notable hill forts along the Cotswold Way include those at **Leckhampton Hill** (see Map 15, p116), **Crickley Hill** (see Map 16, p117), **Haresfield Beacon** (see Map 21, p128) and – just off the trail – **Uley Bury** (see Map 26, p137). Some of the earlier settlements, including the one at Crickley Hill, are at least 5000 years old, although the hill fort there is far more modern, occupied around 500BC. Although little of these sites is visible on the ground today, there are some excellent interpretive panels along the trail, including an artist's impression at Crickley Hill of how a hill fort might have looked.

The thin soil on these sites, and the fact that they have never been ploughed, means not only that it is relatively easy to make out the lines of the forts on the ground, but also that they are particularly rich environmentally, and several – including Painswick Beacon – have been designated as SSSIs (see p61).

❑ Painswick Rococo Garden   Map 19

Not far from the trail, this garden (☎ 01452-813204, 💻 www.rococogarden.org.uk; mid Jan to end Oct daily 11am-5pm; £7) is claimed to be the only complete English Rococo garden still in existence. It was planted in the 1740s, but so quickly did the fashion change that the original was soon replanted and the garden was later abandoned. Over 240 years later, in 1984, restoration was put in hand thanks to a painting made in 1748 showing the original design. Flights of fancy characterise a fairly structured and geometric layout, with fruit and vegetables forming a part of the whole rather than hidden away. A maze created to commemorate the garden's 250th anniversary is an added attraction; the gardens are renowned for their display of snowdrops in early spring, with a bluebell walk added in 2015. Coffee, tea, cakes and light lunches are served in the old coach house.

PAINSWICK   MAP 20a, p126

The small town of Painswick, which harks back to the Domesday Book, may come as something of a surprise for those more familiar with the Cotswold villages further north. The off-white stone of the buildings, many built by wool merchants during the 18th century, comes without the golden hue found to the north and the whole style is more elegant. If you've the energy, count the 99 yew trees in the grounds of **St Mary's Church** (legend has it that the

Devil won't let the 100th one grow), seek out the tea-caddy gravestones, or look for the spectacle stocks by the churchyard wall. And while you're there, note the clock on the tower, erected to celebrate the millennium.

The Arts and Crafts Movement (see box p76) was influential here in the early 20th century and the tradition continues. Today's artists exhibit at **The Painswick Centre** (Tue-Sat 10am-5pm; admission free), on Bisley St, which has regular artists

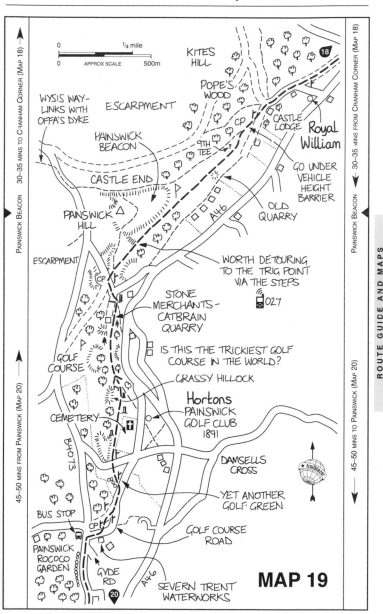

ROUTE GUIDE AND MAPS

30-35 MINS TO CRANHAM CORNER (MAP 18)

PAINSWICK BEACON

45-50 MINS FROM PAINSWICK (MAP 20)

30-35 MINS FROM CRANHAM CORNER (MAP 18)

PAINSWICK BEACON

45-50 MINS TO PAINSWICK (MAP 20)

¼ mile

0

APPROX SCALE

500m

KITES HILL

18

POPE'S WOOD

ESCARPMENT

WYSIS WAY - LINKS WITH OFFA'S DYKE

PAINSWICK BEACON

CP

CASTLE LODGE

Royal William

9TH TEE

CASTLE END

GO UNDER VEHICLE HEIGHT BARRIER

PAINSWICK HILL

A46

OLD QUARRY

ESCARPMENT

CP

WORTH DETOURING TO THE TRIG POINT VIA THE STEPS

027

STONE MERCHANTS - CATBRAIN QUARRY

IS THIS THE TRICKIEST GOLF COURSE IN THE WORLD?

GOLF COURSE

GRASSY HILLOCK

Hortons PAINSWICK GOLF CLUB 1891

CEMETERY

B4073

DAMSELLS CROSS

YET ANOTHER GOLF GREEN

BUS STOP

CP

trailblaze

GOLF COURSE ROAD

PAINSWICK ROCOCO GARDEN

GYDE RD

A46

20

SEVERN TRENT WATERWORKS

MAP 19

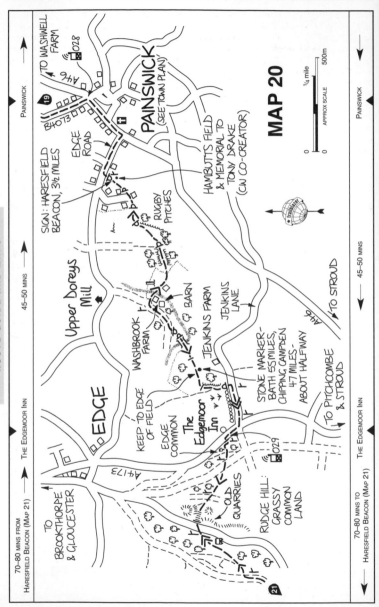

MAP 20

APPROX SCALE

0   ¼ mile

0   500m

70-80 MINS FROM HARESFIELD BEACON (MAP 21) →   THE EDGEMOOR INN   ←   45-50 MINS   →   PAINSWICK

70-80 MINS TO HARESFIELD BEACON (MAP 21)   THE EDGEMOOR INN   45-50 MINS   PAINSWICK

TO WASHWELL FARM

🏕 028

PAINSWICK
(SEE TOWN PLAN)

A46

19

B4073

EDGE ROAD

SIGN: HARESFIELD BEACON, 3½ MILES

HAMBUTTS FIELD & MEMORIAL TO TONY DRAKE (CW CO-CREATOR)

RUGBY PITCHES

Upper Doreys Mill

EDGE

TO BROOKTHORPE & GLOUCESTER

WASHBROOK FARM

KEEP TO EDGE OF FIELD

EDGE COMMON

A4173

BARN

JENKINS FARM

JENKINS LANE

TO STROUD

A46

The Edgemoor Inn

🏕 029

STONE MARKER– BATH 55 MILES, CHIPPING CAMPDEN 47 MILES– ABOUT HALFWAY

TO PITCHCOMBE & STROUD

OLD QUARRIES

RIDGE HILL: GRASSY COMMON LAND

21

in residence and is the focus of Painswick's art festival, Artburst (see box p16), in August. There are also art exhibitions at the Patchwork Mouse (see Where to eat), an art café. If you're here at the weekend, don't miss the **Ashton Beer Collection** (mob ☎ 07828-930050, 🖳 ashtonbeercollection .wix.com/beer#_=_; May-Oct Sun & bank hols 2-5.30pm; £5), housed in the old Christ Church on Gloucester St, whose central window was designed by Sir Edward Burne-Jones and made by William Morris's company. Here, John Ashton Beer has displayed around 600 items from his Arts and Crafts collection, lovingly assembled over four decades. Do phone ahead if you're particularly interested; he will often open by appointment.

Transport
Stagecoach's No 61 **bus** stops outside the church every day. For details, see pp48-50.

For a **taxi**, try JW Goddard (☎ 01452-812240) or A La Carte (☎ 01452-813268).

Services
Painswick's **tourist information centre** (☎ 01452-812278, 🖳 www.painswicktourist info.co.uk; Mar-Oct Mon & Wed-Fri 10am-4pm, Tue & Sat 10am-1pm) is in the Gravedigger's Hut on the south side of St Mary's churchyard and is run by volunteers.

There is no bank in the town, but there's an ATM at the small best-one **supermarket** (Mon-Sat 7am-8pm, Sun 8am-5pm) on St Mary's St. More upmarket foodwise is Olivas **deli** (see p127). Sadly, the **post office** (Wed & Fri 9.30-11.30am) has been moved into the Town Hall from its beautiful half-timbered building on New St, dating back to the 15th century.

There's a doctor's **surgery** (☎ 01452-812545; Mon-Fri 8.30am-6pm) to the north of the town at Hoyland House on Gyde Rd, off Gloucester St, and the handy Painswick **Pharmacy** on New St. Public **toilets** are located by the church and also in the car park on the A46 south of town.

Where to stay
Most of Painswick's places to stay are near the town centre. Three **B&Bs** are close to each other on Gloucester St, along the trail. At *Troy House* (☎ 01452-812339, 🖳 www .troyguesthouse.co.uk; 1T/1D, both en suite; 🍴; WI-FI; 🐾; Ⓛ), where the rooms are in a separate cottage, you'll pay £37.50pp, or £55 for single occupancy.

Opposite is *St Anne's* (☎ 01452-812879, 🖳 www.st-annes-painswick.co.uk; 1T/2D, all en suite; WI-FI; 🐾; Ⓛ), a cottagey place with flowers in the rooms and newly laid eggs for breakfast. They also have drying facilities and may be able to do a clothes wash for you. Rates are £37.50pp, or £50 for single occupancy.

The neighbouring *Ashton House* (☎ 01452-812738, 🖳 www.ashtonhousebed andbreakfast.co.uk; 1S/1T share facilities, 2D en suite; 🍴; WI-FI; Ⓛ) charges from £37.50pp (sgl occ £60) and £55 for the single room.

Also on the trail is the *Falcon* (☎ 01452-814222, 🖳 www.falconpainswick .co.uk, New St; 2T/2D/6D or T/1Qd, all en suite; 🍴; WI-FI; 🐾; Ⓛ), a 16th-century coaching inn with a 21st-century twist. Rooms can be booked online and prices fluctuate considerably, with the highest at weekends, but expect to pay £41-64.50pp (sgl occ full room rate, £109-129 for three or four people sharing).

On the corner at The Cross, there's an air of grandeur about *Cardynham House* (☎ 01452-814006, 🖳 www.cardynham.co .uk; 6D/2Tr/1Qd, all en suite; 🍴; WI-FI), too. Here there are four grades of room, costing £45-110pp (sgl occ £70-100, three/four sharing room rate plus additional £20pp), depending on the day and time of year; for true indulgence, how about the pool room – 'great fun, if expensive' according to one reader – with its own covered, heated swimming pool at £220 for two sharing? Note that wi-fi here is available only in the lounge because of the thick stone walls.

At *Tibbiwell Lodge* (☎ 01452-812748 or mob ☎ 07872-310393, 🖳 www.tibbiwell lodgepainswick.webs.com; 1T private facilities, 1D/1Tr, both en suite; 🍴; WI-FI; 🐾; Ⓛ), a short way down Tibbiwell Lane, there's an interesting choice of rooms, with higher prices charged at weekends. The triple, with a balcony overlooking the valley, costs £37.50-47.50pp (sgl occ £50-95, three sharing room rate plus £15). The double, with a terrace, is £42.50-49.50pp (sgl occ £55-99), and the twin £32.50-37.50pp (sgl occ £40-75). Useful facilities include a drying room and boot wash area.

Top of the range in accommodation terms, *The Painswick* (🖳 www.thepainswick.co.uk; 16 rooms, all en suite; 🐾) is an imposing three-storey stone building on a quiet lane. Formerly Cotswold 88, it is scheduled to re-open in spring 2016, with rooms costing from £150, excluding breakfast.

Where to eat and drink

Painswick is something of a mecca for foodies, so it could be worth timing your walk for a stop here at some stage of the day. Two of the old inns have recently come under new ownership, with very positive results. The *Royal Oak* (☎ 01452-813129; daily noon-2.30pm & 6-9pm), on St Mary's St, remains a proper real-ale pub, cosy and stone built with two bars – one with a piano, the other with sports TV. Standard pub fare is augmented by the likes of beetroot and butternut squash burger with goat's cheese and chips (£10.50), or homemade venison and cranberry pie (£12.95),

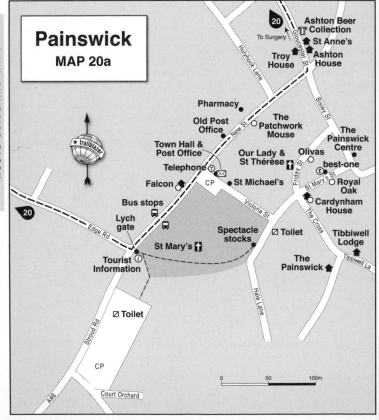

Painswick
MAP 20a

★ trailblazer

ROUTE GUIDE AND MAPS

20
To Surgery
Ashton Beer Collection
St Anne's
Troy House
Ashton House
Holyhock Lane
Gloucester St
Bisley St
Pharmacy
New St
The Patchwork Mouse
The Painswick Centre
Old Post Office
Town Hall & Post Office
Our Lady & St Thérèse
Olivas
Friday St
best-one
Telephone
St Mary's St
Royal Oak
Falcon
CP
St Michael's
Cardynham House
Bus stops
Victoria St
Lych gate
Spectacle stocks
Toilet
The Cross
Tibbiwell Lodge
St Mary's
Tibbiwell La
Tourist Information
Hale Lane
The Painswick
Edge Rd
20
Stroud Rd
Toilet
CP
A46
Court Orchard

0   50   100m

with delicious fish and chips on Fridays.

More stylish is the *Falcon* (see Where to stay; daily noon-2.30pm, Mon-Sat 6.30-9.30pm, Sun to 8.30pm), where you'll dine in relaxed but contemporary surroundings with excellent service. Locals and visitors flock here for a diverse menu (so you may need to book), but many walkers will appreciate their range of pies at £10.95; the aubergine and courgette lasagne (£13.75) was delicious.

Pretty tablecloths set the scene for the **bistro** at *Cardynham House* (see Where to stay; Tue-Sun noon-3pm & Tue-Sat 6.30-9.30pm), which serves everything from baguettes and jacket potatoes at lunchtime, to a regularly changing menu in the evening that will set you back around £25 for two courses with wine.

If you fancy something lighter at lunchtime, search out *Olivas* (☎ 01452-814774; ⌨ olivas.moonfruit.com, Friday St; daily 10.15am-5pm, or earlier in winter). They operate both as a deli and a licensed coffee shop serving soups, salads, spectacular sandwiches and light lunches. If you're travelling in a group of six or more and book ahead, they'll whiz up a tapas evening, too. More informal still is the art café *The Patchwork Mouse* (☎ 01452-812560; ⌨ www.thepatchworkmouse .co.uk; Mon-Fri 8.30am-5pm, Sat-Sun 10am-5pm; WI-FI), on New St. There's pretty china for your coffee or traditional tea and scones but the atmosphere is arty rather than twee, with a 'library room' at the back and regular exhibitions.

Finally, do keep an eye out for the restaurant (and/or the B&B) at St Michael's, which although closed at the time of research, may well resurface over the lifetime of this guide.

For a more rural repast, consider Rococo Gardens (see box p122).

PAINSWICK TO STONEHOUSE   MAPS 20-23

This **8½-mile (13.4km, 4¼-4¾hr)** section marks the halfway point along the Cotswold Way; indeed, you'll pass a milestone stating 'Bath 55' on one side – and 'Chipping Campden 47' on the other. After the open countryside of the first few miles the trail enters a narrow strip of woodland, following the edge of the escarpment as it twists and turns around **Haresfield Beacon**. With unimpeded (not to mention spectacular) views in almost every direction, and sheer slopes on two sides, it's no surprise that it was chosen as the site of an Iron-Age hill fort (see box p122).

The descent through woods and fields to the **Stroudwater (Ebley) Canal**, gives little indication of the urban sprawl to the east that is the town of Stroud. No wonder, then, that the appearance of first the railway, then two busy parallel roads, jars the senses. Yet the canal between these, just a few metres above sea level and the lowest point along the route, is one of the few areas of water along the Cotswold Way and introduces a very different environment.

EDGE   MAP 20, p124

Right on the Cotswold Way on the busy A4173, opposite the entrance to Edge Common (now part of Rudge Hill National Nature Reserve), *The Edgemoor Inn* (☎ 01452-813576, ⌨ www.edgemoorinn.com; food served Mon-Sat noon-2pm & 6.30-8.30pm, Sun sittings at 12.15pm & 2.15pm) could be a good staging post. Expect daily specials on the menu and a range of real ales such as Wickwar's BOB.

Upper Doreys Mill (☎ 01452 812459, ⌨ www.doreys.co.uk; 1D/1T, both en suite; ⌨; WI-FI) is a B&B lying in rural isolation near the bottom of a steep lane, just a short walk from the trail at Washbrook Farm. B&B here is £40pp (sgl occ £70), with a minimum two-night stay; note that they accept credit and debit cards, but not cheques. For an evening meal, there's plenty of choice within half a mile or so.

ROUTE GUIDE AND MAPS

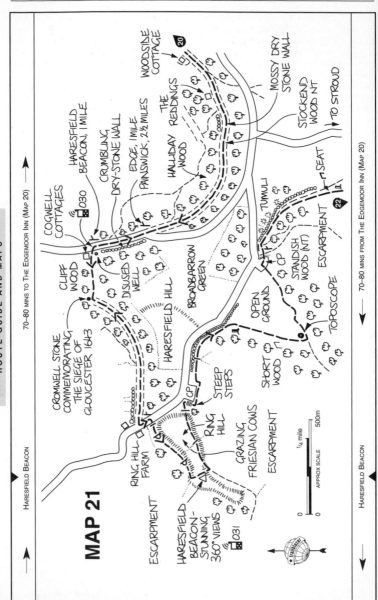

MAP 21

HARESFIELD BEACON

HARESFIELD BEACON

70-80 MINS TO THE EDGEMOOR INN (MAP 20)

70-80 MINS FROM THE EDGEMOOR INN (MAP 20)

WOODSIDE COTTAGE

20

MOSSY DRY STONE WALL

TO STROUD

STOCKEND WOOD NT

THE REDDINGS

HALLIDAY WOOD

HARESFIELD BEACON, 1 MILE

CRUMBLING DRY-STONE WALL

EDGE, 1 MILE
PAINSWICK, 2½ MILES

COGWELL COTTAGES

030

SEAT

22

TUMULI

STANDISH WOOD (NT)

ESCARPMENT

CP

OPEN GROUND

TOPOSCOPE

BROADBARROW GREEN

DISUSED WELL

CLIFF WOOD

HARESFIELD HILL

CROMWELL STONE COMMEMORATING THE SIEGE OF GLOUCESTER 1643

SHORT WOOD

STEEP STEPS

CP

RING HILL

GRAZING FRIESIAN COWS

ESCARPMENT

RING HILL FARM

HARESFIELD BEACON- STUNNING 360° VIEWS

031

ESCARPMENT

¼ mile

500m

0

0

APPROX SCALE

★ trailblazer

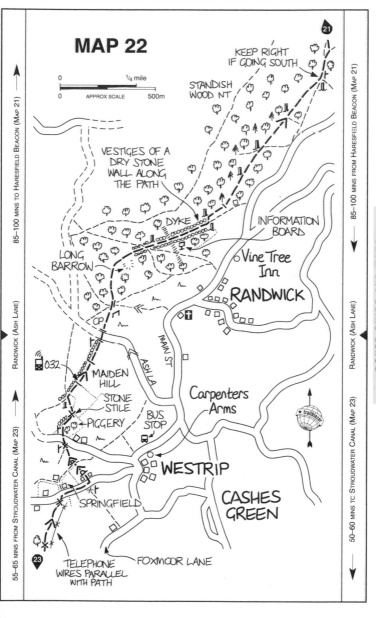

MAP 22

0   ¼ mile

0   APPROX SCALE   500m

KEEP RIGHT
IF GOING SOUTH

STANDISH
WOOD NT

VESTIGES OF A
DRY STONE
WALL ALONG
THE PATH

DYKE

INFORMATION
BOARD

LONG
BARROW

Vine Tree
Inn

RANDWICK

CP

MAIN ST

032

MAIDEN
HILL

ASH LA

STONE
STILE

PIGGERY

BUS
STOP

Carpenters
Arms

trailblazer

WESTRIP

SPRINGFIELD

**CASHES
GREEN**

FOXMOOR LANE

TELEPHONE
WIRES PARALLEL
WITH PATH

85–100 MINS TO HARESFIELD BEACON (MAP 21)

RANDWICK (ASH LANE)

55–65 MINS FROM STROUDWATER CANAL (MAP 23)

85–100 MINS FROM HARESFIELD BEACON (MAP 21)

RANDWICK (ASH LANE)

50–60 MINS TO STROUDWATER CANAL (MAP 23)

ROUTE GUIDE AND MAPS

RANDWICK/WESTRIP MAP 22, p129

On the western outskirts of Stroud are the villages of Randwick and Westrip, a short but steep walk down from the trail. Local **pubs** do a good job of satisfying walkers' hunger pangs – except on Sunday evenings and Monday. Up the hill in **Randwick** is *Vine Tree Inn* (☎ 01453-763748, 🖳 www.thevinetreerandwick.co.uk; Wed-Fri noon-2pm, Tue-Thur 7-9pm, Fri 6-9pm, Sat noon-9pm, Sun noon-3.30pm), where lunchtime ciabattas at £6.50 vie with Hungarian sausage and bread (£7.95), or glazed ham, egg and chips (£8.50).

Cotswold Green's No 230 bus from Stroud stops here; see public transport map and table, pp48-50.

Further south, **Westrip** boasts *The Carpenters Arms* (☎ 01453-762693; 🖳 www.the-carpenters-arms-westrip.co.uk; food Wed-Fri noon-2pm summer only, Sat-Sun noon-2.30pm, Tue-Sat 6-9pm), a real-ale pub where paninis come in from £4.95, or two people can indulge in a main meal such as lasagne or chilli for just £10.

STONEHOUSE MAP 23

As the Cotswold Way emerges into the valley that links Stonehouse to the west and Ebley to the east, there's little to delay the walker. Stonehouse **railway** station, a little over half a mile (1km) from the trail, off the B4008, is served by First Great Western, offering straightforward access to the Cotswold Way at this point.

See box p16 for details of Frocester Beer Festival which is held near here in August.

Stagecoach's **bus** Nos 61, 64, 66E and 66S stop on the B4008. See public transport map and table, pp48-50.

STONEHOUSE TO PENN WOOD MAPS 23-24

At this point, the Cotswold Way offers two alternatives. The **shorter route** of the two, which runs close to King's Stanley, is only 1½ **miles (2.5km)** long, taking about **40-50 minutes** to walk. Predominantly urban with an agricultural fringe, its attractions are of a practical nature, with a couple of B&Bs, a pub and a useful shop in King's Stanley itself.

The more **scenic route**, which follows in part the restored Stroudwater (Ebley) Canal then goes on to cross Selsley Common, is just over **3 miles (5km)**, 1½-1¾hrs), so about twice the distance. Unless time is of the essence, opt for the longer walk; the rewards are infinitely greater, with the common itself one of the trail's highlights. Open and windswept, it offers glorious walking at any time of the year, but is at its best in summer when the grass is thick with orchids and other wild flowers. Both routes converge in Penn Wood, just a quarter of a mile (0.45km) or so above (almost literally) Middleyard.

KING'S STANLEY
(SHORTER ROUTE) MAP 24, p133

Only a short walk west of the trail across playing fields, King's Stanley offers most of the services essential to walkers.

The **Co-op** (Mon-Sat 7.30am-10pm, Sun 9am-9pm) has all the necessities, including a **post office** counter and a useful

ATM. Opposite is a small **newsagent**, Yew Tree Stores.

For **B&B** accommodation, try *Orchardene* (☎ 01453-822684, 🖳 www .orchardene.co.uk; 1T en suite/1D with private bathroom; 🛏; WI-FI; 🐾; (Ⓛ), reached by heading away from the shops along

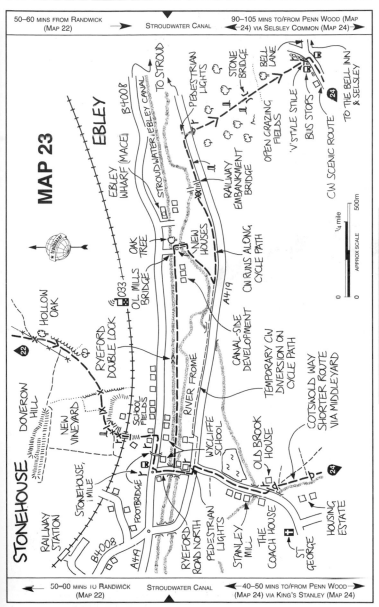

Castle St. A 19th-century stone house down a narrow drive, it's a friendly place, offering local organic food, including homemade bread and their own honey. B&B comes in at £37.50pp, or £50 for single occupancy.

For **food**, pub grub is available at the *King's Head* (☎ 01453-828293; Wed, Fri & Sat noon-3pm & 5-9pm, Thur 5-9pm,

Sun noon-3pm), by the war memorial, with dishes from £5.95 to £9.95. There's also a Chinese takeaway, *Ben's* (☎ 01453-828855; Tue-Sun 4.30-11pm), almost hidden down a narrow street that runs between Shute St and the playing fields.

Stagecoach **bus** No 66S stops daily by the war memorial. For details, see the public transport map and table, pp48-50.

MIDDLEYARD
(SHORTER ROUTE)   MAP 24

The Cotswold Way runs through Middleyard, a small ribbon of old and new stone houses up the hill from King's Stanley, yet within easy walking distance of the larger village's facilities. Backing on to farmland, with direct access clearly signposted from the trail, the aptly named *Valley Views* (☎ 01453-827458, 🖳 www .valley-views.com, 12 Orchard Cl; 1T/2D,

all with private facilities; 🛏; WI-FI; Ⓛ) is a modern, very comfortable house where guests have their own sitting room and sunroom. B&B here costs £34-39pp (sgl occ is from £55), the higher rate being for a large double with its own balcony.

Stagecoach **bus** No 66S stops in the village; see the public transport map and table, pp48-50.

EBLEY
(SCENIC ROUTE)   MAP 23, p131

Less than quarter of a mile (0.4km) east of the oak tree where the re-routed Cotswold Way turns away from Ebley Canal is **Ebley Wharf**, a new development across the bridge from Ebley Mill. If you're after **supplies**, it's worth the detour for a branch of

Mace (Mon-Sat 7am-9pm, Sun 8am-7pm); there are a couple of **cafés** here, too.

Cotswold Green's No 230 service calls at Ebley as do Stagecoach's No 61, 64 & 66E services. See public transport map and table, pp48-50.

SELSLEY   MAP 23, p131 & MAP 24
(SCENIC ROUTE)

The village of Selsley is notable for the Victorian **All Saints' Church**, clearly visible on the hill from the canal and a little way from the heart of the community. The church was influential in the development of the Arts and Crafts Movement (see box p76), its stained-glass windows being one of the first commissions for William Morris's design company. Work was contributed by Dante Gabriel Rossetti and Edward Burne-Jones, as well as by Morris himself. The church lies alongside Selsley Common, itself a haven for any number of wild flowers, including the pyramidal orchid (see p63 and photo opposite p64).

Both lodging and sustenance are on hand in the centre of the village at *The Bell Inn* (off map 23; ☎ 01453-753801; 🖳 www

.thebellinnselsley.com; 2D en suite; WI-FI; 🐾; Ⓛ), a couple of hundred yards (200m) from the trail. A recent makeover has resulted in two classy bedrooms with king-size beds, contemporary bathrooms and plenty of mod cons. **B&B** here is £45pp in the smaller room, or £60pp in the larger, which has a separate living room with sofa bed. For single occupancy you'll pay £85-110; a third person on the sofa bed costs £15. In the restaurant (Mon-Sat noon-2.30pm & 6.30-9.30pm, Sun noon-4pm), roast belly of pork at £12 could be a winner, or – perhaps more manageable at lunchtime – goats' cheese, rocket and red onion pizza for £5.50.

Cotswold Green's No 35 **bus** stops by The Bell Inn and Stagecoach's No 66S stops daily by All Saints' Church. See public transport map and table, pp48-50.

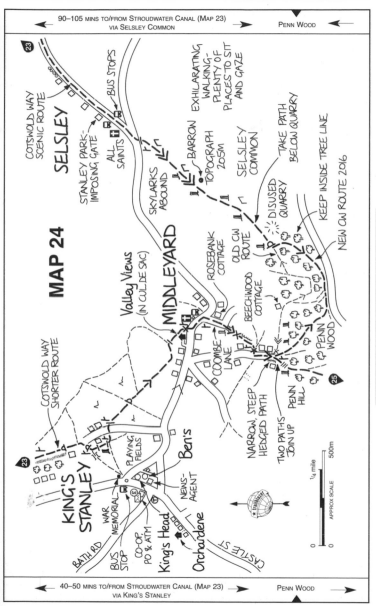

PENN WOOD TO DURSLEY — MAPS 24-27

Further ribbons of steeply banked beech woods characterise this **6½-mile (10.25km, 3¼-4hrs)** stretch, broken up by two significant highlights as well as a couple of interesting long barrows.

The views from **Coaley Peak** (Map 25) look not just west to the Severn, but onward to Cam Long Down and the Tyndale Monument – a taste of things to come. **Cam Long Down** (Map 27) itself is all too short, the steep climb up being richly rewarded with 360° views: a place to be savoured before the descent into Dursley. Be careful up here if the weather is poor, though; there are some sheer drops.

The area is also home to two of the trail's most interesting long barrows (see box p136), at **Nympsfield** and **Uley**, and two very different mansions: **Woodchester Mansion** (see box below) and **Owlpen Manor** (see box p136), although the latter is no longer open to the public.

NYMPSFIELD — off MAP 25

About half a mile (0.8km) off the trail from Coaley Peak, in the heart of the village of Nympsfield, ***The Rose and Crown Inn*** (☎ 01453-860612, 🖳 www.cotswoldcountrypubs.com/theroseandcrown; daily noon-9pm; WI-FI; 🐕) offers a solid menu with daily specials and real ale – or try a combination of the two in their steak and locally brewed ale pie at £12.50.

Cotswold Green's No 35 **bus** service calls here; see public transport map and table, pp48-50.

❑ Woodchester Mansion and Park — Map 25

Despite its imposing architecture, the three-storey Victorian **Woodchester Mansion** (☎ 01453-861541, 🖳 www.woodchestermansion.org.uk; £7.50, NT & English Heritage members £6.50) near Nympsfield was never finished, its rooms being inhabited by five species of bat, but never by humans. It is usually open to the public from Easter to October (Tue-Sun & bank hols 11am-5pm), but do check their website first. Visitors may explore the house, including the drawing room, which was the only room to be completed, and upstairs along boarded corridors. Lunches, tea and coffee in their tea room should help to restore a sense of normality.

The mansion is set in the grounds of **Woodchester Park**, a peaceful wooded valley with a chain of lakes that is owned by the National Trust (☎ 01452-814213, 🖳 www.nationaltrust.org.uk; daily dawn-dusk; parking £3, NT members free). Designated as an SSSI (see p61), the estate is notable not just for the bats, but for a broad diversity of birds and wild flowers. Waymarked trails through the grounds are accessible to the public all year. Visitors arriving on foot can access the mansion along the main drive; otherwise entry is via the National Trust car park to the south, from where it's a 10- to 15-minute walk to the house.

ULEY — MAP 26, p137

Although it's over half a mile (1km) from the Cotswold Way, Uley does at least justify the diversion. Probably many people's idea of a proper village, it boasts a pub, a decidedly imposing church, St Giles, and a **post office cum shop** (Mon-Fri 8am-6pm, Sat 8am-4pm, Sun 9am-noon; post office Mon-Fri 8am-1pm & 2-6pm, Sat 9am-12.30pm); it even has its own brewery and a posh manor house – Owlpen Manor – a

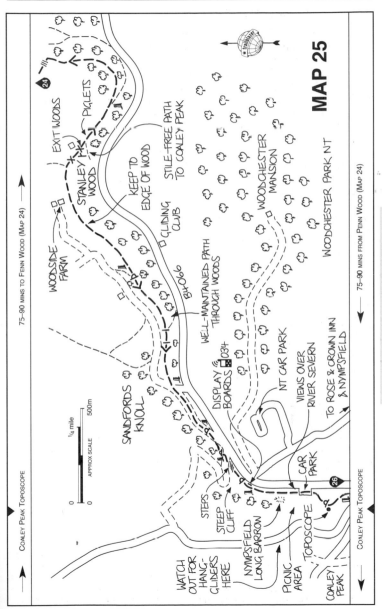

❏ **What is a long barrow?**
Essentially another name for a communal burial ground, the long barrow is known locally as a 'tump'. These were the graveyards of the Neolithic people, early settlers who were the first to farm the land over 5000 years ago. In addition to human remains, archaeologists have identified the remains of fires that indicate some form of ritual or religious activity.

Of almost 100 long barrows in the Cotswolds, several are along the Cotswold Way including the **Nympsfield Long Barrow** near Coaley Peak, dating from 2500BC, and others at Leckhampton Hill and in Standish Wood. Notable among them are **Belas Knap** (see box p101) and – just off this stretch of the route – **Uley Long Barrow**, more evocatively known as **Hetty Pegler's Tump**. Best approached along the road rather than by scrambling up the steep hill through the woods, Hetty Pegler is worth the detour, since here you can crawl inside the chamber itself. You'll need a torch (if not, a camera flash will do) – but don't spend too long, for folklore has it that, if you do, the fairies will start to work their magic on the passing of time.

short distance away. The village is also notable for the hill fort of Uley Bury (see box p122), which is much closer to the trail.

The whitewashed *Old Crown* (☎ 01453-860502, 🖳 www.theoldcrownuley.co.uk; 2T/2D, all en suite; WI-FI; 🐾; ⓛ), with a terrace garden at the rear, does **B&B** at £37.50-42.50p (sgl occ £45). There is a standard **pub menu** (food served Mon-Fri noon-2pm & 6-9pm, Sat & Sun noon-9pm) and plenty of real-ale choices to accompany your meal.

Cotswold Green's No 35 **bus** service stops near the post office; see public transport map and table, pp48-50.

❏ **Owlpen Manor**   **off Map 26**
Almost hidden from view in a valley along a short avenue of trees, Owlpen Manor (☎ 01453-860261, 🖳 www.owlpen.com) is an enchanting Tudor manor house, complete with great hall, dating in part back to 1450. It was abandoned early in the 19th century, but was rescued in 1926 in line with the principles of the Society for the Protection of Ancient Buildings (🖳 www.spab.org.uk), a body formed by William Morris. While most of the furniture and decoration date to an earlier era, the Arts and Crafts Movement founded by Morris is also represented. Outside, the formal gardens with their neatly clipped yews lead to beech woods with a series of walks, while above looms an elaborate Victorian church.

Sadly, the estate, which remains in private hands, is no longer open to the public except for private functions, though if you'd like to explore you could always spend a few days in one of their cottages.

DURSLEY   MAP 27a, p140
Only a few years ago, it was difficult not to echo the sentiments of one local resident, that Dursley had been 'very successfully ruined' by the planning authorities. Now, as houses and shops have materialised on the building sites that marred the centre, so the town has settled into a new phase, marked by a strong sense of community. At one end of the pedestrianised Parsonage St, which boasts a decent range of traditional shops and facilities, stand the pillared Georgian **Market House** and the parish church of **St James the Great**. Cars follow the newer road that runs almost parallel, lined with a

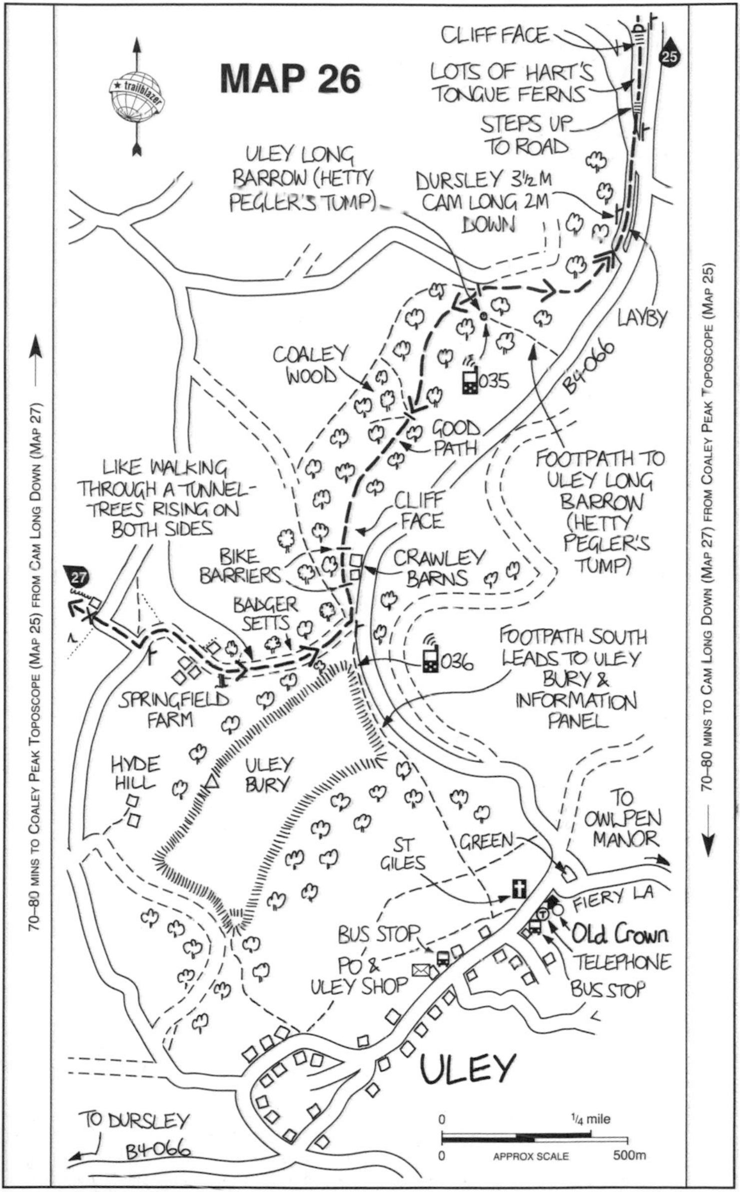
MAP 26
trailblazer
CLIFF FACE
LOTS OF HART'S TONGUE FERNS
STEPS UP TO ROAD
25
ULEY LONG BARROW (HETTY PEGLER'S TUMP)
DURSLEY 3½M CAM LONG 2M DOWN
LAYBY
B4066
COALEY WOOD
035
GOOD PATH
FOOTPATH TO ULEY LONG BARROW (HETTY PEGLER'S TUMP)
LIKE WALKING THROUGH A TUNNEL- TREES RISING ON BOTH SIDES
CLIFF FACE
BIKE BARRIERS
CRAWLEY BARNS
27
BADGER SETTS
036
FOOTPATH SOUTH LEADS TO ULEY BURY & INFORMATION PANEL
SPRINGFIELD FARM
HYDE HILL
ULEY BURY
TO OWLPEN MANOR
ST GILES
GREEN
FIERY LA
Old Crown
TELEPHONE
BUS STOP
BUS STOP
PO & ULEY SHOP
ULEY
TO DURSLEY
B4066
0
¼ mile
0
APPROX SCALE
500m
70–80 MINS TO COALEY PEAK TOPOSCOPE (MAP 25) FROM CAM LONG DOWN (MAP 27)
70–80 MINS TO CAM LONG DOWN (MAP 27) FROM COALEY PEAK TOPOSCOPE (MAP 25)

ROUTE GUIDE AND MAPS

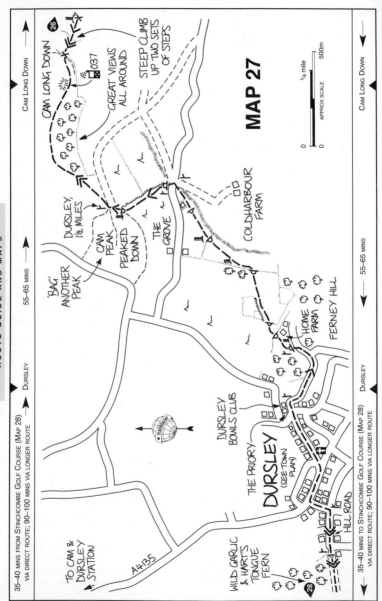

CAM LONG DOWN

55–65 MINS

DURSLEY

35–40 MINS FROM STINCHCOMBE GOLF COURSE (MAP 28)
VIA DIRECT ROUTE; 90–100 MINS VIA LONGER ROUTE

CAM LONG DOWN

26

0037

GREAT VIEWS ALL AROUND

STEEP CLIMB UP TWO SETS OF STEPS

MAP 27

0   ¼ mile
APPROX SCALE
0   500m

DURSLEY, 1½ MILES

'BAG' ANOTHER PEAK

CAM PEAK

PEAKED DOWN

THE GROVE

COLDHARBOUR FARM

HOME FARM

FERNEY HILL

DURSLEY BOWLS CLUB

THE PRIORY

DURSLEY (SEE TOWN PLAN)

TO CAM & DURSLEY STATION

A4135

HILL ROAD

WILD GARLIC & HART'S TONGUE FERN

28

CAM LONG DOWN

55–65 MINS

DURSLEY

35–40 MINS TO STINCHCOMBE GOLF COURSE (MAP 28)
VIA DIRECT ROUTE; 90–100 MINS VIA LONGER ROUTE

supermarket which seems to have given the town a boost, and a leisure complex currently undergoing a facelift. For the walker, Dursley has one further card up its sleeve: the CAMRA award-winning Old Spot pub (see p141), which is one of the best along the trail.

Like many other Cotswold towns, Dursley was founded on the wool trade; today its weaving skills have turned towards billiard-table baizes and the covers for tennis balls. It was also home to the Lister family, of engineering fame, who still have a presence here. To get an idea of the town's history, including its industrial past, pop into the **Heritage Centre** (Tue-Sat 10.30am-12.30pm).

See box p16 for details of the walking festival held here in October.

Transport

First Great Western **trains** (see box p46) run to Cam & Dursley station, nearly three miles (4.8km) north of the town.

The town's bus station is on May Lane, squeezed between the modern, tinted-glass library and the Old Spot – the old and the new. Three **buses** – Cotswold Green's No 35, Severnside Transport's No 87 and Third Sector's No 207 run between the station and Dursley, all stopping at the bus station. Stagecoach's Nos 61, 62/62A and 88 also call at Dursley but not at the railway station. See the public transport map and table, pp48-50.

For **taxi** services, try A to B Taxis (☎ 01453-548483), Jenkins (☎ 01453-542346), or PMD Taxis (mob ☎ 07860-950793).

Services

While the town has no **tourist information** centre as such, staff at the **library** (Mon & Thur 9.30am-5pm, Tue & Fri 9.30am-6.30pm, Sat 9/30am-4pm) are extremely helpful and they have a good selection of leaflets for visitors. Both Lloyds and Barclays **banks** have branches with ATMs in the town; there's an ATM at Sainsbury's, too. The **post office**, with a bureau de change and ATM, is now housed in Baileys News by the Market House, at the end of Parsonage St.

A large Sainsbury's **supermarket** (Mon-Sat 8am-10pm, Sun 10am-4pm) may have brought a new dimension to Dursley, but its traditional shops along the pedestrianised Parsonage St are more than hanging on. This is where you'll find an independent **bakery**, a **butcher** with good cheese and pies, and a florist that doubles as a **greengrocer**. Crisps, sandwiches and drinks can also be bought at Hewitt's, the **newsagent**. A **farmers' market** is held on the second Saturday of each month at the Market House, from 9am to 1pm.

If you've any problems with your **boots**, Dursley Cobblers (☎ 01453-542918; Mon, Tue, Thur & Fri 9am-5pm, Wed & Sat 9am-4pm), on Parsonage St, may be able to repair them, while for **camera** issues try Clifton Cameras (☎ 01453-548128; Mon-Sat 9am-5.30pm) opposite. And while you're at it, you could get to grips with muddy clothes at The Washtub **launderette** on Silver St.

Although there's a branch of Lloyds **pharmacy** attached to the May Lane surgery almost right on the trail about two minutes' walk from the library, more central are two other chemists – Boots and the Co-op – along Parsonage St.

If you've any energy left after a day's walking, you could always try Dursley's **swimming pool** (🖳 www.dursleypool .com). Check online for times of public sessions, which vary according to the time of year.

Where to stay

A shortage of **B&B** accommodation in Dursley itself has been eased with the opening of *Underhill House B&B* (☎ 01453-549617, 🖳 www.dursleybnb.co.uk; 1D/2Tr, all en suite; ➖; WI-FI; Ⓛ). Right next to The Old Spot, they offer evening meals, as well as laundry and drying facilities. B&B costs £32.50-37.50pp (sgl occ £45-50), with £20 for a third bed in either of the two larger rooms.

Well recommended is *The Garden Flat* (☎ 01453-545312; 1T; ➖; WI-FI), a self-contained annexe of **Ormond House**, at 13 Silver St. Large, light and airy, with its own kitchen and bathroom, it looks over

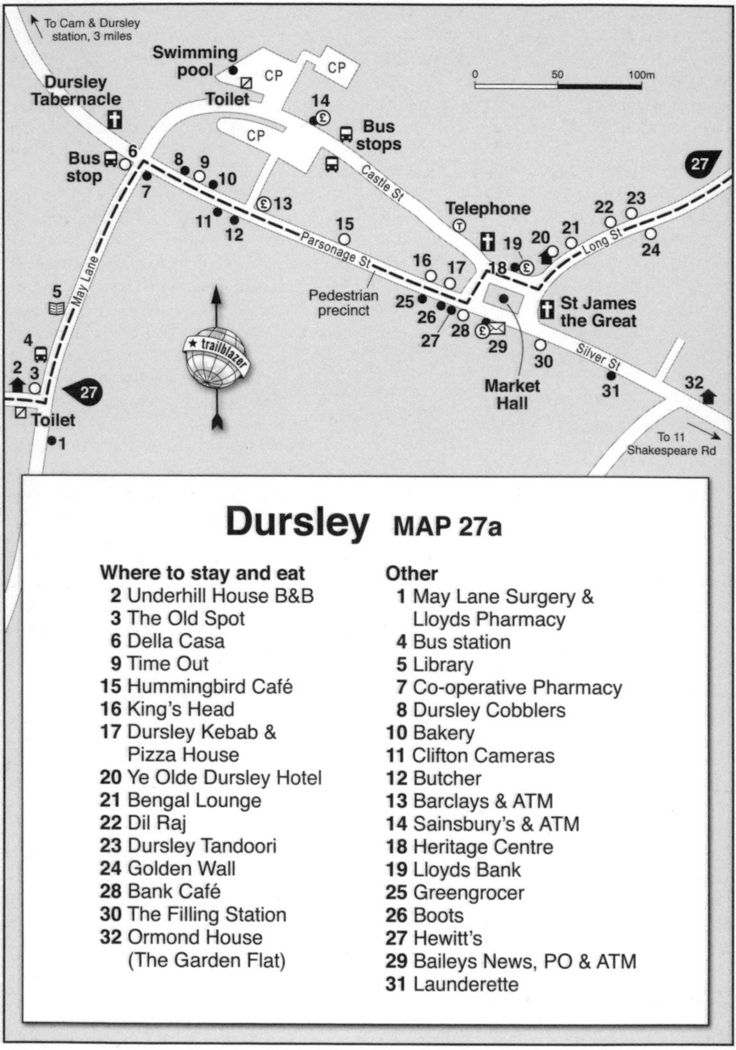

Dursley MAP 27a

Where to stay and eat
- **2** Underhill House B&B
- **3** The Old Spot
- **6** Della Casa
- **9** Time Out
- **15** Hummingbird Café
- **16** King's Head
- **17** Dursley Kebab & Pizza House
- **20** Ye Olde Dursley Hotel
- **21** Bengal Lounge
- **22** Dil Raj
- **23** Dursley Tandoori
- **24** Golden Wall
- **28** Bank Café
- **30** The Filling Station
- **32** Ormond House (The Garden Flat)

Other
- **1** May Lane Surgery & Lloyds Pharmacy
- **4** Bus station
- **5** Library
- **7** Co-operative Pharmacy
- **8** Dursley Cobblers
- **10** Bakery
- **11** Clifton Cameras
- **12** Butcher
- **13** Barclays & ATM
- **14** Sainsbury's & ATM
- **18** Heritage Centre
- **19** Lloyds Bank
- **25** Greengrocer
- **26** Boots
- **27** Hewitt's
- **29** Baileys News, PO & ATM
- **31** Launderette

a pretty garden and costs £35pp (sgl occ £40) for B&B; the fridge is well stocked so that guests can cook their own substantial breakfast. Further out in this direction, at ***11 Shakespeare Road*** (☎ 01453-547080, 🖳 ronnieh@talktalk.net; 2D; ☕; Ⓛ), walkers are welcomed with tea and cake. B&B, with sole use of a bathroom, is £30pp. They don't have wi-fi but internet access is available in one of the rooms. To get there, you can either follow Silver Street into Bull Pitch, turning right at the end, then left on to Byron Rd, left again on to Tennyson Rd and first right on to Shakespeare Rd (passing the New Inn on the way), or phone for directions from the Priory (Map 27). As long as she is free, the owner is happy to collect walkers if it is raining.

Back in town, *Ye Olde Dursley Hotel*, formerly the Old Bell (☎ 01453-542821; 2S/6T/1F, 5 en suite; ✆; WI-FI; ⒧), on Long St, changed hands in September 2015, but apart from the name, little else has changed – yet. You'll pay £30pp for B&B, regardless of room size and number of people sharing. The downside is that rooms are above a busy bar, with a nightclub operating in the latter half of the week.

Where to eat and drink

Arguably one of the best reasons for stopping in Dursley is to pay a visit to *The Old Spot* (☎ 01453-542870, 🖥 www.oldspot inn.co.uk; food Mon-Sat noon-5.45pm, Sun noon-4pm). Regularly featured among the top CAMRA awards, it is a stronghold among ale drinkers (see box p23), such that food is normally served only during the day – albeit with the occasional gourmet evening. That's a shame, but don't let it put you off; their soup and a sandwich at £7.50 is good value, their specials change regularly and their Sunday roast is so popular that it runs to two sittings.

Of the other pubs, the *King's Head* (☎ 01453-297396; 🖥 www.kingsheaddursley .co.uk; Mon-Sat 9.30am-10pm, Sun 11am-9.30pm; WI-FI) boasts a £5 brunch menu which gives way late morning to stone-baked pizzas, sandwiches and salads, whereas at *Ye Olde Dursley Hotel* (see Where to stay; daily 10am-9pm) you're looking at standard pub fare; there's also a beer garden and a games room here.

Heading upmarket, 2015 saw the arrival of *Della Casa* (☎ 01453-549679, 🖥 www.dellacasa.co.uk; Mon-Sat noon-3pm & 5-10.30pm, Sun noon-9pm) on Parsonage St. Cool and classy, it focuses on Italian cuisine, from pizzas and risotto to *bistecca pepe nero* (£7.95-15.95) and business seems to be booming.

For breakfast, lunch or a cup of tea during the day, the choice has burgeoned in recent years. Near the Market House, try *Bank Café* (☎ 01453-543920; Mon-Fri 9am-5pm, Sat 9am-4pm, Sun 10am-4pm; WI-FI), where squashy sofas meet functional chairs and tables in a big old banking hall. The pedestrianised section of Parsonage St also boasts *Hummingbird* (☎ 01453-299276, 🖥 hummingbird-cafe.co .uk; Mon-Sat 9am-4pm), their breakfast, tea and scones offset by Caribbean specialities such as curry goat, rice & peas for £6.50. Next to the bakery is the new *Time Out* (mob ☎ 07986-505424; Mon-Sat 8.30am-3pm), where the emphasis is not surprisingly on fresh bread, cakes and pies, as well as light meals. Then there's the aptly named *Filling Station* (☎ 01453-542609; Mon-Fri 8am-3pm, Sat 9am-2pm), on Silver St, which serves the likes of sandwiches and jacket potatoes.

Indian cuisine is well represented with a trio of restaurants on Long St: *Bengal Lounge* (☎ 01453-519711/2; Sun-Thur 5.30-11pm, Fri & Sat to 11.30pm), *Dursley Tandoori* (☎ 01453-548833; daily 4.30-11.30pm), and *Dil Raj* (☎ 01453-543472; Sun-Thur 5.45-11.30pm, Fri & Sat 5.30pm-midnight). Otherwise you'll be looking at a takeaway, perhaps from the Chinese *Golden Wall* (daily 5-10.30pm), also on Long St, or *Dursley Kebab and Pizza House* (daily 3pm-midnight).

DURSLEY TO WOTTON-UNDER-EDGE MAPS 27-30

The Cotswold Way offers another choice at this stage. The **longer (scenic) route**, a **6¾-mile (11km, 2¼-2¾hrs)** stretch, climbs steeply from Dursley and circumnavigates Stinchcombe Hill – and the golf course – before coming almost full circle. The **more direct route** (just **4½ miles/7.2km, 3¼-3¾hrs**) cuts straight across what looks on the map like the stem of a leaf. Which you choose should depend on time and the weather. On a clear day, the views from

Stinchcombe Hill more than justify the detour, but if you're lumbered with English weather at its worst, going straight across may be the better option. Either way, you'll have the opportunity to climb the **Tyndale Monument**, perhaps to see those views from on high.

STINCHCOMBE HILL   MAP 28

Up on the hill above Dursley, overlooking the golf course, two **B&Bs** right on the Cotswold Way broaden the options in this area. Just beyond the golf club is *Highlands* (☎ 01453-544053, mob ☎ 07974-406798; 1S/2D; WI-FI; Ⓛ), opened in 2014 and well situated for either of the alternative routes. Each of the bedrooms (with a view!) has its own basin, but only the large double is en suite; the other rooms share a shower and toilet. Expect to pay £47.50pp in the en-suite room or £40pp in the smaller double with a 4ft bed, with the single room at £60. Single occupancy of a double comes in at £70. Tea and cake is served on arrival; guests also have the use of a living room.

For *Stinchcombe Hill House* (☎ 01453-543090, mob ☎ 07788-725592, www.stinchcombehillhouse.co.uk; 3D or T, all en suite; ☛; WI-FI; Ⓛ), you'll need to take the longer Cotswold Way route, but you'll be rewarded by a restored Edwardian house, friendly owners and their dogs, and superb views towards Tyndale Monument. B&B costs £42.50pp (£65 sgl occ) and the owners will drive walkers into Dursley for an evening meal.

NORTH NIBLEY   MAP 29, p144

This thriving little village boasts all the essentials – a church, a school, a **grocery shop** with **ATM** (Mon-Fri 7am-6pm, Sat 7am-1pm, Sun 8.30-11am) and **post office** (Mon-Fri 9am-1pm, Sat 9am-noon) as well as a decent pub – not to mention a range of accommodation.

The No 201 **bus** service, run by Mike's Travel; for details, see the public transport map and table, pp48-50.

This is one place where campers don't have to trudge far for the night, as there's a campsite at *Nibley House* (☎ 01453-543108 for camping or ☎ 01453-544632 for B&B, 🖳 www.nibleyhouse.co.uk), just a few yards off the trail towards St Martin's Church. It's a working farm, where **campers** pay £6pp, with an outside toilet and shower, and plenty of space to explore. For £7 a head, they'll even make your breakfast. Those with delusions of grandeur might prefer to lord it over the campers in the Georgian manor house itself, a family home set in extensive flower gardens: the rooms (1T private facilities, 1D or T/1Qd, both en suite; WI-FI; 🐾; Ⓛ) are large and cost £42.50-55pp (sgl occ £45, three/four sharing rates on request) for **B&B**.

The village pub, *The Black Horse Inn* (☎ 01453-543777, 🖳 www.blackhorse-northnibley.co.uk, Barrs Lane; 3D/1Qd, all en suite; WI-FI; 🐾), is right on the Cotswold Way and offers B&B for £35-50pp (£50 sgl occ; three/four sharing around £100), as well as a restaurant and bar. The menu (Mon 6-9pm, Tue-Fri noon-2pm & 6-9pm, Sat noon-3pm & 6-9pm, Sun noon-4pm) includes standard pub fare with some vegetarian options.

After the steep climb through the woods from North Nibley, the additional ascent of the stone **Tyndale Monument** (entry £1) on Nibley Knoll may seem 121 steps too far. It's worth it, though, for some splendid views in every direction. The monument was erected in 1866 to the memory of Sir William Tyndale, who in defiance of the authorities translated the New Testament into English. He was burnt at the stake for heresy in 1536.

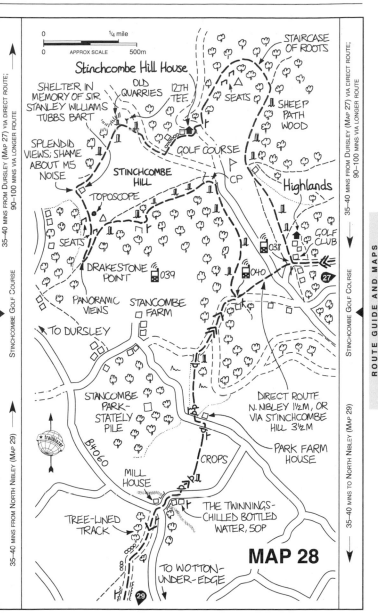

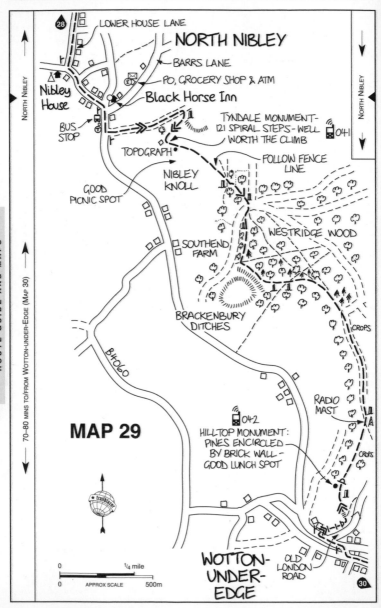

NORTH NIBLEY

NORTH NIBLEY

LOWER HOUSE LANE

28

BARRS LANE

PO, GROCERY SHOP & ATM

Black Horse Inn

Nibley House

BUS STOP

TOPOGRAPH

TYNDALE MONUMENT-
121 SPIRAL STEPS – WELL
WORTH THE CLIMB

041

NIBLEY KNOLL

FOLLOW FENCE LINE

GOOD PICNIC SPOT

SOUTHEND FARM

WESTRIDGE WOOD

BRACKENBURY DITCHES

B4060

CROPS

MAP 29

042

HILLTOP MONUMENT:
PINES ENCIRCLED
BY BRICK WALL –
GOOD LUNCH SPOT

RADIO MAST

CROPS

0   ¼ mile

0   500m
APPROX SCALE

WOTTON-
UNDER-
EDGE

OLD
LONDON
ROAD

30

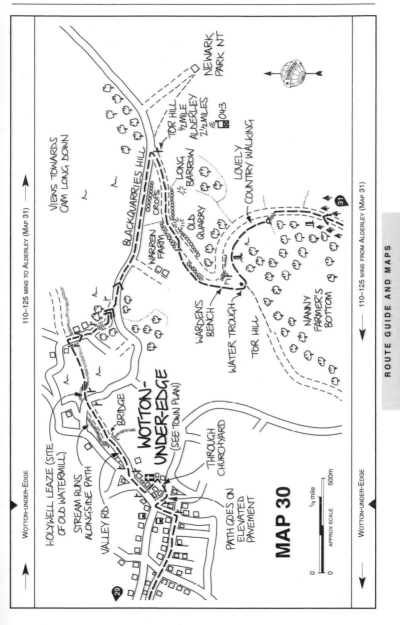

WOTTON-UNDER-EDGE

VIEWS TOWARDS CAM LONG DOWN

NEWARK PARK NT

TOR HILL ½MILE
ALDERLEY 2½MILES

043

LONG BARROW

BLACKQUARRIES HILL

WARREN FARM

WARREN CROFS

OLD QUARRY

LOVELY COUNTRY WALKING

31

WARDENS BENCH

WATER TROUGH

TOR HILL

NANNY FARMER'S BOTTOM

HOLYWELL LEAZE (SITE OF OLD WATERMILL)

STREAM RUNS ALONGSIDE PATH

VALLEY RD

BRIDGE

WOTTON-UNDER-EDGE
(SEE TOWN PLAN)

THROUGH CHURCHYARD

PATH GOES ON ELEVATED PAVEMENT

MAP 30

¼ mile
APPROX SCALE
0   500m

0

29

ROUTE GUIDE AND MAPS

WOTTON-UNDER-EDGE   MAP 30a

It's a friendly place, Wotton-under-Edge, and very community spirited. Almost everything happens on the appropriately named Long St, which morphs from the High St, extending downhill the length of the town. The Cotswold Way runs along this street, passing most of the shops and many pubs and cafés, as well as two of three sets of **almshouses**. One of these, on Church St, incorporates a small chapel, where visitors are welcome.

The trail continues past the 13th-century parish church of **St Mary the Virgin** before rejoining open countryside. More visible than any of these from above the town is the former **Tabernacle Church**, now an auction room.

East of the town, the Cotswold Way passes through the grounds of **Newark Park** (see Map 30; ☎ 01453-842644, 🖳 www.nationaltrust.org.uk; Mar-Oct Wed-Mon 11am-5pm; mid to late Feb Wed-Mon 11am-5pm, early Dec Sat & Sun 11am-4pm; £8.40), with almost direct footpath access from the trail. Built as a Tudor hunting lodge, it has commanding views to the south-west from its ridge-top location. Following a chequered history, during which it was converted to a fashionable house, it was finally abandoned during the war years and was given to the National Trust in 1949. Since then, both house and garden have been restored and the place is once again inhabited, with an eclectic collection of art on view to the public.

See box p15 for details of Wotton's Arts Festival.

Transport

Wessex's No 84 & No 86 **bus** services call here as do Cotswold Green's No 40, Severnside's No 87 and the No 201 operated by Mike's Travel. For details, see the public transport map and table, pp48-50.

For **taxis**, try Al's Taxis (☎ 01453-519354, ☎ 07843-427967) or Coombe Valley Taxis (☎ 01453-845071).

WOTTON-UNDER-EDGE

Where to stay
6 Hawks View
7 Orchard House
14 Swan Hotel

Where to eat and drink
3 Bunter's Café
4 Wotton British Takeaway
5 Royal Oak Inn
14 Swan Hotel
15 Reg's Kebab, Chicken & Pizza
16 The Star
17 Pizza Planet
18 The Edge Coffee Shop
19 Singing Teapot
20 The Ark Coffee Shop
23 The Wotton Coffee Shop
34 The Falcon Steakhouse
35 Hong Kong Kitchen
36 India Palace

Other
1 Former Tabernacle Church (auction rooms)
2 One Stop Shop
8 Chipping Surgery
9 Swimming pool
10 Under the Edge Arts
11 Heritage Centre & Tourist Information
12 Cinema (Electric Picture House)
13 Town Hall
21 Lloyds Pharmacy
22 Parson's Bakery
24 Co-op
25 Relish Deli
26 Tesco Express
27 Cotswold Book Room
28 Lloyds & ATM
29 Barclays & ATM
30 Walkers Bakery
31 Post Office
32 Don Clark Camera Repairs
33 WH Thomas & Son
37 Culverhay Surgery

ROUTE GUIDE AND MAPS

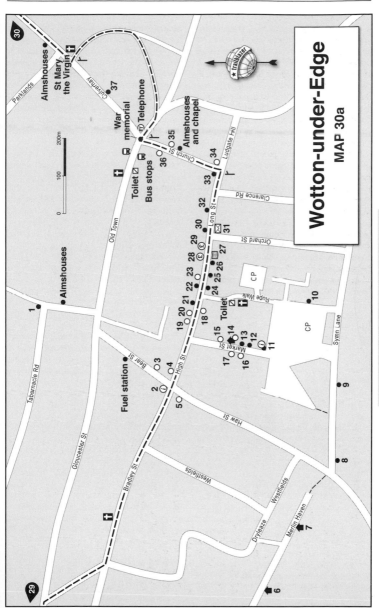

Wotton-under-Edge
MAP 30a

Services

For **tourist information**, find your way to the purpose-built **Heritage Centre** (☎ 01453-521541, 💻 www.wottonheritage .com; Tue, Thur & Fri 10.30am-12.30pm & 2-4pm, Sat 10am-1pm, Sun Apr-Oct 2-5pm), tucked away behind Long St on The Chipping. Run entirely by volunteers, it has good displays relating to the town's history as well as offering all the normal information services. A range of leaflets and tourist information is also available from the council's **One Stop Shop** (Mon-Fri 9am-12.30pm) on the corner of Bradley and Bear streets.

Of the **banks**, Barclays and Lloyds (both with ATMs) are close together on Long St. The **post office** is almost opposite, as is a **bookshop**, Cotswold Book Room. For **waterproofs** and other outdoor clothing, make your way to WH Thomas & Son (closed Wed & Sun), at the bottom of Long St; 'gentleman's outfitters' since 1896, they also have women's sizes. If your **camera** is on the blink, Don Clark Camera Repairs (☎ 01453-842102; Mon-Tue & Thur-Fri 9.30am-4.30pm, Wed 1-4.30pm, Sat 9am-1pm), also on Long St, may be able to help.

The town's main **supermarket**, the Co-op (Mon-Sat 7am-10pm, Sun 10am-4pm), is some way down Long St, with Tesco Express (daily 7am-10pm) just a few yards further on. More personal are the excellent Relish **Deli** (with paninis, salads, pizza and pies for lunch on the way – and space to eat in) and Parson's **bakery**, with a second bakery – Walkers – further down the road. A **farmers' market** is held at 9am-1pm on the first Saturday of each month, except January, in the Town Hall on Market St.

The **pharmacy**, a branch of Lloyds, is here, too, with two **medical surgeries** relatively close by: Chipping Surgery (☎ 01453-842214; Mon 8.30am-7.30pm, Tue, Thur & Fri 8.30am-6.30pm, Wed 8.30am-5pm), on Symn Lane, and Culverhay (☎ 01453-843252; Mon 8am-8pm, Tue, Thur & Fri 8am-6pm, Wed 8am-1pm), on Culverhay. There are public **toilets** south of Long St on both Rope Walk and on Old Town.

The town scores on the entertainment stakes, all run by volunteers. The Electric Picture House **cinema** (☎ 01453-844601, 💻 www.wottoncinema.com), on Market St, has several screenings a week. Close to the car park, **Under the Edge Arts** (💻 www .utea.org.uk), a community venture in Chipping Hall, hosts regular displays and a programme of events throughout the year. There's even a week-long Arts Festival (see box p15) every year at the end of April/ early May.

For a reviving dip at the end of a day's walking, check out the open-air **swimming pool** (☎ 01453-842086, 💻 wottonpool.co .uk; end Apr-mid Sep, Mon-Fri 3.30-5pm & 6.30-8pm, Sat/Sun 2-4pm; times slightly different in school holidays), on Symn Lane.

Where to stay

Accommodation options in Wotton have diminished in recent years, but there's still a good hotel and two B&Bs. Both B&Bs are on Merlin Haven, reached along a footpath to the west of the swimming pool, or by following Westfields into Dryleaze, then turning left and left again into Merlin Haven. At one end of the road is *Orchard House* (☎ 01453-842613, 💻 jchaines@tis cali.co.uk; 1T/1D share bathroom; ▼; WI-FI), which charges £30-40pp (sgl occ £55). At the other, you'll find *Hawks View* (☎ 01453-521441; 1D en suite; WI-FI; Ⓛ), on the left as you're coming from the town. Here B&B is £30pp (sgl occ £60) and, subject to prior arrangement, there's an evening meal option at £10pp.

Back in town, the helpful and welcoming *Swan Hotel* (☎ 01453-843004, 💻 www .swanhotelwotton.com; 2S share bathroom, 3D/1T/4Tr, all en suite; ▼; WI-FI in most rooms; 🐾; Ⓛ), on Market St, has attractive rooms; two of the rooms can be linked for a family or group. B&B rates are £42.50-47.50pp (sgl/sgl occ £75-85, £95-105 for three/four sharing).

Where to eat and drink

Cafés and takeaways dominate the foody outlets in Wotton-under-Edge, but there are some good **pubs** too. Of these, *The*

Star (☎ 01453-844651; food served Mon-Sat noon-2pm) offers a daily homemade special such as curry, chilli or pasta for £5.25, alongside the normal pub basics, and walkers (mud and all) are very welcome.

At the *Royal Oak Inn* (☎ 01453-844366, 🖳 www.theroyaloakwotton.com; daily noon-2.30pm, Mon-Sat 6-9pm), on Haw St, you can eat inside or in their large garden. Their 'lunchtime and OAP' menu (Mon Sat), has plenty of jacket potatoes and pub standards, while a second, 'main' menu boasts dishes such as chargrilled swordfish with avocado, cucumber and sun-blush tomato salsa (£10.95).

Rather smarter is *Swan Hotel* (see Where to stay; Mon-Fri noon-3pm, Mon-Thur 5-9pm, Fri 5-9.30pm, Sat noon-9.30pm, Sun noon-8pm) – 'no muddy boots', please – whose extensive menus include a range of British tapas from £4.50, 'gourmet' burgers from £10, as well as more formal dining.

Right at the bottom of Long St, on the corner of Church St, *The Falcon Steakhouse* (☎ 01453-521894, 🖳 www.falconsteakhouse.com; Mon 6-9pm, Tue-Sun 12-2.30pm & 6-9pm) is a new and very popular venture run by local farmers, so be prepared to book. Concentrating on meat from their own farms, such as an 8oz rump steak (£15.95), they also serve the likes of ploughmans (£7).

Away from the pubs, Long St will serve you well, with breakfast, light lunches and tea served in various styles. Relatively modern is *The Edge Coffee Shop* (☎ 01453-844108; Mon-Fri 9am-5pm term time, or from 10am in holidays, Sat 10am-4pm), whose offerings include soup

(£4), a selection of innovative salads (£5.50) and home-made cakes, including gluten free. On the other side of the road, several smaller places vie for your custom. The tiny *Singing Teapot* (mob ☎ 07769-267455; Tue-Sat 9.30am-4pm) offers tea, cakes and light lunches in a genuinely welcoming environment. Close by is *The Ark Coffee Shop* (☎ 01453-521838; Mon-Fri 9am-noon & 2.45-4.45pm, Sat 9.30am-12.30pm), where a team of Christian volunteers serves up coffee and cakes. And a few doors further down is *The Wotton Coffee Shop* (☎ 01453-520448; Mon-Sat 9am-5pm, Sun 10am-2pm), with plenty of choice and the bonus of a two-course Sunday roast at £8 – though you'll need to book.

If you're tempted by a cooked breakfast, try *Bunter's Café* (Mon-Fri 7.30am-2.30pm, Sat 8.30am-2pm), just off Long St, where the full English will set you back just £5.95. And if you're passing through on a Sunday between April and October, it's worth checking at the **Town Hall**, on Market St, where afternoon tea is usually served 2.30-5pm by one of the local organisations.

Ethnic cuisine comes from *India Palace* (Sun-Thur 5.30-11.30pm, Fri & Sat to midnight), Church St, which has a restaurant as well as a takeaway service, and the nearby *Hong Kong Kitchen* (Tue-Sat 5-10pm, Sun 6-10pm), which also serves fish & chips, but is takeaway only. Closer to home, foodwise, is *Wotton British Takeaway* (Mon-Sat 11.30am-2pm & 5-10pm), on High St, for fish, chicken and pies, or perhaps *Pizza Planet* (Mon-Sat 4.30-11pm, Sun to 10.30pm), on Market St. *Reg's Kebab, Chicken & Pizza* (Sun-Thur 3-11pm, Fri-Sat 3pm-midnight) is also here.

WOTTON-UNDER-EDGE TO OLD SODBURY   MAPS 30-35

This **12¼-mile (19.7km)** section will take about **6-6¾ hours**, passing through open, rolling fields, interspersed with the occasional tract of woodland, and a number of small villages with attractive stone churches. Of these, one of the most intriguing, primarily for its cubed yews, is **St Mary the Virgin** at Hawkesbury (Map 33), but it's a long downhill detour off the Cotswold Way. Similarly, tantalising glimpses through the trees of **Horton Court** (Map 34) might tempt the walker to tackle the very steep path down for closer inspection but see p152 before contemplating this; most will be happy to stick to the trail and the lovely drovers' road south of Hawkesbury. If the walk lacks drama, it certainly makes up for it in nomenclature: who could resist the appeal of a dip that glories in the name of Nanny Farmer's Bottom? And if you find yourself tiring, there's always the prospect of a sandwich or dinner at the Dog Inn in Old Sodbury to act as a spur.

ALDERLEY MAP 31

There's an air of exclusivity about Alderley, from the timeless solidity of the **Church of St Kenelm** to the old stone houses surrounded by well-maintained gardens.

Wessex's No 86 **bus** stops in the village by the church; for details, see the public transport map and table, pp48-50.

HILLESLEY MAP 31

Little more than a cluster of individual stone cottages with a church and a pub, Hillesley is another attractive village around half a mile (1km) from the trail.

The local watering hole, *The Fleece Inn* (☎ 01453-520003, 💻 www.thefleece innhillesley.com; Mon-Thur noon-2.45pm & 6-9pm, Fri noon-2.45pm & 6-9.30pm, Sat noon-3pm & 6-9.30pm, Sun noon-8pm)

reopened as a community pub in 2012. At lunchtime, there's a standard pub menu, while themed evening menus and a Sunday roast offer a wider choice.

Wessex's No 86 **bus** stops in the village by the Church of St Giles; for details, see the public transport map and table, pp48-50.

HAWKESBURY UPTON
MAP 33, p153

Is there no end to the attractive villages in this area? The heart of this one lies about quarter of a mile (0.4km) off the Cotswold Way, but with a pleasant B&B pretty close and a range of other facilities, it has plenty to offer the walker.

Down a quiet lane just east of the trail, *Coombe Farm* (☎ 01454-238202, 💻 karen .hasted@lineone.net; 3T, all en suite; ☞) has compact rooms in a modern annexe and offers B&B for £34pp (sgl occ £44). The room that has a bath also has its own kitchen.

Within half a mile (0.8km) of the farm, the *Beaufort Arms* (☎ 01454-238217, 💻 www.beaufortarms.com; daily noon-2.30pm & 6.30-9.30pm) is very much a village hub, with plenty of real ales and scarcely a nod to the 21st century. Hearty pub meals such as meat pies and Hawkesbury faggots come up in substantial portions, with a 'cheapskates' menu at £4.95 for smaller appetites. Note that the 'old codger's' cod and chips at £7.50 is enough for all but the most ravenous of walkers.

At the far end of the village, about half a mile (0.8km) from the trail, *The Fox Inn* (☎ 01454-238558, 💻 www.flavoursofitaly atthefoxinn.co.uk; 1T/2D/1Tr, all en suite; ☞; WI-FI; 🐾; Ⓛ) has attractive rooms from £36pp (sgl occ £46, £78 for three sharing) including breakfast (served 8-9.30am). As the name suggests, its *Flavours of Italy* restaurant (Tue-Sat noon-2pm & 6-9pm, Sun noon-9pm) specialises in Italian cuisine, from *antipasti* to *gelato*, with pizzas, pasta and much more in between.

Also up this way is the excellent village **shop** (Mon-Sat 8am-6pm, Sun 8am-12.30pm), with all the basics, filled rolls made to order, and a good range of pastries. The **post office** is located a short way beyond the pub.

For **campers**, *Oakfield Farm Camping* (see p154) can be accessed along footpaths to the west of Beaufort Arms; ring them for directions.

Wessex's No 86 **bus** stops in the village. See the public transport map and table, pp48-50, for details.

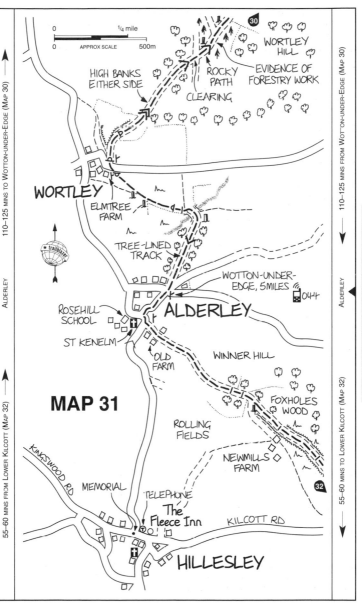

1/4 mile

0 APPROX SCALE 500m

HIGH BANKS EITHER SIDE

ROCKY PATH

EVIDENCE OF FORESTRY WORK

WORTLEY HILL

CLEARING

WORTLEY

ELMTREE FARM

TREE-LINED TRACK

WOTTON-UNDER-EDGE, 5 MILES

044

ALDERLEY

ROSEHILL SCHOOL

ST KENELM

OLD FARM

WINNER HILL

MAP 31

FOXHOLES WOOD

ROLLING FIELDS

NEWMILLS FARM

32

KINGSWOOD RD

MEMORIAL

TELEPHONE

The Fleece Inn

KILCOTT RD

HILLESLEY

110–125 MINS TO WOTTON-UNDER-EDGE (MAP 30)

ALDERLEY

55–60 MINS FROM LOWER KILCOTT (MAP 32)

110–125 MINS FROM WOTTON-UNDER-EDGE (MAP 30)

ALDERLEY

55–60 MINS TO LOWER KILCOTT (MAP 32)

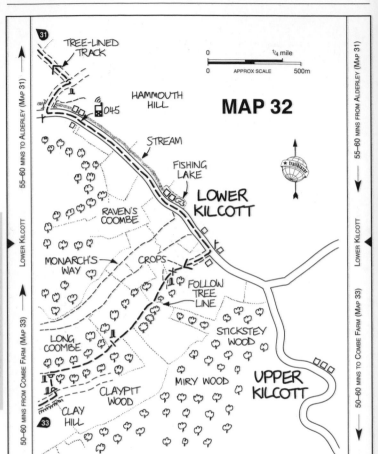

MAP 32

HORTON   MAP 34, p155

While the village of Horton is on the Cotswold Way, most walkers will bypass its main attraction, the National Trust property of **Horton Court** (☎ 01454-814213, 💻 www.nationaltrust.org.uk), which lies at the bottom of a steep footpath off the Cotswold Way (or you could walk back along the road from the village school). However, note that the property will be closed for building repairs during 2016 and is not expected to re-open until autumn 2017.

It's a rather grand name for the seemingly modest but picturesque property that sits in a cottage-style garden close to the church of **St James the Elder**. At its heart is a 12th-century Norman hall, all that remains of what may be the oldest rectory in England. Other parts of the building date to Tudor times, with significant expansion and the addition of an Italianate loggia during the 16th century, and further changes in the 1920s.

MAP 33

32

CROPS

MONUMENT IN
MEMORY OF
GENERAL LORD
ROBERT SOMERSET

046

DROVERS'
POOL

GOOD
SKYLARK
COUNTRY

POOL
FARM

STARVEALL LA

HOME
FARM

Coombe Farm

POST
OFFICE

BUS STOPS

HAWKESBURY
KNOLL

HORTON
2 MILES

BUS STOP

HAWKESBURY

HIGH ST
BUS STOP

SHOP

St MARY THE
VIRGIN WITH
ITS CUBED YEWS

Beaufort
Arms

The Fox Inn &
Flavours of Italy

CHURCH HILL

HAWKESBURY
UPTON

TO OAKFIELD
FARM (CAMPING)

CRICKET PITCH (PATH RUNS
TO RIGHT OF SCOREBOARD)

BROAD HILL

DROVERS' ROAD -
EASY WALKING
ON OPEN FARM TRACK.
GOOD VIEWS EAST & WEST

BIRCH
HILL

HIGHFIELD
FARM

BRICK
SHED

0   ¼ mile

0   APPROX SCALE   500m

34

50–60 MINS TO Lower Kilcott (MAP 32)

COMBE FARM

75–85 MINS FROM HORTON (MAP 34)

50–60 MINS FROM Lower Kilcott (MAP 32)

COMBE FARM

75–85 MINS TO HORTON (MAP 34)

ROUTE GUIDE AND MAPS

Campers are in luck with a friendly site relatively close by at *Oakfield Farm Camping* (☎ 01454-311283, www.oakfield farmcamping.co.uk; May-Oct). About 1¼ miles (2km) from the trail by road, it can also be reached along a footpath from the church, but ring them for directions. For £8pp, you'll have a level site with basic toilet and hot and cold water, or enjoy their camper's breakfast (tea and a bacon roll) for £11pp all in. Do note that the nearest shop is at Hawkesbury Upton. However, Wessex's No 86 **bus** stops here; see the public transport map and table, pp48-50, for details.

LITTLE SODBURY   MAP 34

This pretty village is set apart by the hill-top church of St Adeline, offering a perfect vantage point from which to survey the landscape unrolling ahead.

For **B&B**, try *New Crosshands Farm* (☎ 01454-316366, ☐ www.newcrosshands farm.co.uk; 1T/1D/1D or T private facili-ties/1D en suite; ➳; ⌖; Ⓛ), whose versa-tile accommodation includes a self-con-tained apartment, with a double and a twin room sharing a bathroom and kitchen, that can be booked on a B&B basis during the summer (minimum two-night stay). You'll pay £37pp (sgl occ £45) for B&B but £30pp if self-catering in the apartment. In the evening they'll drive walkers to the Cross Hands (see below) for dinner; they can then walk back or get a taxi. Dogs may stay in the apartment or the stables but not in the rooms in the house.

OLD SODBURY   MAP 35, p156

The trail passes through the grounds of the beautiful **St John the Baptist Church**, up on the hill, before dropping down to the vil-lage itself. In the shadow of its larger neigh-bour to the west, Chipping Sodbury, the vil-lage nevertheless has a lot to recommend it to the walker. Badminton Horse Trials (see box p15) is likely to make accommodation hard to find in early May.

Wessex's No 86 **bus** service stops out-side The Dog Inn. There are also three buses that stop at the Cross Hands Hotel on the A46: Wessex's No 620, Coachstyle's No 41 and Severnside's No 622. See the public transport map and table, pp48-50, for details.

For **taxis**, try Grab-a-Cab (☎ 01454-313883, ☐ www.grab-a-cab-online.co.uk) in Chipping Sodbury.

In the centre of the village, and right on the trail, the popular *Dog Inn* (☎ 01454-312006, ☐ www.the-dog-inn.co.uk; 3D or T/2Tr, all en suite; ➳; WI-FI; ⌖; Ⓛ) offers a welcome respite. **B&B** costs £40pp (sgl occ £57.50, three sharing £100). In the bar, real ales, including Sharp's Doom Bar, and an extensive menu (served Mon-Sat noon-2.30pm & 6-9pm, Sun noon-7pm) are the order of the day. Vegetarians won't go hun-gry – and with a good choice of curries as well as steaks, plenty of fresh fish, pasta and jacket potatoes, nor will anyone else. For £30, a hungry twosome could even tuck into a paella.

Some 300 yards (270m) from the trail is the more upmarket *Sodbury House* (☎ 01454-312847, ☐ www.sodburyhouse.co .uk; 3S/2D/2D or T, all en suite; ➳; WI-FI; Ⓛ), which offers B&B for £46pp (sgl £62, sgl occ £66). In the evening, most guests gravitate towards The Dog Inn for dinner or – in the other direction – The Bell.

Rather over half a mile (1km) in the other direction, on the main A46, the 14th-century *Cross Hands Hotel* (☎ 01454-313000, ☐ www.oldenglishinns.co.uk/old-sodbury; 6S/2T/13D, all en suite; ➳; WI-FI; ⌖) is just by the bus stop. Rates for B&B vary daily and are usually best for online bookings but expect to pay £37-44.50pp (sgl £40-70, sgl occ rates on request). They also have a **restaurant** (daily 11am-10pm).

Cotswold Service Station (Mon-Fri 6.30am-8pm, Sat 8am-6pm), on the other side of the crossroads, is handy for stocking up on drinks and snacks for your walk.

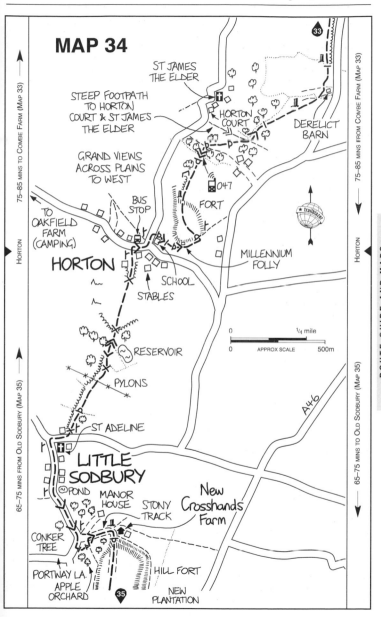

MAP 34

ST JAMES THE ELDER

STEEP FOOTPATH TO HORTON COURT & ST JAMES THE ELDER

HORTON COURT

DERELICT BARN

GRAND VIEWS ACROSS PLAINS TO WEST

047

FORT

TO OAKFIELD FARM (CAMPING)

BUS STOP

HORTON

MILLENNIUM FOLLY

SCHOOL

STABLES

RESERVOIR

0   1/4 mile
APPROX SCALE   500m
0   500m

PYLONS

A46

ST ADELINE

LITTLE SODBURY

POND

MANOR HOUSE

STONY TRACK

New Crosshands Farm

CONKER TREE

PORTWAY LA.
APPLE ORCHARD

HILL FORT

NEW PLANTATION

35

75-85 MINS TO COMBE FARM (MAP 33)

75-85 MINS FROM COMBE FARM (MAP 33)

HORTON

HORTON

65-75 MINS FROM OLD SODBURY (MAP 35)

65-75 MINS TO OLD SODBURY (MAP 35)

33

trailblazer

ROUTE GUIDE AND MAPS

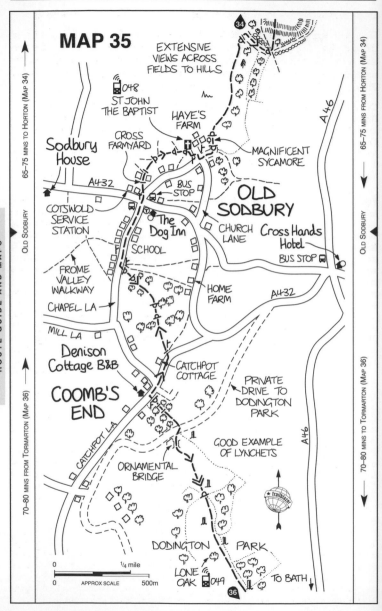

MAP 35

EXTENSIVE VIEWS ACROSS FIELDS TO HILLS

☎ 048 ST JOHN THE BAPTIST

HAYE'S FARM

MAGNIFICENT SYCAMORE

Sodbury House

CROSS FARMYARD

A432

BUS STOP

OLD SODBURY

COTSWOLD SERVICE STATION

The Dog Inn

SCHOOL

CHURCH LANE

Cross Hands Hotel

BUS STOP 🚌

FROME VALLEY WALKWAY

HOME FARM

A432

CHAPEL LA

MILL LA

Denison Cottage B&B

CATCHPOT COTTAGE

PRIVATE DRIVE TO DODINGTON PARK

COOMB'S END

GOOD EXAMPLE OF LYNCHETS

CATCHPOT LA

ORNAMENTAL BRIDGE

★ trailblazer

DODINGTON PARK

LONE OAK ☎ 049

TO BATH

0 ¼ mile
0 APPROX SCALE 500m

← 65–75 MINS TO HORTON (MAP 34)

65–75 MINS FROM HORTON (MAP 34) →

OLD SODBURY

OLD SODBURY

← 70–80 MINS FROM TORMARTON (MAP 36)

70–80 MINS TO TORMARTON (MAP 36) →

OLD SODBURY TO COLD ASHTON   MAPS 35-39

Despite being split in half by the M4, this **8½-mile (13.7km, 4¼-4¾hrs)** part of the walk has much to recommend it. In place of many (but not all!) of the ups and downs further north are broad expanses of farmland, an unexpectedly rewarding walk across **Dodington Park**, and the glimpsed glory of **Dyrham Park** (see p161), which most certainly merits a visit.

COOMB'S END   MAP 35

B&Bs don't come much more conveniently located than the white-washed *Denison Cottage* (☎ 01454-311510, 🖳 susanhol brook2012@btinternet.com; 1T; WI-FI; 🐾; (Ⓛ), which is right on the path. Formerly home to the butler at Dodington Park, it's an attractive place with a two-acre walled garden. A Scandinavian cabin in the garden provides accommodation for guests, who have access to a private shower room in the house. B&B costs £35pp (sgl occ £45).

TORMARTON   MAP 36, p158

In spite of its proximity to the busy M4, the village of Tormarton remains relatively unscathed by noise, or even by the 21st century, so it's an unexpectedly good place to stop for the night. With a welcoming hotel, a pub with rooms, a choice of B&Bs and even a place to camp, there's plenty of choice, too. The village is served by the No 41 **bus**, run by Coachstyle; see pp48-50.

Rather unexpectedly, **campers** can pitch a tent at *The Compass Inn* (☎ 01454-218242, 🖳 www.compass-inn.co.uk) in return for a donation to their charity box. There are no outdoor facilities, but when the hotel is open you can use their toilets. The hotel itself is something of a rabbit warren, independently owned but marketed under the Best Western umbrella, and with extensive gardens. It's about 500m from the village, quite close to the motorway and within in sight of the A46, so noise is a factor, but it's not too bad. **Rooms** (7T/13D/ 4Tr/2Qd, all en suite; 🖢; WI-FI; (Ⓛ) have all the accoutrements of a business hotel, costing £39.75-44.75pp (sgl occ full room rate; three/four adults sharing: full room rate plus £20) plus **breakfast** at £3.95-12.50. Service is formal but friendly and the **food** (Mon-Sat 7am-9.15pm, Sun 8am-9.15pm), served in the bar, restaurant or garden, is a pleasant surprise; good sandwiches at lunchtime, from £5.95, come with a proper salad.

With the Cotswold Way at the bottom of the garden, *Noades House* (☎ 01454-218278, 🖳 www.noadesstudio.co.uk/bandb; 1T/1D both en suite, 1T private bathroom; 🖢; WI-FI; (Ⓛ), on the quiet Old Hundred Lane, is exceptionally well placed. Rates are £37.50-40pp, or £50-60 for single occupancy. Right next door, *Old Hundred Coach House* (☎ 01454-218420, 🖳 dce daveb@yahoo.co.uk; 1T, private bathroom; 🖢; WI-FI; 🐾; (Ⓛ) charges £25pp (sgl occ £30) for B&B.

At a stone's throw from the pub is *Little Smithy* (☎ 01454-218412, 🖳 www.little smithy.com; 1T/1D, both en suite; 🖢; (Ⓛ), where you'll pay £40pp, or from £60 for single occupancy. Breakfast is eaten in the main house, but the rooms, both self-contained, are in an adjoining cottage, where there's also a lounge that guests can share.

In the village centre, *The Major's Retreat* (☎ 01454-218263, 🖳 www.major sretreat.co.uk; 3T, all en suite; WI-FI; 🐾; (Ⓛ) offers B&B in rooms above the pub; contact them for their rates. No-nonsense **pub grub** (daily noon-2.30pm & 7-9.30pm) is excellent value, from £3.95 for a doorstep sandwich. Real ales may include Wickwar, Mole Best from Mole's Brewery, and Castle Coombe.

Up the road and over the crossroads, the rooms at *Chestnut Farm* (☎ 01454-218563, 🖳 www.cfbb.co.uk; 1T/4D/cottage sleeping up to four; all en suite; 🐾; (Ⓛ) are grouped together in a converted barn, or in a separate cottage. You'll pay £30pp (£40 sgl occ; four in the cottage £100), with breakfast taken in the main house.

ROUTE GUIDE AND MAPS

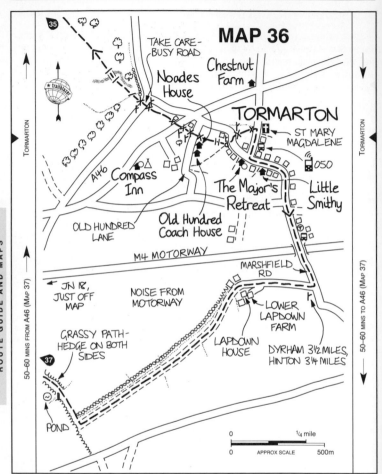

SOUTH OF THE M4   MAP 37

South of Tormarton, on the main A46 about 500 yards (500m) from the trail, **B&B** is available at *The Crown* (☎ 01225-891166, 🖥 www.thecrowntolldown.co.uk; 3D/6D or T, all en suite; 🛏; WI-FI; 🐾; Ⓛ), where rooms are in a separate building behind the pub. The average rate for B&B is 42.50pp, but they do vary – especially during Badminton Horse Trials. Their menu (Mon-Sat noon-3pm & 6-9pm, Sun noon-8pm)

features salads, boards and small plates along with a range of satisfying dishes with a contemporary twist (£10.95-12.95). They also serve sandwiches on Saturday afternoons. On the opposite corner, at Marshfield **Bakery** (Mon-Fri 8am-5pm, Sat 10am-4pm), biscuits and cakes are sold alongside sandwiches and pasties to present the perfect packed lunch.

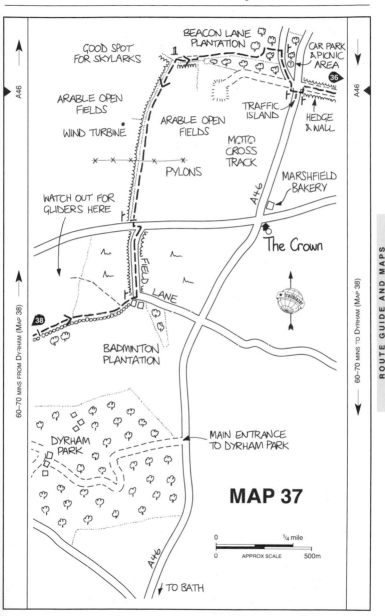

GOOD SPOT
FOR SKYLARKS

BEACON LANE
PLANTATION

CAR PARK
& PICNIC
AREA

ARABLE OPEN
FIELDS

WIND TURBINE

ARABLE OPEN
FIELDS

TRAFFIC
ISLAND

HEDGE
& WALL

MOTO
CROSS
TRACK

× — × — × — ×
PYLONS

A46

MARSHFIELD
BAKERY

WATCH OUT FOR
GLIDERS HERE

The Crown

FIELD LANE

★ trailblazer

BADMINTON
PLANTATION

DYRHAM
PARK

MAIN ENTRANCE
TO DYRHAM PARK

MAP 37

A46

TO BATH

0   ¼ mile

0   APPROX SCALE   500m

60–70 MINS FROM DYRHAM (MAP 38)

60–70 MINS TO DYRHAM (MAP 38)

ROUTE GUIDE AND MAPS

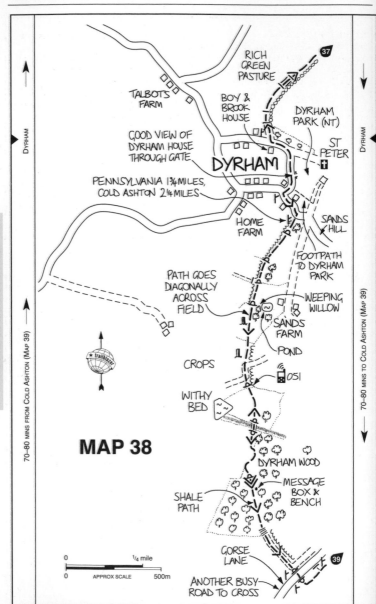

70–80 MINS FROM COLD ASHTON (MAP 39)

70–80 MINS TO COLD ASHTON (MAP 39)

DYRHAM

DYRHAM

RICH GREEN PASTURE

37

TALBOTS FARM

BOY & BROOK HOUSE

DYRHAM PARK (NT)

GOOD VIEW OF DYRHAM HOUSE THROUGH GATE

ST PETER

DYRHAM

PENNSYLVANIA 1¾ MILES, COLD ASHTON 2¼ MILES

SANDS HILL

HOME FARM

FOOTPATH TO DYRHAM PARK

PATH GOES DIAGONALLY ACROSS FIELD

WEEPING WILLOW

SANDS FARM

POND

CROPS

051

WITHY BED

DYRHAM WOOD

MESSAGE BOX & BENCH

SHALE PATH

MAP 38

0   ¼ mile
0   APPROX SCALE   500m

GORSE LANE

39

ANOTHER BUSY ROAD TO CROSS

trailblazer

❑ **Dyrham Park**   **Map 37, p159 & Map 38**

As the Cotswold Way wends through the tiny village of Dyrham, it passes the ornamental gates of Dyrham Park (☎ 0117-937 2501, 🖳 www.nationaltrust.org.uk; park
daily 10am-5pm or dusk; garden mid Feb-Dec daily 10am-5pm, Jan-early Feb 10am-
4pm; house Mar-Oct daily 10am-5pm; admission house, garden & park £12.50, garden & park only £5.20, NT members free), affording a splendid vista up the long
drive to the house and church. Or at least, that's the normal view; at the time of
research, the building was undergoing substantial repairs to the roof, opening a great
opportunity for visitors to explore the rooftop on a guided tour. If you're not pushed
for time it's well worth getting sidetracked.

Familiar to many film buffs as the set location for *Remains of the Day*, the
Baroque-style house nestling at the bottom of a steep valley was built at the end of
the 17th century. A strong Dutch influence pervades the original décor and furnish-
ings, and the Victorian kitchens give an indication of how life must have been for
those below stairs. The church alongside, however, is medieval and the estate itself
dates back to Saxon times. Visitors can explore both the house and the formal gardens
as well as 274 acres (110 hectares) of rolling parkland.

MAP 39

PENNSYLVANIA   **MAP 39, p161**

Just off the main A46 at Pennsylvania, yet still relatively peaceful, *Cornflake Cottage* (☎ 01225-892592, 💻 www.cornflakecottagebandb.co.uk; 1D/1T; ☞; WI-FI; Ⓛ) is new on the scene. Its two rooms share a bathroom, but these are not normally rented out separately unless to family or friends travelling together. The cost for B&B is £40pp, or £50-60 for single occupancy.

On the main road itself there's a **fuel station** (daily 6am-10pm) with a branch of Londis that sells drinks, sandwiches and other snacks.

COLD ASHTON
        MAP 39, p161 & Map 40, p164

With its location between the busy A420 and the even busier A46, Cold Ashton might seem to be blighted, but the reality is entirely different. Most of the village lies along a quiet lane to the south, beyond the church, and its cluster of small stone houses stands peacefully against a backdrop of rolling fields.

When the village pub closed, the neighbouring *Folly End Farm* (☎ 01225-891849, café ☎ 01225-891681, 💻 wineto you@live.co.uk; Mon-Fri 8.30am-3pm, Sat & Sun 9am-3pm) came to the rescue, offering breakfast, lunch, tea and home-made cakes every day. They also provides homely evening meals by prior arrangement for those staying at local B&Bs. The café is licensed and, as an added bonus, they will drive walkers back to their accommodation after dinner. **Campers** don't miss out, either; you can pitch a tent here for free with access to hot and cold water and an outside toilet.

In a peaceful setting opposite the church, and backing onto farmland, the stone-built *Laburnum Cottage* (☎ 01225-891669, 💻 www.laburnumcottage.info; 1T/1D, both en suite; WI-FI; Ⓛ) is well placed for **B&B**, yet only a short walk to the main road for an evening meal. Rooms here are £40pp (sgl occ £50).

Sheltered at the bottom of the steep Greenway Lane, *Hill Farm* (Map 40; ☎ 01225-891952, 💻 www.hillfarmbath.com; WI-FI; Ⓛ; £40pp, sgl occ £55) is a real find, where Lucy Coade's attention to detail is exceptional. Up to four guests stay either in the **Shepherd's Hut** (1D or T), a self-contained traditional wagon on wheels with en suite facilities and a kitchen area, or – rather more conventional – in the **Trough** (1D or T), a converted barn with en suite facilities and a private kitchen/dining area. Either way, everything is set up for near-effortless self-catering with the makings for breakfast and – with advance notice – dinner (£15pp including a glass of wine or

---

❏ **Battle of Lansdown**   **Map 40, p164 & Map 41, p165**

If it were not for the signboards and the monument to Sir Bevil Grenville, the walker on the Cotswold Way might cross the field at the top of Freezing Hill without a second glance. Yet little has changed since the night of 5 July 1643 when the final stages of the Battle of Lansdown were played out between two almost equally matched armies of the Royalists and the Parliamentarians.

In command of the opposing forces were two friends of long standing: Sir William Waller in charge of the Parliamentarian defence of Bath against Sir Ralph Hopton leading a Royalist attack. It was a bloody affair, with 'legs and arms flying all over the place', during which the Royalist Grenville was mortally wounded, having led the Cornish infantry in the charge up Lansdown Hill. While the battle itself was indecisive, casualties were severe. The Parliamentarians withdrew under cover of darkness, and the Royalists were thwarted in their pursuit of capturing Bath and moving on to the richer prize of Bristol.

beer). Best of all is the stunning view from the terrace, where guests are free to enjoy a drink or dinner.

About half a mile (1km) south of the trail to the right of the busy A46, *Whiteways* (off Map 39; ☎ 01225-891333, 🖳 white waysbedandbreakfast.co.uk; 2D/2Qd, all en suite; ☞; WI-FI in house only; 🐾 in annexe room only; Ⓛ) is surprisingly well insulated from the traffic that thunders past. You'll find two very big and well-equipped rooms sleeping up to four people in a purpose-built annexe and two in the main house. B&B costs £30-35pp (sgl occ £60, three/four sharing room rate plus £15pp). Guests can benefit from the evening meal option at Folly End Farm (see opposite).

COLD ASHTON TO BATH   MAPS 39-43

After Cold Ashton comes the final **10-mile (16km, 5-5¾hrs)** stretch towards Bath. Leaving behind the busy A46, the Cotswold Way returns to rolling hills dotted with cattle and sheep, the noise of traffic replaced with birdsong. It's a gradual climb to the top of Lansdown Hill, where the trail crosses the very field where the **Battle of Lansdown** (see box opposite) took place in 1643. The area is clearly demarcated with orange 'flags' and informative signboards, as well as a memorial; it doesn't take much to conjure up the chaos that must have ensued that summer evening. As you pass Bath racecourse, do make time to stop at **Prospect Stile** (now a kissing gate!), which at 230m (755ft) affords superb views across Bath (albeit marred by the gasworks) and over the Severn estuary. The last couple of miles of the trail beyond **Weston** see some unexpected ups and downs as the route twists to make the most of open terrain, before the final descent past Lansdown Crescent to the grandeur of Bath Abbey.

If you'd rather stay on the downward slope, you could cut across the golf course to Lansdown Road and follow this straight into Bath, taking in **Beckford's Tower** (see box below) as you go and ending up with Lansdown Crescent on your right.

❏ Beckford's Tower   **off Map 41, p165**
Although the Cotswold Way passes a couple of miles to the west of Beckford's Tower (☎ 01225-460705, 🖳 beckfordstower.org.uk; early Mar-Oct Sat, Sun & bank hol Mon 10.30am-5pm; £4.50), you can't miss its distinctive outline and no trip to Bath would be complete without a brief nod towards William Beckford (1760-1844). Beckford's grandfather was a 17th-century plantation owner and his father three times Lord Mayor of London; Beckford himself inherited a cool £2 million, no mean fortune in the 18th century. Having built Fonthill Abbey near Salisbury, he retired to Lansdown Crescent in Bath, where he set about building the tower as a personal retreat. The land around it was consecrated as a cemetery in 1848 and is where Beckford was laid to rest.

The tower is now owned by Bath Preservation Trust, but part of it is leased to the Landmark Trust (see p62) so it's possible to stay here for a few days. For walkers it's more important to know that, when it's open, the views from the top are worth the climb. There's also an interesting museum focusing on Beckford's colourful life. If you fancy the detour – it's nearly two miles (3km) from the Cotswold Way – you could walk from the golf course to the main road, then downhill along the pavement to the tower.

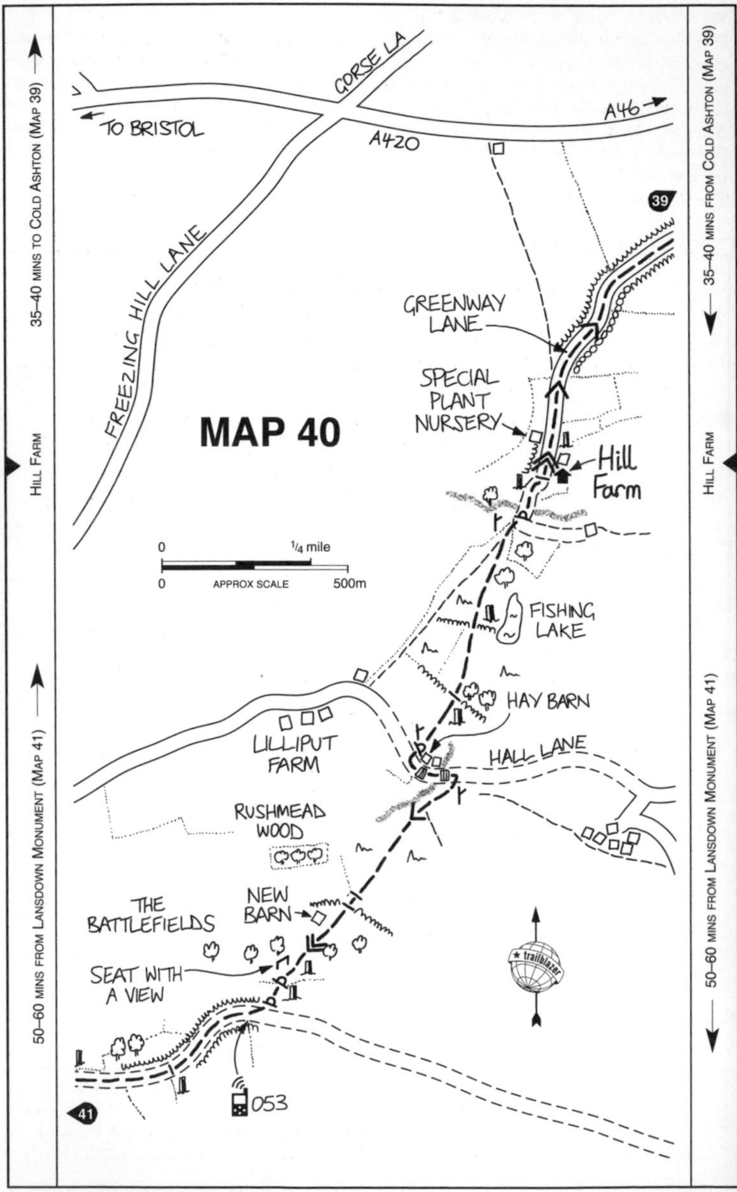

35–40 MINS TO COLD ASHTON (MAP 39)

35–40 MINS FROM COLD ASHTON (MAP 39)

50–60 MINS FROM LANSDOWN MONUMENT (MAP 41)

50–60 MINS FROM LANSDOWN MONUMENT (MAP 41)

ROUTE GUIDE AND MAPS

HILL FARM

HILL FARM

CORSE LA

TO BRISTOL

A420

A46

39

GREENWAY LANE

SPECIAL PLANT NURSERY

Hill Farm

FREEZING HILL LANE

MAP 40

0   ¼ mile
0   APPROX SCALE   500m

FISHING LAKE

HAY BARN

LILLIPUT FARM

HALL LANE

RUSHMEAD WOOD

THE BATTLEFIELDS

NEW BARN

SEAT WITH A VIEW

trailblazer

053

41

WESTON   MAP 43, p167

Heading south, the walk down to Weston culminates in a return to a more urban world, but there are bonuses in practical terms. Well-placed for walkers is *Little Nanny's Kitchen* (☎ 01225-465922; daily 9am-4pm), which serves breakfast, including pancakes, as well as soups, burgers etc. There's a branch of Boots **pharmacy** just

across the road; a little further in the other direction is a small **supermarket**, Tesco Express (Mon-Sat 7am-11pm, Sun 11am-5pm).

First's No 1 **bus** operates between here and the centre of Bath, so if you can't face the steep climbs there is an alternative. See the public transport table, pp48-50.

ROUTE GUIDE AND MAPS

❑ **Important note – walking times**
All times in this book refer only to the time spent walking. You will need to add 20-30% to allow for rests, photography, checking the map, drinking water etc.

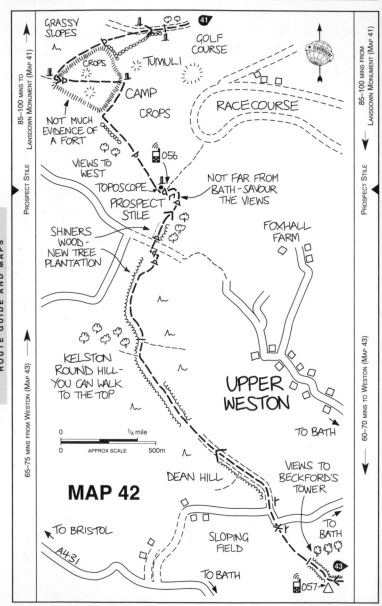

GRASSY SLOPES

CROPS

TUMULI

GOLF COURSE

41

★ trailblazer

CAMP CROPS

RACECOURSE

NOT MUCH EVIDENCE OF A FORT

056

VIEWS TO WEST

TOPOSCOPE

PROSPECT STILE

NOT FAR FROM BATH – SAVOUR THE VIEWS

FOXHALL FARM

SHINERS WOOD – NEW TREE PLANTATION

KELSTON ROUND HILL – YOU CAN WALK TO THE TOP

UPPER WESTON

TO BATH

0   ¼ mile

0   APPROX SCALE   500m

VIEWS TO BECKFORD'S TOWER

MAP 42

DEAN HILL

TO BATH

TO BRISTOL

A431

SLOPING FIELD

TO BATH

057

43

85–100 MINS TO LANSDOWN MONUMENT (MAP 41)

PROSPECT STILE

65–75 MINS FROM WESTON (MAP 43)

85–100 MINS FROM LANSDOWN MONUMENT (MAP 41)

PROSPECT STILE

60–70 MINS TO WESTON (MAP 43)

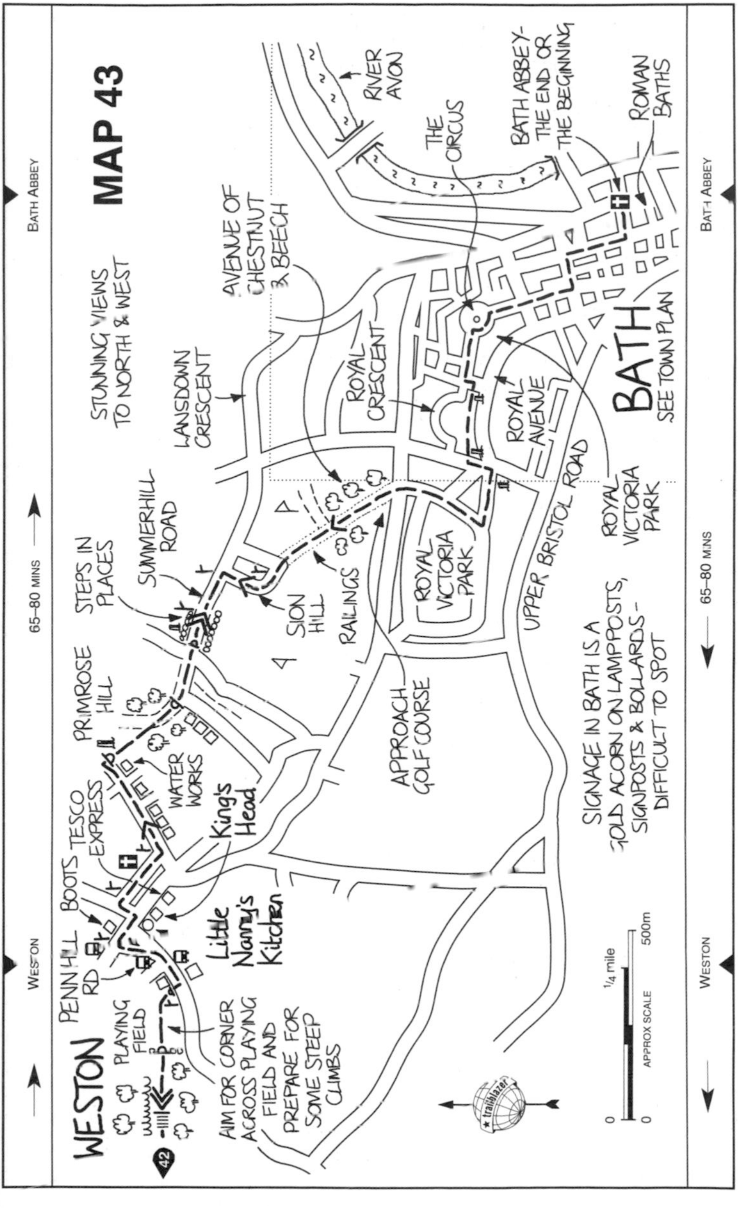

MAP 43

BATH ABBEY

WESTON

65-80 MINS →

RIVER AVON

STUNNING VIEWS TO NORTH & WEST

AVENUE OF CHESTNUT & BEECH

THE CIRCUS

BATH ABBEY- THE END OR THE BEGINNING

ROMAN BATHS

LANSDOWN CRESCENT

ROYAL CRESCENT

BATH
SEE TOWN PLAN

ROYAL AVENUE

SUMMERHILL ROAD

STEPS IN PLACES

SION HILL

RAILINGS

ROYAL VICTORIA PARK

UPPER BRISTOL ROAD

ROYAL VICTORIA PARK

PRIMROSE HILL

WATER WORKS

King's Head

APPROACH GOLF COURSE

SIGNAGE IN BATH IS A GOLD ACORN ON LAMPPOSTS, SIGNPOSTS & BOLLARDS - DIFFICULT TO SPOT

WESTON

PENN HILL RD

BOOTS TESCO EXPRESS

PLAYING FIELD

Little Nanny's Kitchen

AIM FOR CORNER ACROSS PLAYING FIELD AND PREPARE FOR SOME STEEP CLIMBS

42

¼ mile
APPROX SCALE
500m

trailblazer

65-80 MINS →

WESTON

BATH ABBEY

BATH ABBEY

WESTON

BATH   **MAP 43a, pp110-1**

'Oh, who can ever be tired of Bath?'

Catherine Morland in **Jane Austen**'s *Northanger Abbey,* published in 1817

Not so long ago, as the train drew into the station at Bath, the announcer would intone in measured voice, 'Bath Spa'. It's that word 'spa' that has brought fortune to this western town, attracting 18th-century royalty to take the waters and serving as the catalyst for the construction of what we know today as Georgian Bath.

The city predates Roman times, when it was known as Aquae Sulis, but it is the Georgian buildings that are today revered, and which have been protected as a World Heritage Site since 1987. Although George III (1738-1820) moved his allegiance to Cheltenham, sparking another building frenzy, Bath has never really fallen out of favour.

Today's visitors come not just to bathe in the waters at the smart new Thermae Spa, but to explore the city's history at the Roman Baths, and to marvel at the soaring roof of Bath Abbey. They come, too, to investigate its museums, and – rather more prosaically – to try out any number of restaurants, hotels and bars that are around every corner. All that against a background of architecture that cannot fail to attract even the least-interested observer.

For the walker, the focal point of the city is the culmination of the trail, Bath Abbey, where you'll be greeted by an engraved limestone circle, sibling to the one in Chipping Campden (see p75). Those unfamiliar with the city will need to keep a sharp eye out for the Cotswold Way signs, which have been reduced to discreet roundels featuring the National Trail acorn in a stylish metallic paint on black. Look out for these on lamp posts and bollards; nothing so rustic as a wooden fingerpost here!

See box pp14-16 for details of festivals in Bath.

Arrival and departure

Whether Bath is the grand finale of your walk, or a historic starting point, there is no shortage of ways to get to and from the city.

For more details, see the map and information on public transport, pp48-50.

● **By train** Bath Spa railway station is at the end of Manvers St, near the river, just a few minutes' walk south of the abbey (and thus the end – or beginning – of the trail). First Great Western trains call here en route between London Paddington and Bristol/Weston-super-Mare. The station is also on the route between London Waterloo and Bristol, operated by South West Trains. For details see box p46.

● **By coach** The coach/bus station is located on Dorchester St, close to both the railway station and the new SouthGate shopping centre which dominates the southern part of the city.

National Express's No 403 service calls here; for details see box p47.

● **By bus** Wessex's No 620 and First's No 1 services call at the bus station (see pp48-50).

● **By car** Bath is about half-an-hour's drive from junction 18 of the M4.

● **By air** The nearest airport with both domestic and international flights is Bristol; see box p44. The Airdecker bus (🖳 www .airdecker.com; daily 1-2/hr) operates between the airport and Bath.

If you want to abandon your rucksack or other luggage so you can explore the city, you can leave it with Bath Backpackers (see p172) for £3 a bag per day.

Local transport

The centre of Bath is sufficiently compact that most visitors are happy to wander the streets on foot. Cyclists, however, can pick up a **bike** from any of the 12 nextbike docking stations around the city, and drop it back later. For the visitor, most useful are the five stations close to the city centre: at the railway station [95]; Green Park [60]; Holburne Museum [21]; Orange Grove [68]; and Charlotte St car park [49]. You'll need to download the app or obtain an access card from 🖳 www.nextbike.co.uk/ en/bath, or to call ☎ 020-8166 9851. Rentals cost £1 per half hour, up to a maximum of £10 per 24 hours, with a £10 credit deposit required at the time of registration.

At the other end of the energy spectrum, open-top **buses** encircle the tourist areas of the city, anathema to some but a great relief from blistered feet for others.

For details of both these and horse-drawn carriages, see pp180-1.

Registered **taxis**, easily spotted by the light on the roof, can be hailed on the streets. Others, such as *Abbey Taxis* [87] (☎ 01225-444444), which is behind the abbey, and many of those run by *V-Cars* (☎ 01225-464646) must be prebooked. There's also a taxi rank in front of the railway station.

Services

● Tourist information

The Visitor Information Centre [70] (☎ 01225-322442, ☐ visitbath.co.uk; Abbey Chambers, Abbey Church Yard; Mon-Sat 9.30am-5.30pm, Sun 10am-4pm) has a prime spot next to the abbey. It's a large, modern space, with knowledgeable staff, numerous leaflets, a range of maps and guidebooks, and an accommodation-booking service. Note, though, that it can get very crowded, so allow plenty of time, particularly at weekends and in the height of the tourist season.

● Money matters

All the main high street **banks** have branches with **ATMs** across the city. The most central are on Milsom St, where there are branches of Lloyds [34] and HSBC [33], there is also a branch of Lloyds [63] on Lower Borough Walls; both Barclays [90] and HSBC [91], on Southgate, also have ATMs. **Foreign currency** is handled by these and other banks, or at the main **post office** [29] on the corner of Broad and Green streets.

● Shopping

Arguably the most central of the **supermarkets** for those seeking supplies is Waitrose [26] (Mon-Fri 7.30am-9pm, Sat 7.30am-8pm, Sun 11am-5pm), which is in the Podium on Northgate St. There's a large branch of Sainsbury's [59] (daily 7am-11pm) behind the old Green Park Station, and smaller Sainsbury's Locals (daily 7am-11pm) on Monmouth St [45] and opposite the bus station [94]. More interesting by far are some of the smaller, **independent shops**, where you can taste the cheese to go in your lunch before buying. Two to tempt your palate are The Fine Cheese Co [27] (☎ 01225-483407, ☐ www .finecheese.co.uk; Mon-Sat 8am-5pm), on

Walcot St opposite the Podium, and Chandos Deli [11] (☎ 01225-314418, ☐ www.chandosdeli.com; Mon-Fri 8am-5.30pm, Sat 9am-7pm, Sun 9am-5pm), on George St. Both have their own licensed cafés serving sandwiches prepared to order and lots of other goodies. There are also several food outlets in the **Guildhall Market** [67] (☐ www.bathguildhallmarket .co.uk) and an excellent **farmers' market** [58] in the old Green Park Station in front of Sainsbury's every Saturday (9am-4pm).

For **outdoor supplies**, such as walking boots, poles and clothing, there are several outlets: BCH Camping & Leisure [92] on Southgate St; Blacks [77] and Cotswold Outdoor [76] on Abbey Gate; Millets [32] on High St; and The North Face [89] in SouthGate shopping centre. All are open on a Sunday as well as during the week.

Bath is an easy place to lose a bibliophile, with an excellent independent **bookshop**, Topping & Company [15] (The Paragon, ☐ www.toppingbooks.co.uk; daily 9am-8pm), at the top of Broad St, where tea and coffee are always on the go. They have a good range of maps and guides, too, as does the large branch of Waterstone's [35] (Mon-Sat 9am-6pm, Sun 10.30am-5pm) on Milsom St.

● Health

The Royal United **Hospital** (☎ 01225-428331) is at Combe Park, about 1½ miles (2.4km) west of the city centre. **Pharmacies** include Boots [93] in the SouthGate centre and the independent Luther Wilson [2] right on the trail on Brock St near The Circus

Where to stay

While there's plenty of accommodation close to the end of the trail, by the abbey, much of it is on the expensive side. The suggestions given on p172 and pp174-6 include some more reasonable options, many of them grouped together in one or two areas to the south-east and west of the city, and all within easy reach of the trail.

Although seemingly limitless, Bath's accommodation can get booked up very early during Bath Festival (end May-June) and in the summer. (cont'd on p172)

ROUTE GUIDE AND MAPS

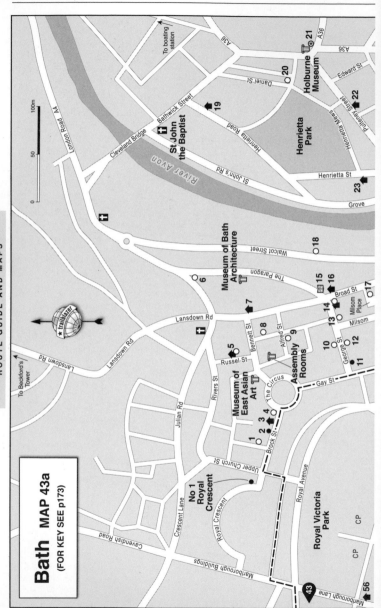

Bath MAP 43a
(FOR KEY SEE p173)

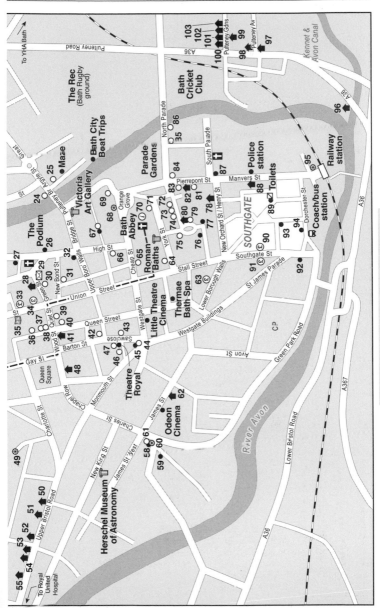

(cont'd from p169) Prices almost everywhere vary considerably, taking into account the time of year, the day of the week, the length of stay, and what is going on in the city; those given below are necessarily for guidance, primarily based on a single night midweek during the summer. At weekends, usually defined as Friday and Saturday night, and bank holidays, many places also insist on a **minimum two-night stay**, especially for advance bookings.

● **Hostels** Basic hostel accommodation that is also central comes in various guises (though campers will be out of luck). The largest option, sleeping over 200 people in two different buildings, is the **YMCA** [16] (☎ 01225-325900, 🖳 www.bathymca.co .uk/what-we-do/accommodation; WI-FI), on Broad Street Place. Dorm accommodation (one 10-, two 12-, two 15- & one 18-bed dorm) is in the original 135-year-old building; one of the 15-bed dorms is only for women and one of the 12-bed dorms is men only. The newer building has the private rooms (10S/5D/29T/6Tr/7Qd). Staying at the YMCA costs £14-23pp in a dormitory, with private rooms for £19-36pp; all rates, include a continental breakfast and at the weekend a cooked option (£3.50) is available. There's a laundry for guests' use, a left-luggage facility (small charge), and a gym (at a reduced rate for residents) – though that's unlikely to be of interest at the beginning or end of a 102-mile hike!

For something more personal, head for the privately run **Bath Backpackers** [82] (☎ 01225-446787, 🖳 www.hostels.co.uk/bath .php; 72 beds; WI-FI), at 13 Pierrepont St, where there's a self-catering kitchen, lounge with satellite TV, and internet facilities. Accommodation, in 4-, 8-, 10-, or 12-bed dormitories, costs £14-24pp.

A further option is the hostel at **St Christopher's Inn** [28] (☎ 01225-481444, 🖳 www.st-christophers.co.uk/bath-hostels; 54 dorm beds, 1D or T/2D; WI-FI), at 9 Green St. Beds in 6- to 12-bed dorms (one of them female only) are £15-20pp and their twin and doubles (one en suite) are £27.50pp (sgl occ full room rate); booking online though is recommended as the rates

are generally lower. On the down side, it's above the noisy Belushi's pub. The plus? All rates include a continental breakfast, with a cooked breakfast (£3.95) available if requested in advance.

The city's youth hostel, **YHA Bath** (reservation ☎ 01629-592700, or ☎ 0800 0191 700, hostel ☎ 01225-465674, 🖳 www .yha.org.uk/hostel/bath; 121 beds inc some 2-/3-/4-bedded en suite rooms and 4-/6-/8-/ 10-bedded dorms; WI-FI; (Ⓛ), is over a mile (1.6km) east of the centre on Bathwick Hill. If you don't mind the walk, and fancy staying in an Italianate mansion, it could be worth considering. Pricing is dynamic and fluctuates widely, but members can expect to pay in the range of £15-26pp for a dorm bed, or £39-51 for two sharing a private en suite twin room. Laundry facilities and meals are available, and the hostel is licensed.

● **Guesthouses and B&Bs**
Central Right on the Cotswold Way as you walk into Bath, near The Circus, is **Brocks** [3] (☎ 01225-338374, 🖳 www.brocks guesthouse.co.uk, 32 Brock St; 1T or D/ 2D/2Tr/1Qd, all en suite; ▼; WI-FI), where a room costs £49.50-64.50pp (sgl occ £99-115, three/four sharing room rate plus £40pp). Not far from here, at 7 Belmont, a pedestrian walkway that runs parallel to but above Lansdown Rd, you'll find **The Belmont** [7] (☎ 01225-423082, 🖳 www.bel montbath.co.uk; 1S/2T/3D, most en suite; ▼; WI-FI), a traditional B&B run by Archie Watson. The single costs from £45 with a shared bathroom, or it's £30-40pp (sgl occ £55-65) for two sharing.

At the other end of town, close to the railway station, **The Henry Guest House** [78] (☎ 01225-424052, 🖳 www.thehenry .com; 1S private shower facilities, 2T/3D/ 1Qd all en suite; ▼; WI-FI) offers contemporary rooms in a Georgian townhouse at £50-72.50pp (sgl £80-95, three sharing £170-185 plus £35 for fourth person), with a minimum two-night stay at weekends. They are happy to do a wash & dry for £12.

Similarly convenient for the railway station, albeit rather noisy, is **Anabelle's** [88] (☎ 01225-330133, 🖳 www.anabelles guesthouse.co.uk; 4D/5T; ▼; WI-FI), where

BATH – MAP KEY (see map pp170-1)

Where to stay
3 Brocks
5 The Queensberry
7 The Belmont
14 Travelodge Bath Central
16 YMCA
19 Chestnuts House
22 Edgar Townhouse
23 Kennard
28 St Christopher's Inn
41 Harington's Hotel
48 Francis
50 The Bath House
51 Dorset Villa
52 The Albany
53 Crescent Guesthouse
54 Waltons
55 Bay Tree House
56 Marlborough House
62 Premier Inn
78 The Henry Guest House
80 3 Abbey Green
82 Bath Backpackers
88 Anabelle's
96 Travelodge Bath
Waterside
97 Radnor Guesthouse
98 Memblard Guesthouse
99 White Guest House
100 Avon Guesthouse
101 Lynwood
102 Apple Tree
103 Brindley's

Where to eat and drink
1 Rustico Bistro Italiano
4 The Circus
5 The Olive Tree
6 The Star Inn
8 Casani's
9 Woods
10 Clayton's Kitchen
12 Martini
13 Loch Fyne
14 Wagamama
17 Côte Brasserie
18 Schwartz Bros
20 The Pulteney Arms
24 Rajpoot
25 Ponte Vecchio
30 The Old Green Tree
31 Volunteer Rifleman's
Arms
36 Salamander
37 Firehouse Rotisserie
38 Olé Tapas
39 The Eastern Eye
40 The Raven
42 Gascoyne Place
43 Schwartz Bros
44 Thai Balcony
46 Garrick's Head
47 Ciao Ciao
61 Green Park Brasserie
64 Pump Room
65 The Roman Baths
Kitchen
66 Pâtisserie Valerie
67 Market Café
69 Browns
71 The Real Italian Pizza Co
72 Sally Lunn's
73 Tilleys Bistro
74 Acorn Vegetarian
Kitchen
75 Crystal Palace
79 The Bath Bun
81 Yak Yeti Yak
83 Salathai
84 The Green Rocket
85 Sotto Sotto
86 OPA

Other
2 Luther Wilson (chemist)
11 Chandos Deli
15 Topping & Company
21 nextbike
26 Waitrose (in
The Podium)
27 Fine Cheese Co
29 Post Office
32 Millets
33 HSBC Bank & ATM
34 Lloyds Bank & ATM
35 Waterstone's
45 Sainsbury's Local
49 nextbike
58 Farmers' Market
59 Sainsbury's
60 nextbike
63 Lloyds Bank & ATM
67 Guildhall Market
68 nextbike
70 Visitor Info Centre
76 Cotswold Outdoor
77 Blacks
87 Abbey Taxis
89 The North Face
90 Barclays Bank & ATM
91 HSBC & ATM
92 BCH Camping & Leisure
93 Boots
94 Sainsbury's Local
95 nextbike

you'll pay £30-35pp for B&B sharing a bathroom, or £35-42.50 en suite (sgl occ £45-£55). Two of the doubles and one twin are en suite; the rest share three bathrooms.

The more central *3 Abbey Green* [80] (☎ 01225-428558, ☐ www.threeabbey green.com; 4D/4D or T/2Qd, all en suite; ☛; WI-FI) is a family-run guesthouse occupying a listed townhouse just behind the abbey. Charges vary considerably, but expect to pay £50-90pp (sgl occ £90-162, four sharing £180-220). They also have one self-contained apartment (sleeping up to three people) costing £140-160 per night. In the apartment they have a minimum two-night stay all the time but in the guesthouse only at weekends. However, if there is availability at short notice they would consider a one-night stay.

Across Pulteney Bridge on Henrietta Rd is *Chestnuts House* [19] (☎ 01225-334279, ☐ www.chestnutshouse.co.uk; 4D/1Tr, all en suite; ☛; WI-FI; 🐾) – a stone-built house with rooms for £40-67.50pp (sgl occ £75-115, £100-140 for three sharing).

East of the city Outside the immediate centre, there are two gluts of predominantly terraced B&Bs in residential areas that are within easy walking distance of the trail. The first, about 10 minutes' walk east of the abbey across the railway, and a short stroll from the Kennet and Avon Canal, runs along **Pulteney Rd and up Pulteney Gardens**. Of these, three are right on the main road, so potentially quite noisy. Colourful flowers enliven *Radnor Guesthouse* [97] (☎ 01225-316159, ☐ www.radnorguesthouse.co.uk; 9 Pulteney Terrace; 1S/2D/1T, all en suite; WI-FI), with B&B at around £35-50pp (sgl/sgl occ £65-70).

Opposite is *Membland Guesthouse* [98] (☎ 01225-839847, mob ☎ 07958-599572, ☐ www.memblandguesthouse.co.uk; 3D, all en suite; WI-FI), where rooms cost £35-47.50pp (sgl occ from £70). Then on the corner of Pulteney Gardens, *Avon Guesthouse* [100] (☎ 01225-313009, ☐ www.avonguesthousebath.co.uk; 2D/3D or T/1Qd, all en suite; ☛; WI-FI) charges £34-45pp (sgl occ £60-90), or – in the quad

which has a bath – £90-120/100-140 for three/four guests.

Pulteney Gardens itself harbours several Victorian homes offering B&B. At No 23, B&B at *White Guest House* [99] (☎ 01225-426075, ☐ www.whiteguesthouse .co.uk; 1S/1T/3D, all en suite; WI-FI) will set you back £32.50-40pp, or £45-55 for a single/single occupancy.

On the opposite side at No 6 is *Lynwood* [101] (☎ 01225-426410, ☐ www .lynwood-house.com; 2S with private facilities, 2D/1Tr, all en suite; WI-FI), with accommodation for £37.50-41.50pp (from £45 for the single/sgl occupancy, around £100 for three sharing). Note that the rate does not include breakfast but this can be delivered from a local café or they will advise you on local places to go. Right next door, at *Apple Tree* [102] (☎ 01225-337642, ☐ www.appletreeguesthouse.co .uk, No 7; 3D/1Tr, all en suite; WI-FI) you'll pay £45-80pp (sgl occ £80-150, and room rate plus £30 for three sharing).

At the end on the corner, and in another class entirely, is the self-styled 'boutique B&B' *Brindley's* [103] (☎ 01225-310444, ☐ www.brindleysbath.co.uk; 1T or D/5D, all en suite; WI-FI). With French-inspired décor, its rooms – four with king-size beds – cost £60-95pp (sgl occ £90-160).

West of the city A second clutch of guest-houses and B&Bs is at **Crescent Gardens**, an elevated section of the **Upper Bristol Rd** that's just a few minutes' walk from the trail – and the centre of Bath. Closest of these is *The Bath House* [50] (mob ☎ 07711-119847, ☎ 0117-937 4495, ☐ www .thebathhouse.org; 1T or D/4D; ☛; WI-FI), at No 40, a self-styled 'boutique B&B' where rooms with en suite king-size or four-poster beds are £39.50-64.50pp (sgl occ £72-113). They also have two self-catering **apartments**, about 100 yards away on James St. One sleeps up to three people (1T or D plus a sofa bed; £49.50-64.50pp, sgl occ £82-113; extra £20 for three sharing); the other up to five (2T or D/1S; £139-229 for four people sharing, extra £20 for additional person). In both apartments a complimentary continental breakfast is provided for the first morning. Down the road at No 31, rates at *Dorset Villa* [51] (☎ 01225-425975; 2T/2D/one room sleeping up to five people; all en suite; ☛; WI-FI) vary dramatically, from £29.50 to £47.50pp (sgl occ £35-53; rates on request for three to five people sharing). About half of their rooms have baths; the rest have showers.

Rooms at *The Albany* [52] (☎ 01225-313339, ☐ www.albanybath.co.uk, No 24; 1T/1T or D/2D/1Tr and one room sleeping up to five; WI-FI) are all en suite, except one with a private shower, and cost £35-47.50pp (rates on request for single occupancy, or three or more sharing).

At *Crescent Guesthouse* [53] (☎ 01225-425945, ☐ www.crescentbath.co.uk, No 21; 1S/1T/3D, all en suite; WI-FI) you can expect to pay £35-47.50pp and £55-85 for single occupancy.

Rates at *Waltons* [54] (☎ 01225-426528, ☐ www.waltonsguesthouse.co.uk, No 17; 2S/4D/1Tr, all en suite; WI-FI) are £40-45pp, £50-55 for a single, £120-135 for three sharing.

Last up is *Bay Tree House* [55] (☎ 01225-483699, ☐ www.baytreehousebath.co.uk, No 12; 1T/3D/1Tr, most en suite; ☛; WI-FI), with B&B for £37.50-47.50pp (sgl occ £65-85, £125 for three sharing).

Further up, a turning to the right leads into **Marlborough Lane**, where the elegant *Marlborough House* [56] (☎ 01225-318175, ☐ www.marlborough-house.net; 2D/1T or D/2Tr/1Qd; all en suite; WI-FI; ☛) is in a class of its own. For £47.50-77.50pp (sgl occ £95-135) you can have a room, perhaps with a four-poster or Louis XIV king-size bed; three/four sharing will pay £115-175/185. The toiletries in the rooms are organic as are the ingredients for breakfast.

● **Hotels** With B&Bs climbing steadily up the price ladder, it's not unreasonable to shop around for one of the cheaper hotels, especially if you're happy to find a café for breakfast. Relatively new on the scene is a *Premier Inn* [62] (☎ 0871-527 9454, ☐ www.premierinn.com; 23D/31Tr/44Qd, all en suite; ☛; WI-FI), on James St. Rates start

at around £50 for the room, regardless of occupancy, but vary considerably.

In similar mould are two branches of **Travelodge** (☐ www.travelodge.co.uk) here: the older *Bath Central* [14] (☎ 0871-984 6219; 51D/4D or T/19Tr, all en suite; ☛; WI-FI; ☛) is indeed central, above a nightclub on George St, whereas the more peaceful *Bath Waterside* [96] (☎ 0871-984 6407, Rossiter Rd; 19T/97D/4Tr, all en suite; ☛; WI-FI; ☛) is in more tranquil surroundings to the south, on the Kennet and Avon Canal. Walk-in rates start from £56 for a double room without breakfast but can be double that and can vary hugely from day to day. The best rates, however, are found online; with at least 21 days' notice, rooms can come in as low as £39. Note that dogs are charged at £20 per stay, not per night; and wi-fi costs £3 for 24 hours.

To the east of the abbey, over the river, are several small hotels. These include *Edgar Townhouse* [22] (☎ 01225-420619, ☐ www.edgar-townhouse.co.uk; 2S/3T/12D/1Qd, all en suite; WI-FI), at 64 Great Pulteney St, which offers B&B for £41-79.50pp (sgl £72-75, sgl occ £96-135, and £160-170/195 for three/four sharing).

Round the corner at the *Kennard* [23] (☎ 01225-310472, ☐ www.kennard.co.uk; 2S/1T/8D/1Tr; WI-FI), 11 Henrietta St, the single rooms share shower facilities but the others are all en suite. You'll pay £65-80pp for B&B, £65-70 for a single and £150-170 for three sharing.

Grandly located on the southern side of Queen Square, the *Francis* [48] (☎ 01225-424105, ☐ www.mgallery.com, 12S/33T/53D, all en suite; some ☛; WI-FI) is one of the city's most established hotels. Rebuilt in 1953 after being damaged in the Blitz, and restored in 2012 as part of the Accor chain's Mgallery Collection, it is traditional in style, with elegance veering towards the ornate. Prices for B&B start at £66.50pp, topping out at £125pp (sgl from £123, sgl occ rates on request).

Equally central but far more personal is *Harington's Hotel* [41] (☎ 01225-461728, ☐ www.haringtonshotel.co.uk, 8-10 Queen St; 10D/1D or T/3Tr; ☛; WI-FI), just off the square, where B&B costs

£39.50-92.50pp (sgl occ £85-165, while three sharing pay the room rate plus £35). All rooms are en suite but some have a bath rather than a shower, so do make it clear when booking if you have a preference.

At the top end of the scale, one boutique hotel stands out: *The Queensberry* [5] (☎ 01225-447928, 🖳 www.thequeensberry .co.uk; 29D, all en suite; ➡; WI-FI) on Russel St, off The Circus. Stylish and contemporary, its rooms come in at £65-230pp (sgl occ full room rate) excluding breakfast (continental/English £10/17.50).

Where to eat and drink

Eating out in Bath is easy. The problem lies in choosing where to go from the broad array of pubs, restaurants, cafés and fast-food joints whose menus demand attention at every turn. The following, then, is no more than a selection of options within easy reach of the centre. Others abound, especially around Kingsmead Square, so you'll be spoiled for choice.

● **Traditional and contemporary** As you walk into (or out of) Bath along the Cotswold Way, you'll pass *The Circus* [4] (🖳 www.thecircuscafeandrestaurant.co.uk; Mon-Sat 10am-10.30pm), aptly located near The Circus on Brock St. You can have breakfast, elevenses, lunch or tea here, or dine in style. Whatever your choice, the décor is pleasantly informal and the menus seasonal; they even make a 'power salad' at £9.70 sound appealing, though 'whim wham' for dessert could prove your undoing!

In a prime location right in front of the abbey, and hugely popular with tourists, is *The Roman Baths Kitchen* [65] (🖳 sear cys.co.uk/venues/roman-baths-kitchen; Sun-Thur 8.30am-8pm, Fri-Sat 8.30am-9pm). Separate daytime and dinner menus have a fairly broad range of dishes, from small and large and sharing plates to grills and salads.

Long a local favourite is *Green Park Brasserie* [61] (☎ 01225-338565, 🖳 www .greenparkbrasserie.com, Charles St; daily noon-2.45pm, Tue-Thur 6-8.45pm, Fri & Sat 6-9.45pm), where there's the added buzz of live jazz in the evening from Wednesday to Saturday. Rather grandly located in the old booking hall of the restored Green Park Station, it spills over on to the old station concourse. Come at lunch for satisfying doorstop sandwiches (£4-7) and sharing boards, enjoy a set menu (lunch & 5.30-7pm, two courses £13), or indulge à la carte on dishes such as salmon and king prawn skewers marinated in rum, chilli & brown sugar with saffron yoghurt, tarragon & shaved fennel salad (£15). However, be aware that they are sometimes closed for a private function so it is best to call in advance to check.

Following a stylish makeover, *Clayton's Kitchen* [10] (🖳 theporter.co.uk/ claytons-kitchen; Mon-Sat 8am-3pm, Mon-Thur 6-10pm, Fri-Sat 6-10.30pm, Sun 9am-4pm & 6-9pm), on George St, has emerged from a former vegetarian restaurant. From sandwiches to deli boards and locally sourced mains, it has plenty of choice, though is probably not a place for a rushed lunch.

Just off Queen Square, *Firehouse Rotisserie* [37] (🖳 www.firehouserotisserie .co.uk, John St; Mon-Fri noon-2.30pm & 6-11pm, Sat-Sun noon-10pm) is a light and convivial spot that presents a range of innovative 'small plates' along with grills and pizzas from about £9.95.

Close to the nextbike rack on Orange Grove, *Browns* [69] (🖳 www.browns-res taurants.co.uk; Mon-Sat 8.30am-11pm, Sun 9am-11pm; full menu from noon) could be a good spot to abandon a bike for lunch. The atmosphere is buzzing, the menu broad and prices (mains from £10) affordable.

Racing paraphernalia adorns the walls of the established *Woods* [9] (🖳 www .woodsrestaurant.com; Tue-Sun noon-2.30pm, Tue-Sat 5.30-9.30pm), a family-run place on Alfred St, opposite the Assembly Rooms. Come for their bar menu with goodies such as provençal fish soup (£8.50); a two-course fixed-price menu at lunch or early dinner (5.30-7pm); or with plenty of time to select from dishes that might include seared Gressingham duck breast with root vegetables, fresh thyme and claret jus (£19.50).

If celebration is in order, a classy

venue could be appropriate. Round the corner from Woods, on Russel St, **The Olive Tree** [5] (🖳 olivetreebath.co.uk; Tue-Sun noon-2pm, daily 7-10pm) is the exclusive and top-quality restaurant at The Queensberry Hotel (see Where to stay), exuding calm and contemporary style. There's a two-course lunch menu at £21, but tasting menus from £55 are strictly for specials; booking is recommended.

● **Mediterranean** For classic French cuisine with a contemporary twist, try **Casani's** [8] (🖳 www.casanis.co.uk; Wed, Fri & Sat noon-1.30pm, Tue-Thur 6-9pm, Fri & Sat 6-9.30pm), at 4 Savile Row, near the Assembly Rooms. Think *parfait de chêvre* for starters, or mains such as *magret de canard* (£22). There's more than a passing nod to French café culture at *Côte Brasserie* [17] (🖳 www.cote-restaurants.co.uk; Mon-Fri 8am-11pm, Sat 9am-11pm, Sun 9am-10.30pm) in Milsom Place, too, where *moules marinières* at £6.50 jostle for space on the menu with *poulet breton* (£10.50); outside seating adds to the ambience.

At **Tilleys Bistro** [73] (🖳 www.tilleys bistro.co.uk; Tue-Sat noon-3pm & 5-9pm, or 9.30pm on Sat, Sun 5.30-9pm), on North Parade Passage, the spread is more European, with influences from Spanish and Italian through French to British. There are set menus, too, including a two-course lunch or early dinner for £15.95.

For Italian cuisine in many guises, you'll be spoiled for choice. Combine your meal with a touch of history at the stylish Italian **Ciao Ciao** [47] (🖳 www.ciaociaoris torante.co.uk; Mon-Sat noon-2.30pm & 5.30-10pm), which occupies the house where Beau Nash lived and died, next to the theatre on Barton St.

At the riverside **Ponte Vecchio** [25] (🖳 www.pontevecchiobath.com; Mon-Fri noon 3pm & 6-10pm, Sat & Sun noon-10pm), in a prime position overlooking the weir, next to The Rec, it's all about the setting. Dine inside or out in their wood and stainless-steel take on a traditional boathouse from an Italian menu with pizzas and pasta from £8.95; other mains from £13.50.

Rather less scenic is the long-standing **Martini** [12] (🖳 www.martinirestaurant.co .uk; Mon-Fri noon-2.30pm & 6-10.30pm, Sat noon-10.30pm, Sun noon-2.30pm & 6-10pm), on George St. The décor may not be up to much, but traditional food and an old-fashioned Italian welcome bring punters back for more. Italian is on the menu at 2 Margaret's Buildings, too, where **Rustico Bistro Italiano** [1] (🖳 www.rusticobistro italiano.co.uk; Tue-Sun noon-2.30pm & 6-10pm) serves hearty helpings of Italian classics. But if you're just after a pizza, beat a path to the unpretentious but popular **Real Italian Pizza Co** [71] (🖳 www.real italianpizza.co.uk; daily 11am-11pm), on York St, where busy chefs do wonders with

---

❏ **Bath specialities**

● **Bath bun** Created in the 17th century by Sally Lunn, the original Bath bun is a light bread roll, akin to a large French brioche and still served at the eponymous Sally Lunn's (see p179) in Bath. Later, though, the term 'Bath bun' became associated with a sweetened roll sprinkled with sugar and this is now the more widely known of the two.

● **Bath Oliver** The plain savoury biscuit served as an accompaniment to cheese was the creation of one Dr Oliver, who practised in Bath during the 18th century. It's widely available in supermarkets and delicatessens.

● **Bath chap** The breadcrumbed boiled cheek of a pig, these normally come in a cone shape. Find them at the Guildhall Market in Bath.

● **Bath soft cheese** An old Bath recipe is said to lie behind the creation of this cheese, which is available at the city's Saturday morning farmers' market.

● **Bath asparagus** Not so much a culinary speciality as a rare summer delicacy, Bath asparagus grows wild in the hills around the city, the locations a closely guarded secret. As you might expect, it is strictly protected.

a wood-fired pizza oven. For the latest Italian success story, though, make your way down to the grotto-like setting of *Sotto Sotto* [85] (☎ 01225-330236, 🖳 www.sotto sotto.co.uk; daily noon-2pm & 5-10pm), on North Parade. Come for the (slightly noisy) atmosphere and for dishes such as *pollo e salsiccia*: strips of chicken and Italian sausage in white wine with hot cherry peppers, garlic, rosemary and aged balsamic vinegar (£13.75), and be prepared to book.

Tapas are on hand at *Olé Tapas* [38] (☎ 01225-466440, 1 John St; Sun-Thur noon-10pm, Fri-Sat noon-11pm), a buzzing little place with offerings of fish, chorizo, aubergine and more, at £2.50-8 per dish. And then there's Greek cuisine, as defined at *OPA* [86] (🖳 www.opabath.com; Mon-Sat noon-2am), also on North Parade.

● **World cuisines** A must for the setting alone is *The Eastern Eye* [39] (☎ 01225-422323, 🖳 www.easterneye.com, 8a Quiet St; Mon-Fri noon-2.30pm & 6-11.30pm, Sat-Sun noon-11.30pm), even if you're not a huge fan of Indian cuisine – though it's good. Occupying the first floor of a 19th-century building adorned with sculptures of 'Commerce' and 'Genius', it sits beneath a magnificent three-domed ceiling.

Arguably the best Indian food in Bath, however, is to be had below stairs on Argyle St to *Rajpoot* [24] (🖳 www.rajpoot .com; daily noon-2.30pm & 6-11pm, weekends to 11.30pm).

Rather less smart is the irresistibly named *Yak Yeti Yak* [81] (🖳 www.yak yetiyak.co.uk; daily noon-2pm, Sun-Thur 6-10pm, Fri-Sat 5-10.30pm), on Pierrepont St, where Nepalese mains are around £6 for vegetarian dishes, and £8.50 for others; they also have a three-course lunch menu for £10.50.

Just a few steps up the road you can be transported to the Far East at *Salathai* [83] (🖳 www.salathai-bath.co.uk; daily noon-2.30pm & 6-10.30pm, to 10pm on Sun), where set menus cost from £16.95, or £14.95 for vegetarian.

There's also the tranquil setting of *Thai Balcony* [44] (🖳 www.thai-balcony .net, 1 Seven Dials; daily noon-2.30pm,

Sun-Thur 6-10pm, Fri-Sat 6-10.30pm), above the Sainsbury's Local on Sawclose.

For a reliable source of good, inexpensive food with plenty of noodles, you can't beat the relaxed *Wagamama* [14] (🖳 www .wagamama.com/restaurants/bath; Mon-Sat noon-11pm, Sun noon-10pm) next to the Travelodge on the corner of George and Broad streets; it's great for vegetarians, too.

● **Vegetarian and fish** Vegetarians and vegans beat a path to *Acorn Vegetarian Kitchen* [74] (🖳 www.acornvegetarian kitchen.co.uk, 2 North Parade Passage; daily noon-3pm & 5.30-9.30pm), close to the abbey, and go no further. Formerly the popular Demuths, it has gone up a notch, with a two-course early evening menu at a rather pricey £17.95. But then, with dishes such as seared braised fennel with pistachio paté, chickpeas in a smoked tomato sauce, green olives and a saffron lemon gel (£11.95) on the à la carte menu, you'll be spoiled for choice.

Simpler is *The Green Rocket Café* [84] (🖳 www.thegreenrocket.co.uk, corner North Parade & Pierrepont St; Mon-Sat 9am-4.30pm, Thur-Sat 6-9.30pm, Sun 10am-4.30pm), which also offers a take-away service. Freshly squeezed juices complement a well-chosen lunch menu, from sandwiches to noodles, mezze, and preserved lemon, tomato and chickpea stew (£4.50-9.50), with dinner mains up to £13.50 for a thali. Check out, too, the places listed under 'world cuisines' above, or try the veggie options listed by almost all mainstream restaurants.

For fish lovers, *Loch Fyne* [13] (☎ 01225-750120, 🖳 www.lochfyneseafood andgrill.co.uk/locations/bath; Mon-Fri 7.30am-10.30pm, Sat & Sun 8am-10.30pm) needs little introduction having become familiar on many a British high street in recent years. With fresh fish cooked in open kitchens it remains a popular concept and the place can get very busy.

● **Bars, pubs and pub grub** For the most part, opening hours quoted in this section relate to when food is served; almost all venues serve drinks outside these hours.

The trend towards gastro-pubs has claimed many an erstwhile local and Bath is no exception. Among these is *Gascoyne Place* [42] (💻 www.gascoyneplace.com; Mon-Fri noon-2.30pm, Sun noon-4pm, daily 5.30-10pm), opposite the Theatre Royal on the corner of Sawclose and Barton St. Trendily low key and with a varied menu, it also has live jazz every Sunday evening, and blues or folk on a Friday evening.

In a similar location, just behind the theatre, the *Garrick's Head* [46] (💻 www .garricksheadpub.com; daily noon-3pm, Sun-Tue 5.30-9pm, Wed-Sat 5.30-10pm, earlier in winter) retains the atmosphere of a pub, with a good bar menu and more. Somewhat quirkily it marks the start of the city's ghost walk (see p180) – so presumably Banquo could be among the guests.

Despite the onslaught of modernisation, plenty of pubs remain unscathed. For a quiet drink and well-prepared food, *Crystal Palace* [75] (💻 www.crystalpalace pub.co.uk; Apr-Dec Mon-Sat 11am-9.30pm, Sun noon-9pm, Jan-Mar Mon-Sat to 9pm), on Abbey Green, is absolutely central; the walled garden behind is an added bonus for lunch in the summer months – that's in a good year, of course. Rather less peaceful is *The Pulteney Arms* [20] (💻 www.thepulteneyarms.co.uk, corner Daniel St and Sutton St; Mon-Fri noon-2.30pm & 6-9pm, Sat noon-3pm & 6-9pm, Sun noon-3pm), behind Great Pulteney St. This is the 'rugby' pub, frequented by players and spectators, and heaving when Bath are playing just across the river at The Rec.

There's simple, no-nonsense fare at *The Raven* [40] (💻 www.theravenofbath.co.uk; Mon-Fri noon-3pm & 5-9pm, Sat noon-9pm, Sun 12.30-8.30pm), on Queen St, a no-frills, CAMRA award-winning pub which concentrates on pies – pork pies, steak pies, vegetarian pies, even Heidi pies (about £9.20) – all washed down with real ale.

If you're after nothing more complicated than a good pint, you'll be spoiled for choice (hours given here are pub hours, not those for food). Claiming to be the smallest pub in Bath, the *Volunteer Rifleman's Arms* [31] (☎ 01225-425210; daily 11am-11pm) is centrally located on New Bond

Street Place. They do serve food here, but for many it's all about the beer. Close by there's *The Old Green Tree* [30] (☎ 01225-448259, Green St; Mon-Sat noon-2.30pm), then you could move on to *Salamander* [36] (💻 www.bathales.com/our-pubs/pid/ the-salamander; Mon-Thur noon-3pm & 6-9.30pm, Fri & Sat noon-9.30pm, Sun noon-7.30pm), on John St, for a more Victorian atmosphere, and round off the evening at *The Star Inn* [6] (💻 www.abbeyales.co .uk/www.star-inn-bath.co.uk; Mon-Fri noon-2.30pm & 5.30-11pm, Sat noon-11pm, Sun noon-10.30pm), with its four small bars, where real ale is drawn straight from the barrel.

● **Teahouses and cafés** Walking the Cotswold Way throws up its fair share of trials, from steep hills to unpredictable rain and cold, when a cup of tea is rarely more welcome. Bath doesn't disappoint. Perhaps this is the time to dress up and treat yourself to afternoon tea at the *Pump Room* [64] (☎ 01225-444477; 💻 www.romanbaths.co.uk/ pump-room-restaurant; daily Mar-Dec 9.30am-5pm, Jan & Feb from 10am; note that they may close an hour or so earlier if there is a festival or special occasion), one of the great institutions of Bath. Built between 1795 and 1797, the Pump Room exudes the elegance of the era, with its grand chandeliers and classical music played by the Pump Room Trio. Although you can take morning coffee or lunch here, it's at teatime that it comes into its own. You don't have to have the full works of sandwiches, scones, cakes and pastries (£22.50pp) – but it's certainly tempting. Tables may be reserved during the week and for lunch (noon-2.30pm) on Sunday, but not at other times; at busy periods expect to queue for 20-40 minutes. If you just want to marvel at the building, you can combine it with a visit to the Roman Baths (see p182).

Old-fashioned tea doesn't have to be quite so posh, though. The oldest house in Bath, at 4 North Parade Passage, dates back to around 1482 and houses *Sally Lunn's* [72] (💻 www.sallylunns.co.uk; Mon-Thur 10am-9.30pm, Fri & Sat 10am-10pm, Sun

10am-9.30pm; dinner from 5.30pm). This is the home of the Bath bun (see box on p177), which was created by Ms Lunn when she lived here in the 17th century. Just round the corner (with another entrance on North Parade Passage), the name has been taken up at *The Bath Bun* [79] (🖳 www.thebathbun.com; Tue-Sat 9.30am-5pm, Sun & Mon 11am-5pm), where pretty china and colourful cup cakes are proving very popular. Try their cream tea for £6.50, or traditional high tea at £14.50. Or indulge continental style at *Pâtisserie Valerie* [66] (🖳 www.patisserie-valerie .co.uk, 20 High St; daily 9am-7pm), where cream cakes, iced cakes, chocolate cakes and sticky gateaux provide plenty of sweet treats.

● **Cheap eats and fast food** It's not difficult to find some form of fast food among the many outlets around the city, not to mention the occasional 'greasy spoon' joint where you can get a standard fry up and any number of sandwich bars.

First stop should be the indoor **Bath Guildhall Market** [67] (Mon-Sat 8am-5pm) where – among the pashminas and second-hand books – you'll find the *Market Café* [67]. A full English breakfast here will set you back between £5.45 and £6.65, depending on how hungry you are. Other stalls sell sandwiches and pies – including Bath chaps (see box p177).

One of the best proponents of the burger is *Schwartz Bros* (🖳 www.schwartzbros .co.uk, with a branch on **Walcot St** [18] (Tue & Wed 5.30-11pm, Thur 5.30pm to midnight, Fri & Sat noon-3am, Sun noon-10pm), and another on **Sawclose** [43] (Mon & Tue noon-11.30pm, Wed & Thur noon-midnight, Fri & Sat noon-3am, Sun noon-11pm.

What to see and do

For most walkers on the Cotswold Way, the first sense of the city comes from the glimpse of Lansdown Crescent as you descend Lansdown Hill. Royal Crescent follows, leading to the smart gates of **Royal Victoria Park**, which in themselves represent a symbolic entrance to the city.

Although it is primarily Georgian Bath that draws the crowds, there are hints of medieval times in the ruins of the **city walls** along Upper Borough Walls and Barton St, north of the abbey, while no trip to Bath would be complete without visiting the **Roman Baths** (see p182).

To get a real feel for the city, join one of the two-hour **walking tours** that are run by volunteers from outside the Pump Room [83], right next to the Roman Baths. Tours depart at 10.30am and 2pm Sunday to Friday, and just at 10.30am on Saturday; in the summer, between May and September, there's an additional evening walk at 7pm on Tuesday and Friday. There is no charge – and no tips are accepted. Is this one of Bath's best-kept secrets?

A city with this sort of heritage must have the odd ghost hovering in the shadows. If you fancy being scared out of your wits, join a guided **ghost walk** (🖳 www. ghostwalksofbath.co.uk; year-round Thur-Sat 8pm; £8 per person), lasting just short of two hours. To take part, just turn up at the allotted time outside the Garrick's Head pub [46] (see p179), though groups of 10 or more need to pre-book.

For those who prefer to guide themselves, there's a **city trail** beneath your feet – quite literally: it's marked out with plaques on the pavements. There's no accompanying map, but for an upbeat interpretation, see 🖳 www.bath.co.uk/city-trail. Broadly, the trail starts near the abbey, taking in the Roman Baths and the Pump Room, before moving on to Queen Square, The Circus and the Assembly Rooms, then back towards Pulteney Bridge and Parade Gardens, finishing at Abbey Green.

Further afield, the National Trust (🖳 www.nationaltrust.org.uk/bath-skyline/) have devised a 6-mile (10km) **Bath Skyline walk** and a shorter version, **Walk to the View**; both can be downloaded from the website. Those who would like to complete the **Cotswold Way in stages** should consider signing up for the walks led by the Cotswold Voluntary Wardens, some of them based from Bath; for details, see p29.

If you've had enough of walking, there are always the double-decker **sightseeing** buses (⌨ www.city-sightseeing.com/bath) which operate hop-on, hop-off tours for £14 a head, with a commentary; tickets are valid for 24 hours. Alternatively, you can use the buses as a shuttle service, paying £2.50 for each leg of the journey, without the commentary. Buses set off from the end of Cheap St, behind Bath Abbey.

Or you could try a **horse-drawn tour** (⌨ www.courtyardcarriages.com) which takes in the architectural highlights of Pulteney Bridge, Royal Crescent and The Circus. Trips (£11pp, 25-30 mins) start from Cheap St, opposite Parade Gardens.

When planning your trip, note that several establishments, including the Roman Baths, stop selling tickets up to an hour before closing time, so do be sure to give yourself plenty of time.

● **Bath Abbey** One of England's most glorious churches, Bath Abbey (⌨ www .bathabbey.org; summer Mon 9.30am-5.30pm, Tue-Fri 9am-5.30pm, Sat 9am-6pm, Sun 1-2.30pm & 4.30-5.30pm; Nov-Mar closes every day at 4.30pm; £2.50 donation requested) is the third church to occupy this site. Visitors are welcome to tour the building, with its magnificent flying buttresses and fan-vaulted rafters, but it is during a service, or a concert, that you can best appreciate the architecture as the sound of choral music soars skywards. Tower tours (£6) are offered hourly (Mon-Sat, 10am-5pm), except in bad weather.

Over the years, three separate buildings have occupied the site of the abbey. The first, an Anglo-Saxon church, was replaced by the Normans at the end of the 11th century. When this fell into ruin at the end of the 15th century, the present abbey church was founded, but was abandoned in 1539 at the time of Henry VIII's order for the dissolution of the monasteries. The Gothic church here now was rebuilt during the reign of Elizabeth I and completed in 1616. Today, the Development Project seeks to address the needs of the 21st century – and while this is ongoing, the **Vaults Heritage Museum** is closed.

Take a look at the abbey doors and you'll see the sacred heart and crown of thorns that proclaim its earlier foundation as a Catholic church. To each side of the doors are statues of St Peter and St Paul, to whom the Norman church was dedicated. The statue to the left was decapitated by Roundheads during the reign of Charles I, with the face recarved at a later date to restore the balance – at least in part. The abbey church itself is dedicated to St Peter.

● **Bath Assembly Rooms** Built in 1771, the lavishly designed Assembly Rooms (⌨ www.national trust.org.uk/bath-assembly-rooms/; daily 10.30am-5pm; admission free, except for Fashion Museum), on Bennett St, were the creation of John Wood the Younger, and *the* place to be seen in fashionable Georgian society. Significant damage was caused by a bomb in 1942, but the Assembly Rooms have since been fully restored. Note that the building is sometimes closed for private functions. On the lower-ground floor is the **Fashion Museum** (⌨ www.fashionmuseum.co.uk; daily Mar-Oct 10.30-5pm, Nov-Feb 10.30am-4pm; £8.25, free to NT members). If you neither know nor care how Georgian formality compares with 20th-century designer chic, perhaps you'd be better off in the chain shops on Stall St. If you do, stay put; you'll even get the chance to try on corsets and crinolines. A combined ticket with the Roman Baths (see p182) and Victoria Art Gallery (see p183) costs £20.

● **Herschel Museum of Astronomy** Dedicated to five generations of the Herschel family, this museum (⌨ herschelmuseum.org.uk, 19 New King St; mid Jan-mid Dec Mon-Fri 1-5pm, Sat/Sun and bank hols 11am-5pm; £6) is as much about the interior of an 18th-century townhouse as about astronomy. Already established as a musician, William Herschel moved here in 1777 with his sister, the astronomer Caroline Herschel. As a form of relaxation, he took up astronomy himself, building his own telescope and going on to discover the planet Uranus from this garden in 1781. Among the exhibits relating to everyday life is a 7ft (210cm) scale model of his 40ft (12m) telescope. Herschel went on to be appointed Astronomer Royal, forcing a move to Datchet in 1782. He died in 1823 and is buried in Berkshire, in the churchyard of St Lawrence, Upton.

● **Holburne Museum of Art** Following substantial restoration and extension, this museum (☎ 01225-388569, 🖳 www.holburne.org; Mon-Sat 10am-5pm, Sun/bank hol 11am-5pm; admission free except special exhibitions), at the end of Great Pulteney St, has emerged with a new sense of light and space. Established in 1893 to showcase the collection of Sir William Holburne, it is a major provincial gallery with a particularly strong emphasis on Georgian portraiture. To miss the rest of the collection would be a shame, however. Do take a look at the smaller exhibits tucked away in drawers – and allow time for a breather in the contemporary café.

● **Museum of Bath Architecture** The setting for this fascinating museum (🖳 museumofbatharchitecture.org.uk, The Vineyards, The Paragon; mid Feb-Nov, Tue-Fri 2-5pm, Sat-Sun & bank holiday Mon 10.30am-5pm; entry £5) is the **Countess of Huntingdon's Chapel**, built in 1765 and in use as a place of worship until 1981. The building is interesting in itself, but the real reason for visiting is to find out why – and how – Georgian Bath was built. Work your way through the grand designs of the architects, including the city's principal visionary John Wood, who designed Queen Square, and his son, also John, who was the inspiration behind both The Circus and Royal Crescent. Discover the challenges faced by the stonemasons, carpenters and roofers, then learn about the interior décor, such as applying gold leaf to the ceiling mouldings. Intricate scale models show how the interiors of the houses were constructed – and depict what went on in each of the rooms. Other museums might shout louder, but this is the one to put at the top of your list.

● **Museum of East Asian Art** This museum (🖳 www.meaa.org.uk, 12 Bennett St; Tue-Sat 10am-5pm, Sun noon-5pm; admission £5), based on the personal collection of a Hong Kong lawyer, offers more of an introduction to Asian art than any great insight. Among the exhibits are ceramics, bamboo carvings and an extensive collection of Chinese jade. Find it off The Circus, just a stone's throw from the Cotswold Way as it enters Bath.

● **Parade Gardens** Right in the centre of Bath, the Parade Gardens (Easter-end Sep; admission £1.50) is a peaceful place to enjoy the colour of an English formal garden. Bands play here regularly in summer.

● **Roman Baths and Pump Room** Probably the single greatest attraction for visitors is the **Roman Baths** (🖳 www.romanbaths.co.uk, Stall St; daily Mar-Jun & Sep-Oct 9am-5pm, Jul-Aug 9am-9pm, Nov-Feb 9.30am-5.30pm; £14, or £14.50 in Jul-Aug; combined ticket with Victoria Art Gallery & Fashion Museum £20). Dating to between the 1st and 5th centuries AD, and constructed of stone, the colonnaded great bath was built to take advantage of a natural spring from which waters rise at a constant temperature of around 46°C. If the changing rooms, saunas and plunge pools are reminiscent of a modern-day spa, the temple dedicated to the goddess Sulis Minerva, puts the whole thing firmly back into context. Included in the admission price is entry to the Georgian **Pump Room**, where the spring water may be sampled. For details of afternoon tea at the Pump Room, see p179.

● **Royal Crescent and Lansdown Crescent** At the far right of Royal Crescent, **No 1** (🖳 no1royalcrescent.org.uk; Feb-mid Dec Mon noon-5.30pm, Tue-Sun & bank holidays 10.30am-5.30pm; admission £9) was the first house to be constructed, built in the Palladian style by John Wood the Younger. Following refurbishment and enlargement to encompass the servants' quarters in the neighbouring No 1A, it reopened in 2013. Today's visitor will gain an insight into life both upstairs and downstairs in fashionable Georgian society; don't miss the kitchens or the cabinet of curiosities. Royal Crescent may get all the accolades, but it is **Lansdown Crescent** (see Map 43, p167) that is first seen by those heading south on the Cotswold Way. With sheep grazing on the grassy hill in front, and fine views over the city, it arguably runs its more famous neighbour very close.

● **Victoria Art Gallery** Facing Pulteney Bridge (itself designed by Adam and one of only three river bridges in Europe with shops that are integral to the bridge) is Victoria Art Gallery (⌨ www.victoriagal .org.uk; Tue-Sat 10am-5pm, Sun 1.30-5pm; admission free but special exhibitions £3.50), built at a time of civic pride to show off the city's attributes. While the name tends to suggest that it focuses on Victorian art, the reality is a far broader mix, from the 17th century to the contemporary, and including a couple of Gainsborough paintings and Rex Whistler's glorious incarnation of British insularity, *The Foreign Bloke*. Some are linked to the city, but most were donated by wealthy Bath residents, or formed part of their collections. Displays also include sculpture, ceramics, glass, porcelain and pottery. The room downstairs plays host to a series of changing exhibitions. On a practical note, there's a self-service machine dispensing hot drinks into china cups (yes, really!). And if you're nursing sore feet, note that there is plenty of comfortable seating down the centre of the gallery.

Entertainment

Bath does culture very well, but there's light relief on the agenda too. A great place to ease all those post-walk aches and pains, or to get yourself in a relaxed frame of mind before setting off, is **Thermae Bath Spa** (⌨ www.thermaebathspa.com; daily except 25-26 Dec & 1 Jan, 9am-9.30pm; pools closed 9pm) on the gloriously named Hot Bath St. At £32 a head (£35 at weekends) for just a couple of hours, it's expensive – some would say extortionate – but at least the price now includes a towel, robe and slippers. If you don't fancy shelling out for the open-air spa at the New Royal Bath (no

children under 16), or indeed for one of their 50 treatments and therapies, there's the satellite **Cross Bath** (daily 10am-8pm, last entry 6.30pm), just across the road, which is open air but without the view; a 1½-hour session here costs £18, or £20 at weekends.

Bath's **Theatre Royal** (⌨ www.the atreroyal.org.uk), on Sawclose, stages a wide range of high-quality productions, and – for theatre buffs – shouldn't be missed. If you've a preference for the silver screen, try the multi-screen Odeon **cinema** (⌨ www.odeon.co.uk/cinemas/bath) just below Kingsmead Square, or – for more offbeat offerings – the **Little Theatre Cinema** (⌨ www.picturehouses.com/cine ma/The_Little), on St Michael's Place.

River trips can be organised with Bath City Boat Trips (⌨ www.bathcity boattrips.net; Apr-Sep daily 11am-5pm), with 50-minute trips at £9.95 per adult. On the *Pulteney Princess* (⌨ www.pulteney princess.co.uk; Apr-Oct), which plies the Avon between Pulteney Weir and Bathampton Mill up to seven times a day, a round trip of about an hour costs £8; one-way trips are also possible. If you'd rather set off under your own steam, rowing boats, canoes and punts can be hired from Bath Boating Station (⌨ www.bathboating.co .uk; early Apr-late Sep daily 10am-6pm), whose base is at the end of Forester Rd, north-east of Great Pulteney St (off map 43a). Boats cost £7 per person for the first hour, and £4 for every hour after that (£18 for full day).

Taking to the skies is a great way to see the city as a whole, though on a **balloon trip** it's pot luck as to which way you will fly – assuming the weather is calm enough to take off. Several companies organise trips: try Bath Balloons (⌨ www.bathbal loons.co.uk, Mar-Oct), whose balloons take off from Royal Victoria Park and cost £110-145 a head, depending on the day.

Spectators rather than participants can check out what's on at **The Rec** (⌨ www .bathrugby.com), home to Bath Rugby Club – though it's a small ground by today's standards, and tickets can be hard to come by. The Rec is also used for concerts.

Map key

🕮 Library/bookstore   ● Other

♠ Where to stay

@ Internet   CP Car park

O Where to eat and drink

🕮 Museum/gallery   🚌 Bus station/stop

Δ Campsite

✝ Church/cathedral   —🚃— Rail line & station

⊠ Post Office

☏ Public telephone   Park

Ⓔ Bank/ATM

⊠ Public toilet   📱082 GPS waypoint

ⓘ Tourist Information

☐ Building

Cotswold Way path	Gate	Water
Other path	Stile	Trees/forest
4 x 4 track	Kissing gate	Trig point
Road	Bridge	Guide post
Steps	Hedge	CP Car park
Slope/steep slope	Fence	26 Map continuation

Symbols used in text   🐕 Dogs allowed subject to prior arrangement
🛁 Bathtub in at least one room   Ⓛ packed lunch available if requested in advance

APPENDIX A – GPS WAYPOINTS

Each GPS waypoint was taken on the route at the reference number marked on the map as below.

MAP	REF	GPS WAYPOINT	DESCRIPTION
Map 1	001	N52° 03.018' W01° 46.913'	start of Cotswold Way, Chipping Campden
Map 1	002	N52° 03.525' W01° 47.752'	kissing gate on Dover's Hill
Map 2	003	N52° 01.862' W01° 49.687'	Fish Hill – toposcope
Map 3	004	N52° 01.458' W01° 50.165'	Broadway Tower
Map 3	005	N52° 02.197' W01° 51.172'	junction of road, Broadway
Map 3	006	N52° 01.678' W01° 52.427'	Broadway Coppice guidepost
Map 4	007	N52° 00.332' W01° 52.842'	Shenberrow – cattle grid
Map 4	008	N52° 00.003' W01° 53.040'	Shenberrow Hill
Map 5	009	N52° 00.403' W01° 54.146'	corner of road, Stanton
Map 5	010	N51° 59.377' W01° 54.748'	gate to Stanway House
Map 6	011	N51° 58.322' W01° 53.473'	Stumps Cross
Map 6	012	N51° 58.070' W01° 54.563'	Beckbury Camp monument
Map 7	013	N51° 58.157' W01° 55.655'	Hailes Abbey
Map 8	014	N51° 57.218' W01° 57.825'	corner of North St, Winchcombe
Map 9	015	N51° 55.690' W01° 58.255'	Belas Knap
Map 10	016	N51° 56.542' W02° 01.018'	Cleeve Hill car park
Map 10	017	N51° 56.160' W02° 01.328'	Cleeve Hill toposcope
Map 11	018	N51° 55.600' W02° 01.325'	Cleeve Hill fort, marking track to Southam
Map 13	019	N51° 52.606' W02° 01.227'	bridge over spill by Dowdeswell Reservoir
Map 14	020	N51° 51.827' W02° 02.207'	guidepost and bench, Wistley Hill
Map 14	021	N51° 51.193' W02° 02.865'	junction with Hartley Lane, Seven Springs
Map 15	022	N51° 51.822' W02° 04.550'	Leckhampton trig point
Map 15	023	N51° 50.987' W02° 04.925'	track meets road
Map 16	024	N51° 50.598' W02° 05.783'	Air Balloon pub
Map 16	025	N51° 50.073' W02° 06.893'	The Peak
Map 18	026	N51° 49.922' W02° 09.312'	Cooper's Hill
Map 19	027	N51° 48.358' W02° 11.518'	steps to trig point, Painswick Hill
Map 20	028	N51° 47.205' W02° 11.592'	junction with A46, Painswick
Map 20	029	N51° 46.808' W02° 13.120'	The Edgemoor Inn
Map 21	030	N51° 47.008' W02° 14.685'	junction of road and track by disused well (Cliff Wood)
Map 21	031	N51° 46.691' W02° 15.745'	Haresfield Beacon
Map 22	032	N51° 45.325' W02° 15.522'	gate on Maiden Hill
Map 23	033	N51° 44.395' W02° 15.192'	Oil Mills Bridge
Map 25	034	N51° 42.702' W02° 18.037'	Nympsfield display boards
Map 26	035	N51° 41.908' W02° 18.355'	Uley Long Barrow (Hetty Pegler's Tump)
Map 26	036	N51° 41.527' W02° 18.610'	Uley Bury
Map 27	037	N51° 41.617' W02° 19.482'	Cam Long Down
Map 28	038	N51° 40.818' W02° 22.037'	Stinchcombe Hill Golf Club
Map 28	039	N51° 40.803' W02° 22.938'	Drakestone Point (scenic route)
Map 28	040	N51° 40.725' W02° 22.247'	convergence of paths, Stinchcombe Hill
Map 29	041	N51° 39.528' W02° 22.353'	Tyndale Monument
Map 29	042	N51° 38.492' W02° 21.555'	hilltop monument above Wotton-under-Edge

MAP	REF	GPS WAYPOINT		DESCRIPTION
Map 30	043	N51° 38.347'	W02° 19.310'	Blackquerries Hill signpost
Map 31	044	N51° 37.033'	W02° 19.995'	Alderley, Wotton-under-Edge 5-mile sign
Map 32	045	N51° 36.318'	W02° 19.025'	Lower Kilcott
Map 33	046	N51° 35.220'	W02° 19.780'	Somerset Monument
Map 34	047	N51° 33.663'	W02° 20.453'	wood near Horton Court
Map 35	048	N51° 32.070'	W02° 21.275'	St John the Baptist, Old Sodbury
Map 35	049	N51° 30.906'	W02° 21.032'	lone oak, Dodington Park
Map 36	050	N51° 30.427'	W02° 20.087'	Tormarton bus stop
Map 38	051	N51° 28.200'	W02° 22.735'	kissing gate above withy bed
Map 39	052	N51° 27.245'	W02° 21.698'	Cold Ashton church
Map 40	053	N51° 25.875'	W02° 23.392'	kissing gate at top of hill
Map 41	054	N51° 25.787'	W02° 24.892'	Hanging Hill
Map 41	055	N51° 25.405'	W02° 24.317'	turn by Lansdown Golf Course
Map 42	056	N51° 24.782'	W02° 24.832'	Prospect Stile
Map 42	057	N51° 23.720'	W02° 24.062'	Weston trig point

APPENDIX B – WALKING WITH A DOG

WALKING THE COTSWOLD WAY WITH A DOG

Many are the rewards that await those prepared to make the extra effort required to bring their best friend along the Cotswold Way. You shouldn't underestimate the amount of work involved, though. Indeed, just about every decision you make will be influenced by the fact that you've got a dog: how you plan to travel to the start of the trail, where you're going to stay, how far you're going to walk each day, where you're going to rest and where you're going to eat in the evening etc.

If you're also sure your dog can cope with (and will enjoy) walking, say, 12-14 miles or more a day for several days in a row, you need to start preparing accordingly. Extra thought also needs to go into your itinerary. The best starting point is to study the village and town facilities table on pp34-7 (and the advice below), and plan where to stop and where to buy food.

Looking after your dog

To begin with, you need to make sure that your own dog is fully **inoculated** against the usual doggy illnesses, and also up to date with regard to **worm pills** (eg Drontal) and **flea preventatives** such as Frontline – they are, after all, following in the pawprints of many a dog before them, some of whom may well have left fleas or other parasites on the trail that now lie in wait for their next meal to arrive. **Pet insurance** is also a very good idea; if you've already got insurance, do check that it will cover a trip such as this.

On the subject of looking after your dog's health, perhaps the most important implement you can take with you is a **plastic tick remover**, available from vets for a couple of quid. These removers, while fiddly, help you to remove ticks safely (ie without leaving the head behind buried under the dog's skin).

Being in unfamiliar territory also makes it more likely that you and your dog could become separated. For this reason, make sure your dog has a **tag with your contact details on it** (a mobile phone number would be best if you are carrying one with you); you could also consider having it microchipped for further security.

When to keep your dog on a lead

● **On the edge of the escarpment** It's a sad fact that, every year, a few dogs lose their lives falling over the edge of steep slopes.

● **When crossing farmland** This is particularly important in the lambing season (around February to May) when your dog can scare the sheep, causing them to lose their young. During this time, most farmers would prefer it if you didn't bring your dog at all. Farmers are allowed by law to shoot at and kill any dogs that they consider are worrying their sheep. Dogs running free in standing crops can also cause damage, so do take care to prevent this. The exception to the 'dogs on leads' rule is if your dog is being attacked by cows. A few years ago there were three deaths in the UK caused by walkers being trampled as they tried to rescue their dogs from the attentions of cattle. The advice in this instance is to let go of the lead, head speedily to a position of safety (usually the other side of the field gate or stile) and call your dog to you.

● **Around ground-nesting birds** It's important to keep your dog under control when crossing an area inhabited by ground-nesting birds, which are usually active between March and June; a dog on the loose at this time could inadvertently destroy the nest, or frighten the adult birds away. Most dogs love foraging around in the woods but make sure you have permission to do so; some woods are used as 'nurseries' for game birds and dogs are only allowed through them if they are on a lead.

What to pack

You've probably already got a good idea of what to bring to keep your dog alive and happy, but the following is a checklist:

● **Food/water bowl** Foldable cloth bowls are popular with walkers, being light and taking up little room in a rucksack. You can get also get a water-bottle-and-bowl combination, where the bottle folds into a 'trough' from which the dog can drink.

● **Lead and collar** An extendable one is probably preferable for this sort of trip. Make sure both lead and collar are in good condition – you don't want either to snap on the trail, or you may end up carrying your dog through sheep fields until a replacement can be found.

● **Medication** You'll know if you need to bring any lotions or potions.

● **Bedding** A simple blanket may suffice, or you can opt for something more elaborate if you aren't carrying your own luggage.

● **Poo bags** Essential.

● **Hygiene wipes** For cleaning your dog after it's rolled in stuff.

● **A favourite toy** Helps prevent your dog from pining for the entire walk.

● **Food/water** Remember to bring treats as well as regular food to keep up the mutt's morale. That said, if your dog is anything like mine the chances are they'll spend most of the walk dining on rabbit droppings and sheep poo anyway.

● **Corkscrew stake** Available from camping or pet shops, this will help you to keep your dog secure in one place while you set up camp/doze.

● **Tick remover** See above.

● **Raingear** It can rain!

● **Old towels** For drying your dog.

When it comes to packing, I always leave an exterior pocket of my rucksack empty so I can put used poo bags in there (for deposit at the first bin I come to). I always like to keep all the dog's kit together and separate from the other luggage (usually inside a plastic bag inside my rucksack). I have also seen several dogs sporting their own 'doggy rucksack', so they can carry their own food, water, poo etc – which certainly reduces the burden on their owner!

Cleaning up after your dog

It is extremely important that dog owners behave in a responsible way when walking the path. Dog excrement should be cleaned up. In towns, villages and fields where animals graze or which will be cut for silage, hay etc, you need to pick up and bag the excrement.

Staying with your dog

In this guide we have used the symbol 🐕 to denote where a hotel, pub, B&B or campsite welcomes dogs, although this always needs to be arranged in advance. Some places make an additional charge (usually per night but occasionally per stay), while others may require a deposit, which is refundable if the dog doesn't make a mess. Hostels (both YHA and independent) do not permit dogs unless they are an assistance (guide) dog. Before you turn up, always double check whether there is space for your dog; many places have only one or two rooms that they deem suitable, and in some dogs need to sleep in a separate building.

When it comes to **eating**, most landlords allow dogs in at least a section of their pubs, though very few restaurants do. Make sure you always ask first, then ensure that your dog doesn't run around the pub but is secured to your table or a radiator.

Henry Stedman

INDEX

Page references in **bold** type refer to maps

access 53-6
accidents 57
accommodation 18-22, 35, 37, 74
see also place name
bookings 18-19, 28
Alderley 150, **151**
Airbnb 22
annual events 14-16
areas of outstanding natural beauty (AONBs) 60
art galleries
see place name
Arts and Crafts Movement 43, 75, 76, 81, 108, 122, 132, 136
Ashbee, CR 76, 108
Ashmolean Museum, Broadway 81, **87**
ATMs 25, 26, 34, 36, 41
Austen, Jane 43, 168

Backpackers' Club 42
Badminton Horse Trials 15, 71
baggage carriers 26-8
bank holidays 26
banks 26, 41
Bath **167**, 168-9, **170, 171**, 172-83
Abbey 181
accommodation 169, 172, 174-6
Assembly Rooms 181
bars/pubs 178-9
cafes 179-80
entertainment 183
festivals 14-16
food specialities 177
Lansdown Crescent 183
markets 169, 180
museums & galleries 181-3
restaurants 176-8, 180
Roman Baths 182
Royal Crescent 182-3
services 169
sights 180-3
taxis 169

Bath *(cont'd)*
teahouses 179-80
Thermae Bath Spa 183
tourist information 169
transport 168-9, 183
walking tours 180
Battle of Lansdown 162, 163, **164, 165**
Beckbury Camp 89, **93**
Beckford's Tower 163
bed and breakfast (B&Bs) 20-1, 30
beer 16, 23
Belas Knap 101, **102**, 136
Bill Smyllie Reserve 62, 105
Birdlip **118**, 119
birds 66-70
blisters 56
boots 39
Broadway 76, 81, **84**, 85-6, **87**, 88-9
Broadway Tower **84**, 85
Buckholt Wood 66, **121**
budgeting 29-30
bus services 45, 48, **49**, 50
business hours 26
butterflies 66
Butterfly Conservation 62, 66

Cam Long Down 134, **138**
Campaign to Protect Rural England 62
campaigning organisations 61-2
camping 19, 29-30
camping gear 41
campsites 35, 37
cash machines *see* ATMs
cattle 54, 71
cell phones *see* mobile phones
Charlton Kings 112
Charlton Kings Common 105, **114**
cheese rolling 15, 119, **121**
Cheltenham 14, 15, 16, 76, 105, 108, **109**, 110

Cheltenham Gold Cup 15, 71
Cheltenham Racecourse 101, **107**, 108, **109**
chemists *see* pharmacies
Chipping Campden 16, 75-80, **79**, **82**
churches 27
see also place name
Cleeve Hill 71, 102-3, **104**, 105
Cleeve Hill Common 101, **106**
clothes 39-40
coach services 44, 46, 47
Coaley Peak 63, 134, **135**
Coaley Wood 62, 65, **137**
Cold Ashton **161**, 162
compasses 41
Conservation Volunteers, Trust for 62
conservation 59-62
organisations 61-2
Coomb's End **156**, 157
Cooper's Hill 16, 119, **121**
costs 19, 21, 22, 23, 29-30
Cotswold Beer Festival 16
Cotswold Hills Geopark 61
Cotswold Olimpick Games 16, 81
Cotswold Voluntary Wardens 29, 60, 96, 180
Cotswold Way National Trail Office 42
Cotswold Way Relay 16, 31
Cotswolds AONB 8, 60
Cotswolds Conservation Board 25, 29, 60
Countryside and Rights of Way Act 54-6
Countryside Code 55
Cranham Corner 120, **121**
credit cards 24, 41
Crickley Hill 63, 115, **117**, 122
Crickley Hill Country Park 115, **117**

Davies, WH 44, 53

day walks 36-7
daylight hours 15
debit cards 24, 41
dehydration 56
Devil's Chimney 105, **116**
difficulty of walk 12
digital mapping 18
direction of walk 31-2
disabled access 25
distance chart 186-7
Dodington Park **156**, 157
dogs 25, 54, 55, 74, 187-8
Dover's Hill 16, 81, **82**
Dowdeswell Reservoir
  112, **113**
Drakestone Point **143**
drinks 23, 24
driving 44, 46-7
dry-stone walls 10, 51, 60
duration of walk 12
Dursley 16, 44, 136, **138**,
  139-41, **140**
Dyrham Park **159**, **160**, 161

Ebley **131**, 132
Ebley Canal 127, 130, **131**,
  132
economic impact 51-2
Edge **124**, 127
emergency services 27
emergency signals 57
English Heritage 61, 96, 134
environmental impact 52-3
equipment 38-42
erosion 52-3
exchange rates 26
European Health Insurance
  Cards (EHICs) 26-7

farm animals 71
fauna 66-72
festivals 14-16
field guides 43
first-aid kit 40
Fish Hill **82**
flashlights *see* torches
Flecker, James Elroy 44
flights 44
flowers 63-6
food 22-4, 41, 177
footwear 39
Frocester Beer Festival 16

geology 10-11
geoparks 61
Gloucestershire Geology
  Trust 11, 61
Gloucestershire Old Spot
  pigs 71
Gloucestershire
  Warwickshire Steam
  Railway **95**, 96
Gloucestershire Way 32
Gordon Russell Design
  Museum, Broadway 81, **87**
GPS 17-18, 41
  waypoints 18, 185-6
Great Witcombe Villa 63,
  118, 120
group walking tours 28-9
guesthouses 20-1, 30
guided walks 28-9, 96, 180
Guild of Handicrafts 76
Gurney, Ivor 13, 44, 63
Gustav Holst Way 105, 108

Hailes 94, **95**
Hailes Abbey 89, **95**, 96
Ham Hill 110, **111**, 112
Haresfield Beacon 122,
  127, **128**
Hartley Hill **114**
Hawkesbury Upton 150,
  153
health 56-7
health insurance 16-7
heat exhaustion 57
heat stroke 57
Hetty Pegler's Tump 136,
  137
Hidcote Manor Gardens 76
highlights 36-8
hill forts 122
Hillesley 150, **151**
history of trail 8
holiday cottages 22
holidays 26
Holst, Gustav 108, 120
  see also Gustav Holst Way
horses 71
Horton 152, 154, **155**
Horton Court 152, **155**
hostels 19-20, 30, 35, 37
hotels 21
hyperthermia 57

hypothermia 57

inn*s see* pubs
itineraries 32, 33

Kimsbury Camp 122
King's Stanley 130, 132,
  133

Landmark Trust 22, 62, 75,
  163
Leckhampton Hill 63, 105,
  116, 122
Lee, Laurie 43, 66, 119
Leisure, poem 53
Lineover Wood 62, 63, 105,
  113
litter 52, 55
Little Sodbury 154, **155**
Little Witcombe 120, **120**
long barrows 101, **129**, 136,
  137
Long Distance Walkers'
  Association, The 42
Lower Kilcott **152**
Lyme disease 58

mammals 70-2
map key 184
maps 42-3, 73-4
Masts Field 62, 105
medical services 25
  see also place name
Middleyard 132, **133**
minimum impact 51-6
mobile phones 27, 41
money 24-5, 26, 41
Monarch's Way 33, **152**
Morris, William 76, 85,
  132, 136
museums and galleries
  see place name

Nanny Farmer's Bottom
  145, 150
national holidays 26
national nature reserves
  (NNRs) 61
national trails 8, 17, 53, 60
National Trust 42, 61, 75,
  89, 96, 134, 146, 152,
  161, 180, 181

Natural England 60
Newark Park **145**, 146
North Farmcote **93**, 94
North Nibley 142, **144**
Nympsfield 134
Nympsfield Long Barrow
   135, 136

Old Sodbury 154, **156**
Olimpick Games 16, 81
Owlpen Manor 76, 136

Painswick 16, 76, 119,
   122, **124**, 125-7, **126**
Painswick Beacon 63, 119,
   122, **123**
Painswick Hill 120, **123**
Painswick Rococo
   Garden 122, **123**
Penn Wood 62, 65, 130,
   133
Pennsylvania **161**, 162
pharmacies 25
pigs 71
post offices 25, 26, 34, 36,
   41
Postlip 101, **103**
Postlip Hall 16, 101, **103**
Prescott Speed Hill Climb
   14
Prestbury Hill Reserve 62,
   63, 66, 105, **106**, 110
Prinknash Abbey **121**
Prinknash Bird & Deer
   Park 120, **121**
Prospect Stile 163, **166**
public holidays 26
public transport 45-8, **49**,
   50, 53
pubs 21, 23-4, 26, 30
   see also place name
Pump Room, Bath 179, 182

rail services 44, 45, 46, **49**
rainfall chart 14
Ramblers 9, 42, 43
Randwick **129**, 130
reading, recommended 43-4
real ale 23
reptiles 72
restaurants 23, 24
   see also place name

right to roam 54
rights of way 53-4
Roman Baths, Bath 182
route finding 17
Rowling, JK 44
rucksacks 38-9
Ruskin, John 76

safety, outdoor 58
Sally Lunn's, Bath 177,
   179-80
school holidays 26
Scuttlebrooke Wake 81
seasons 13-14
self-catering 24
self-guided holidays 28
Selsley 76, 132, **133**
Selsley Common 63, 132,
   133
Seven Springs **114**, 115
Shenberrow Hill **90**, 92
sheep 71
shops 25, 26, 35, 37
side trips 32
sites of special scientific
   interest (SSSIs) 61, 122,
   134
smoking 27
Snowshill Manor 89
Stanley Wood 62, 71, **135**
Stanton 89, **91**, 92
Stanway **91**, 92, 94
Stanway House **91**, 92
Stinchcombe Hill 142, **143**
Stonehouse 130, **131**
Stroudwater (Ebley) Canal
   127, 130, **131**
Sudeley Castle **97**, 98
sunburn 56

taxis 27, 45
   see also place name
telephones 25, 27, 41
temperature chart 14
time 27
toilets 53
Tope, Rebecca 44
torches 40, 57
Tormarton 157, **158**
tourist information centres
   34, 36, 42
town facilities 34-7

trail information 42
trail maps 73-4, key 184
train services 44, 45, 46, **49**
transport 45-8, **49**, 50, 53
travel insurance 26-7, 41
trees 62-3
Tyndale Monument 142,
   144

Uley 134, 136, **137**
Uley Bury 122, **137**
Uley Long Barrow 136,
   137
Ullenwood 115, **116**

village facilities 34-7

walkers' organisations 42
walking alone 30, 58
walking companies 26-9
walking poles/sticks 41, 56
walking times 73
Warden's Way 32
water 24, 56
water bottles/pouches 40
waymarks 17
waypoints 18, 185-6
weather 13-14
weather information 58
weekend walks 38
weights and measures 27
Weston 165, **167**
Westrip **129**, 130
whistles 40, 57
wild camping 19
wildlife 53, 66-72
Winchcombe 16, 32, 96,
   97, 98-101, **99**
Winchcombe Way 32, **91**,
   97, **102**
Windrush Way 32
Witcombe Wood 69, **118**
Wood Stanway **93**, 94
Woodland Trust 62
Woodchester Mansion and
   Park 71, 134, **135**
Wotton-under-Edge 15,
   144, **145**, 146, **147**, 148-9
Wysis Way 32, **123**

Youth Hostels Association
   (YHA) 20

TRAILBLAZER'S LONG-DISTANCE PATH (LDP) WALKING GUIDES

We've applied to destinations which are closer to home Trailblazer's proven formula for publishing definitive practical route guides for adventurous travellers. Britain's network of long-distance trails enables the walker to explore some of the finest landscapes in the country's best walking areas. These are guides that are user-friendly, practical, informative and environmentally sensitive.

● **Unique mapping features** In many walking guidebooks the reader has to read a route description then try to relate it to the map. Our guides are much easier to use because walking directions, tricky junctions, places to stay and eat, points of interest and walking times are all written onto the maps themselves in the places to which they apply. With their uncluttered clarity, these are not general-purpose maps but fully edited maps drawn by walkers for walkers.

● **Largest-scale walking maps** At a scale of just under 1:20,000 (8cm or 3$\frac{1}{8}$ inches to one mile) the maps in these guides are bigger than even the most detailed British walking maps currently available in the shops.

● **Not just a trail guide – includes where to stay**, **where to eat and public transport** Our guidebooks cover the complete walking experience, not just the route. Accommodation options for all budgets are provided (pubs, hotels, B&Bs, campsites, bunkhouses, hostels) as well as places to eat. Detailed public transport information for all access points to each trail means that there are itineraries for all walkers, for hiking the entire route as well as for day or weekend walks.

Coast to Coast *Henry Stedman*, 7th edition, £11.99
ISBN 978-1-905864-74-4, 268pp, 110 maps, 40 colour photos

Cornwall Coast Path (SW Coast Path Pt 2) 5th edition, £11.99
ISBN 978-1-905864-71-3, 3526pp, 142 maps, 40 colour photos

Cotswold Way *Tricia & Bob Hayne* 3rd edition, £11.99
ISBN 978-1-905864-70-6, 204pp, 53 maps, 40 colour photos

Dales Way *Henry Stedman* 1st edition, £11.99 – **due June 2016**
ISBN 978-1-905864-78-2, 192pp, 50 maps, 40 colour photos

Dorset & South Devon (SW Coast Path Pt 3) *Stedman & Newton*, £11.99
ISBN 978-1-905864-45-4, 336pp, 88 maps, 40 colour photos

Exmoor & North Devon (SW Coast Path Pt I) *Stedman & Newton*, £11.99
ISBN 978-1-905864-43-0, 192pp, 68 maps, 40 colour photos

Hadrian's Wall Path *Henry Stedman*, 4th edition, £11.99
ISBN 978-1-905864-58-4, 224pp, 60 maps, 40 colour photos

Offa's Dyke Path *Keith Carter*, 4th edition, £11.99
ISBN 978-1-905864-65-2, 240pp, 98 maps, 40 colour photos

Peddars Way & Norfolk Coast Path *Alexander Stewart*, £11.99
ISBN 978-1-905864-28-7, 192pp, 54 maps, 40 colour photos

Pembrokeshire Coast Path *Jim Manthorpe*, 4th edition, £11.99
ISBN 978-1-905864-51-5, 224pp, 96 maps, 40 colour photos

Pennine Way *Stuart Greig*, 4th edition, £11.99
ISBN 978-1-905864-61-4, 272pp, 138 maps, 40 colour photos

The Ridgeway *Nick Hill*, 3rd edition, £11.99
ISBN 978-1-905864-40-9, 192pp, 53 maps, 40 colour photos

South Downs Way *Jim Manthorpe*, 5th edition, £11.99
ISBN 978-1-905864-66-9, 192pp, 60 maps, 40 colour photos

Thames Path *Joel Newton*, 1st edition, £11.99
ISBN 978-1-905864-64-5, 256pp, 99 maps, 40 colour photos

West Highland Way *Charlie Loram*, 6th edition, £11.99
ISBN 978-1-905864-76-8, 208pp, 60 maps, 40 colour photos

'The same attention to detail that distinguishes its other guides has been brought to bear here'.
THE SUNDAY TIMES

Distances chart. Each cell shows two values: the upper (roman) figure and the lower (italic) figure.

	Chipping Campden	Broadway	Stanton	Wood Stanway	Hailes	Winchcombe	Cleeve Hill	Dowdeswell Reservoir	Seven Springs	Crickley Hill	Birdlip
Broadway	6 / *9.5*										
Stanton	10.5 / *17*	4.5 / *7.5*									
Wood Stanway	12.5 / *20*	6.5 / *10.5*	2 / *3*								
Hailes	16 / *25.5*	10 / *16*	5.5 / *8.5*	3.5 / *5.5*							
Winchcombe	18 / *29*	12 / *19.5*	7.5 / *12*	5.5 / *9*	2 / *3.5*						
Cleeve Hill	24 / *38.5*	18 / *29*	13.5 / *21.5*	11.5 / *18.5*	8 / *13*	6 / *9.5*					
Dowdeswell Res'voir	29 / *46.5*	23 / *37*	18.5 / *29.5*	16.5 / *26.5*	13 / *21*	11 / *17.5*	5 / *8*				
Seven Springs	32 / *51*	26 / *41.5*	21.5 / *34*	19.5 / *31*	16 / *25.5*	14 / *22*	8 / *12.5*	3 / *4.5*			
Crickley Hill	37 / *59*	31 / *49.5*	26.5 / *42*	24.5 / *39*	21 / *33.5*	19 / *30*	13 / *20.5*	8 / *12.5*	5 / *8*		
Birdlip	39.5 / *63*	33.5 / *53.5*	29 / *46*	27 / *43*	23.5 / *37.5*	21.5 / *34*	15.5 / *24.5*	10.5 / *16.5*	7.5 / *12*	2.5 / *4*	
Cranham Cnr	43.5 / *69.5*	37.5 / *60*	33 / *52.5*	31 / *49.5*	27.5 / *44*	25.5 / *40.5*	19.5 / *31*	14.5 / *23*	11.5 / *18.5*	6.5 / *10.5*	4 / *6.5*
Painswick	46 / *73.5*	40 / *64*	35.5 / *56.5*	33.5 / *53.5*	30 / *48*	28 / *44.5*	22 / *35*	17 / *27*	14 / *22.5*	9 / *14.5*	6.5 / *10.5*
Stonehouse	54.5 / *87*	48.5 / *77.5*	44 / *70*	42 / *67*	38.5 / *61.5*	36.5 / *58*	30.5 / *48.5*	25.5 / *40.5*	22.5 / *36*	17.5 / *28*	15 / *24*
Selsley Common	56 / *89.5*	50 / *80*	45.5 / *72.5*	43.5 / *69.5*	40 / *64*	38 / *60.5*	32 / *51*	27 / *43*	24 / *38.5*	19 / *30.5*	16.5 / *26.5*
Dursley	63.5 / *101.5*	57.5 / *92*	53 / *84.5*	51 / *81.5*	47.5 / *76*	45.5 / *72.5*	39.5 / *63*	34.5 / *55*	31.5 / *50.5*	26.5 / *42.5*	24 / *38.5*
North Nibley	68.5 / *109.5*	62.5 / *100*	58 / *92.5*	56 / *89.5*	52.5 / *84*	50.5 / *80.5*	44.5 / *71*	39.5 / *63*	36.5 / *58.5*	31.5 / *50.5*	29 / *46.5*
Wotton-u-Edge	70.5 / *113*	64.5 / *103.5*	60 / *96*	58 / *93*	54.5 / *87.5*	52.5 / *84*	46.5 / *74.5*	41.5 / *66.5*	38.5 / *62*	33.5 / *54*	31 / *50*
Hawkesbury Upton	78 / *125*	72 / *115.5*	67.5 / *108*	65.5 / *105*	62 / *99.5*	60 / *96*	54 / *86.5*	49 / *78.5*	46 / *74*	41 / *66*	38.5 / *62*
Little Sodbury	81.5 / *130.5*	75.5 / *121*	71 / *113.5*	69 / *110.5*	65.5 / *105*	63.5 / *101.5*	57.5 / *92*	52.5 / *84*	49.5 / *79.5*	44.5 / *71.5*	42 / *67.5*
Old Sodbury	83.5 / *133.5*	77.5 / *124*	73 / *116.5*	71 / *113.5*	67.5 / *108*	65.5 / *104.5*	59.5 / *95*	54.5 / *87*	51.5 / *82.5*	46.5 / *74.5*	44 / *70.5*
Coomb's End	84 / *134.5*	78 / *125*	73.5 / *117.5*	71.5 / *114.5*	68 / *109*	66 / *105.5*	60 / *96*	55 / *88*	52 / *83.5*	47 / *75.5*	44.5 / *71.5*
Tormarton	85.5 / *137*	79.5 / *127.5*	75 / *120*	73 / *117*	69.5 / *111.5*	67.5 / *108*	61.5 / *98.5*	56.5 / *90.5*	53.5 / *86*	48.5 / *78*	46 / *74*
Pennsylvania	91.5 / *146.5*	85.5 / *137*	81 / *129.5*	79 / *126.5*	75.5 / *121*	73.5 / *117.5*	67.5 / *108*	62.5 / *100*	59.5 / *95.5*	54.5 / *87.5*	52 / *83.5*
Cold Ashton	92 / *147*	86 / *137.5*	81.5 / *130*	79.5 / *127*	76 / *121.5*	74 / *118*	68 / *108.5*	63 / *100.5*	60 / *96*	55 / *88*	52.5 / *84*
Bath	102 / *163*	96 / *153.5*	91.5 / *146*	89.5 / *143*	86 / *137.5*	84 / *134*	78 / *124.5*	73 / *116.5*	70 / *112*	65 / *104*	62.5 / *100*

Cotswold Way
DISTANCE CHART

(route via Selsley Common and Stinchcombe Hill)

miles/*kilometres* (approx)

	Cranham Corner	Painswick	Stonehouse	Selsley Common	Dursley	North Nibley	Wotton-under-Edge	Hawkesbury Upton	Little Sodbury	Old Sodbury	Coomb's End	Tormarton	Pennsylvania	Cold Ashton
Painswick	2.5 / *4*													
Stonehouse	11 / *17.5*	8.5 / *13.5*												
Selsley Common	12.5 / *20*	10 / *16*	1.5 / *2.5*											
Dursley	20 / *32*	17.5 / *28*	9 / *14.5*	7.5 / *12*										
North Nibley	25 / *40*	22.5 / *36*	14 / *22.5*	12.5 / *20*	5 / *8*									
Wotton-under-Edge	27 / *43.5*	24.5 / *39.5*	16 / *26*	14.5 / *23.5*	7 / *11.5*	2 / *3.5*								
Hawkesbury Upton	34.5 / *55.5*	32 / *51.5*	23.5 / *38*	22 / *35.5*	14.5 / *23.5*	9.5 / *15.5*	7.5 / *12*							
Little Sodbury	36 / *61*	33.5 / *57*	27 / *43.5*	25.5 / *41*	18 / *29*	13 / *21*	11 / *17.5*	3.5 / *5.5*						
Old Sodbury	40 / *64*	37.5 / *60*	29 / *46.5*	27.5 / *44*	20 / *32*	15 / *24*	13 / *20.5*	5.5 / *8.5*	2 / *3*					
Coomb's End	40.5 / *65*	38 / *61*	29.5 / *47.5*	28 / *45*	20.5 / *33*	15.5 / *25*	13.5 / *21.5*	6 / *9.5*	2.5 / *4*	0.5 / *1*				
Tormarton	42 / *67.5*	39.5 / *63.5*	31 / *50*	29.5 / *47.5*	22 / *35.5*	17 / *27.5*	15 / *24*	7.5 / *12*	4 / *6.5*	2 / *3.5*	1.5 / *2.5*			
Pennsylvania	48 / *77*	45.5 / *73*	37 / *59.5*	35.5 / *57*	28 / *45*	23 / *37*	21 / *33.5*	13.5 / *21.5*	10 / *16*	8 / *13*	7.5 / *12*	6 / *9.5*		
Cold Ashton	48.8 / *77.5*	46 / *73.5*	37.5 / *60*	36 / *57.5*	28.5 / *45.5*	23.5 / *37.5*	21.5 / *34*	14 / *22*	10.5 / *16.5*	8.5 / *13.5*	8 / *12.5*	6.5 / *10*	0.5 / *0.5*	
Bath	58.5 / *93.5*	56 / *89.5*	47.5 / *76*	46 / *73.5*	38.5 / *61.5*	33.5 / *53.5*	31.5 / *50*	24 / *38*	20.5 / *32.5*	18.5 / *29.5*	18 / *28.5*	16.5 / *26*	10.5 / *16.5*	10 / *16*

TRAILBLAZER TITLE LIST

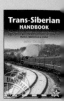

Adventure Cycle-Touring Handbook
Adventure Motorcycling Handbook
Australia by Rail
Azerbaijan
Coast to Coast (British Walking Guide)
Cornwall Coast Path (British Walking Guide)
Corsica Trekking – GR20
Cotswold Way (British Walking Guide)
The Cyclist's Anthology
Dales Way (British Walking Guide) – due mid 2016
Dolomites Trekking – AV1 & AV2
Dorset & Sth Devon Coast Path (British Walking Gde)
Exmoor & Nth Devon Coast Path (British Walking Gde)
Hadrian's Wall Path (British Walking Guide)

Himalaya by Bike – a route and planning guide
Inca Trail, Cusco & Machu Picchu
Japan by Rail
Kilimanjaro – the trekking guide (includes Mt Meru)
Moroccan Atlas – The Trekking Guide
Morocco Overland (4WD/motorcycle/mountainbike)
Nepal Trekking & The Great Himalaya Trail
New Zealand – The Great Walks

Offa's Dyke Path (British Walking Guide)
Overlanders' Handbook – worldwide driving guide
Peddars Way & Norfolk Coast Path (British Walking Gde)
Pembrokeshire Coast Path (British Walking Guide)
Pennine Way (British Walking Guide)
Peru's Cordilleras Blanca & Huayhuash – Hiking/Biking
The Railway Anthology
The Ridgeway (British Walking Guide)
Sahara Overland – a route and planning guide
Scottish Highlands – The Hillwalking Guide
Siberian BAM Guide – rail, rivers & road
The Silk Roads – a route and planning guide
Sinai – the trekking guide

South Downs Way (British Walking Guide)
Thames Path (British Walking Guide)
Tour du Mont Blanc
Trans-Canada Rail Guide
Trans-Siberian Handbook
Trekking in the Everest Region
The Walker's Anthology
The Walker's Haute Route – Mont Blanc to Matterhorn
West Highland Way (British Walking Guide)

For more information about Trailblazer and our
expanding range of guides, for guidebook updates or
for credit card mail order sales visit our website:

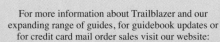

www.trailblazer-guides.com

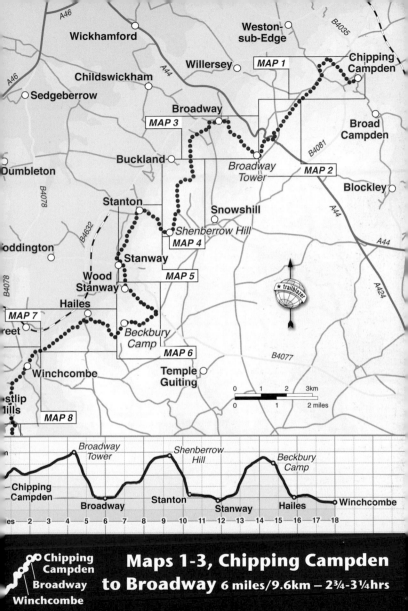

Maps 1-3, Chipping Campden to Broadway 6 miles/9.6km – 2¾-3¼hrs

Maps 3-8, Broadway to Winchcombe
12 miles/19.3km – 5½-6½hrs
NOTE: Add 20-30% to these times to allow for stops

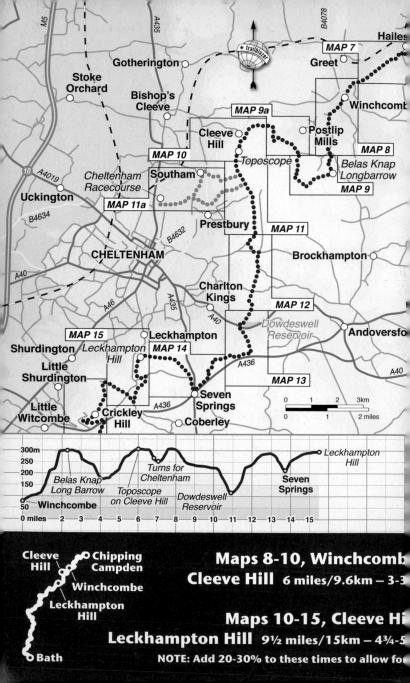

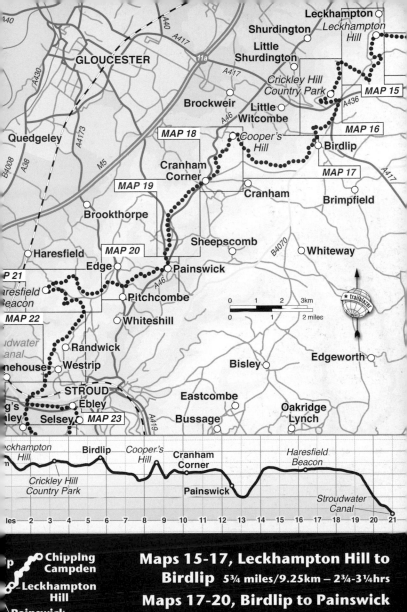

Maps 15-17, Leckhampton Hill to Birdlip 5¾ miles/9.25km – 2¾-3¼hrs

Maps 17-20, Birdlip to Painswick 6¾ miles/10.9km – 3¼-3¾hrs

Maps 20-23, Painswick to Stonehouse 8½ miles/13.4km – 4¼-4¾hrs

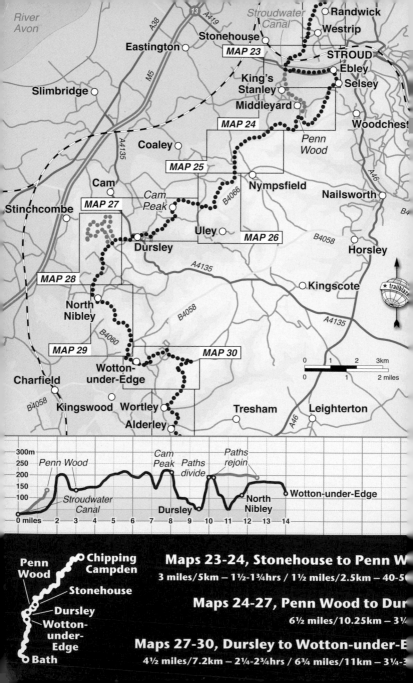

River
Avon

Stroudwater Canal ● **Randwick**
● **Westrip**

Eastington **Stonehouse**
MAP 23 **STROUD**
Ebley
Selsey
Slimbridge **King's Stanley**
Middleyard **Woodchest**
MAP 24
Penn Wood
Coaley **MAP 25**
Nailsworth
Cam **Nympsfield**
Cam Peak **MAP 27**
Stinchcombe **B4066**
Uley **MAP 26**
Dursley **Horsley**
A4135
MAP 28 **Kingscote**
North Nibley **B4058**
A4135
B4060
MAP 29 **MAP 30**
Wotton-under-Edge
Charfield
Kingswood **Wortley** **Tresham** **Leighterton**
Alderley

★ trailblazer

0 1 2 3km
0 1 2 miles

300m
250
200
150 *Penn Wood*
100 *Stroudwater Canal* *Cam Peak* *Paths divide* *Paths rejoin*
Wotton-under-Edge
Dursley **North Nibley**
0 miles 1 2 3 4 5 6 7 8 9 10 11 12 13 14

Penn Wood ○ **Chipping Campden** ## Maps 23-24, Stonehouse to Penn W

3 miles/5km – 1½-1¾hrs / 1½ miles/2.5km – 40-5

Stonehouse ## Maps 24-27, Penn Wood to Dur

Dursley 6½ miles/10.25km – 3¼

Wotton-under-Edge ## Maps 27-30, Dursley to Wotton-under-E

Bath 4½ miles/7.2km – 2¼-2¾hrs / 6¾ miles/11km – 3¼-3

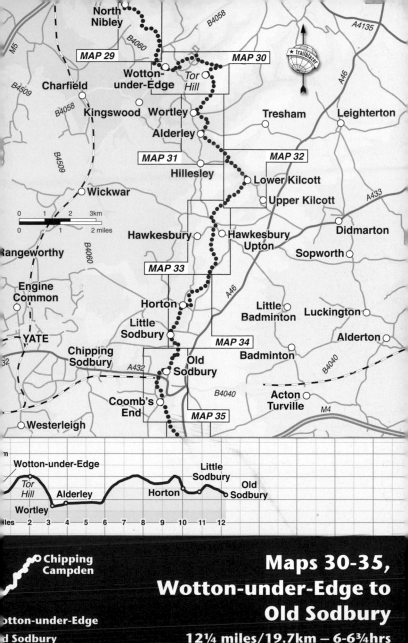

North Nibley

B4058

B4060

MAP 29

MAP 30

★ trailblazer

Charfield

Wotton-under-Edge

Tor Hill

B4509

B4058

Kingswood

Wortley

Tresham

Leighterton

A4135

A46

Alderley

MAP 31

MAP 32

A433

B4509

Hillesley

Lower Kilcott

Upper Kilcott

Wickwar

0 1 2 3km
0 1 2 miles

B4060

Hawkesbury

Hawkesbury Upton

Didmarton

Sopworth

MAP 33

Rangeworthy

Engine Common

A46

Horton

Little Badminton

Luckington

YATE

Little Sodbury

MAP 34

Alderton

Chipping Sodbury

A432

Old Sodbury

Badminton

B4040

2

Coomb's End

B4040

Acton Turville

M4

MAP 35

Westerleigh

m

Wotton-under-Edge

Little Sodbury

Tor Hill

Alderley

Horton

Old Sodbury

Wortley

les 2 3 4 5 6 7 8 9 10 11 12

Chipping Campden

otton-under-Edge

d Sodbury

th

Maps 30-35,
Wotton-under-Edge to
Old Sodbury

12¼ miles/19.7km – 6-6¾hrs
NOTE: Add 20-30% to these times to allow for stops

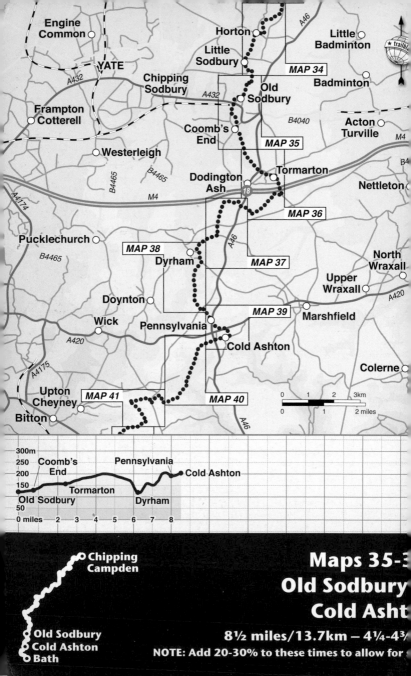

Engine Common

Little Badminton

YATE

A432

Horton

A46

Little Sodbury

Chipping Sodbury

A432

Old Sodbury

Badminton

Frampton Cotterell

MAP 34

B4040

Acton Turville

M4

Coomb's End

MAP 35

Westerleigh

B4465

B4465

M4

Dodington Ash

Tormarton

Nettleton

B4

A4174

18

MAP 36

Pucklechurch

B4465

MAP 38

A46

Dyrham

MAP 37

North Wraxall

Upper Wraxall

A420

Doynton

Wick

A420

Pennsylvania

MAP 39

Cold Ashton

Marshfield

A4175

MAP 41

Upton Cheyney

MAP 40

Colerne

Bitton

A46

| 0 | 1 | 2 | 3km |
| 0 | | 1 | 2 miles |

300m
250
Coomb's End
Pennsylvania
200
150
Tormarton
Cold Ashton
Old Sodbury
Dyrham
50

0 miles 2 3 4 5 6 7 8

Chipping Campden

Maps 35-3

Old Sodbury

Cold Asht

Old Sodbury
Cold Ashton
Bath

8½ miles/13.7km – 4¼-4³/

NOTE: Add 20-30% to these times to allow for

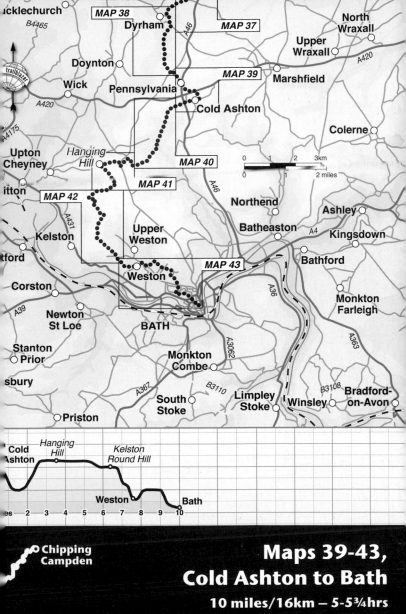

MAP 38
Dyrham
MAP 37
North Wraxall
Upper Wraxall
Doynton
MAP 39
Marshfield
Wick
Pennsylvania
Cold Ashton
Colerne
Upton Cheyney
Hanging Hill
MAP 40
MAP 41
Northend
MAP 42
Batheaston
Ashley
Kelston
Upper Weston
Kingsdown
Bathford
Corston
MAP 43
Monkton Farleigh
Newton St Loe
Weston
BATH
Stanton Prior
Monkton Combe
Priston
South Stoke
Limpley Stoke
Winsley
Bradford-on-Avon

Cold Ashton
Hanging Hill
Kelston Round Hill
Weston
Bath
2 3 4 5 6 7 8 9 10

Chipping Campden

Maps 39-43,
Cold Ashton to Bath

10 miles/16km – 5-5¾hrs

NOTE: Add 20-30% to these times to allow for stops

Ashton

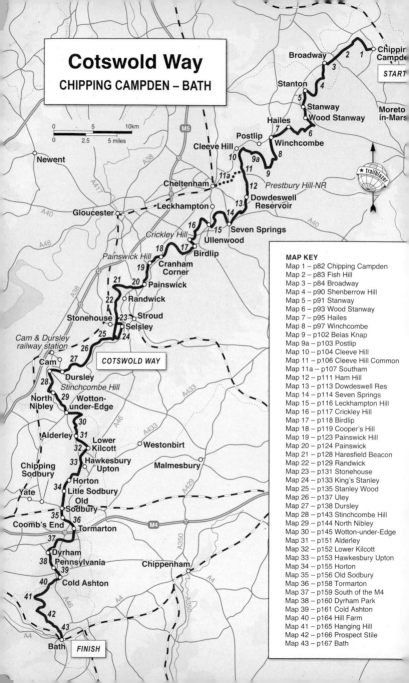

Cotswold Way
CHIPPING CAMPDEN – BATH

Newent

Gloucester

Cheltenham

Leckhampton

Crickley Hill

Painswick Hill

Cranham
Corner

Painswick

Randwick

Stonehouse

Stroud

Selsley

Cam & Dursley
railway station

Cam

COTSWOLD WAY

Dursley

Stinchcombe Hill

North
Nibley

Wotton-
under-Edge

Alderley

Lower
Kilcott

Westonbirt

Chipping
Sodbury

Hawkesbury
Upton

Malmesbury

Yate

Horton

Little Sodbury

Old
Sodbury

Coomb's End

Tormarton

Dyrham

Pennsylvania

Chippenham

Cold Ashton

Bath FINISH

Broadway

Chippin
Campde

START

Stanton

Stanway

Wood Stanway

Moreto
in-Mars

Hailes

Postlip

Winchcombe

Cleeve Hill

Southam

Prestbury Hill-NR

Dowdeswell
Reservoir

Seven Springs

Ullenwood

Birdlip

trailblazer

MAP KEY
Map 1 – p82 Chipping Campden
Map 2 – p83 Fish Hill
Map 3 – p84 Broadway
Map 4 – p90 Shenberrow Hill
Map 5 – p91 Stanway
Map 6 – p93 Wood Stanway
Map 7 – p95 Hailes
Map 8 – p97 Winchcombe
Map 9 – p102 Belas Knap
Map 9a – p103 Postlip
Map 10 – p104 Cleeve Hill
Map 11 – p106 Cleeve Hill Common
Map 11a – p107 Southam
Map 12 – p111 Ham Hill
Map 13 – p113 Dowdeswell Res
Map 14 – p114 Seven Springs
Map 15 – p116 Leckhampton Hill
Map 16 – p117 Crickley Hill
Map 17 – p118 Birdlip
Map 18 – p119 Cooper's Hill
Map 19 – p123 Painswick Hill
Map 20 – p124 Painswick
Map 21 – p128 Haresfield Beacon
Map 22 – p129 Randwick
Map 23 – p131 Stonehouse
Map 24 – p133 King's Stanley
Map 25 – p135 Stanley Wood
Map 26 – p137 Uley
Map 27 – p138 Dursley
Map 28 – p143 Stinchcombe Hill
Map 29 – p144 North Nibley
Map 30 – p145 Wotton-under-Edge
Map 31 – p151 Alderley
Map 32 – p152 Lower Kilcott
Map 33 – p153 Hawkesbury Upton
Map 34 – p155 Horton
Map 35 – p156 Old Sodbury
Map 36 – p158 Tormarton
Map 37 – p159 South of the M4
Map 38 – p160 Dyrham Park
Map 39 – p161 Cold Ashton
Map 40 – p164 Hill Farm
Map 41 – p165 Hanging Hill
Map 42 – p166 Prospect Stile
Map 43 – p167 Bath